7/98

Discarded by rary

D0687604

796.352
A passion for golf : the
best of golf writing /
1998.

98 99 02 10 JUL10

ILL AUG 03

GAYLORD MG

l98

A PASSION FOR GOLF

A PASSION FOR
GOLF

The Best of Golf Writing

FOREWORD BY ARNOLD PALMER

INTRODUCTION BY JOHN GARRITY

EDITED BY SCHUYLER BISHOP

ST. MARTIN'S PRESS ☙ NEW YORK

A THOMAS DUNNE BOOK
An Imprint of St. Martin's Press

A PASSION FOR GOLF. Copyright © 1998 by The Reference
Works and Schuyler Bishop. All rights reserved. Printed in the
United States of America. No part of this book may be used
or reproduced in any manner whatsoever without written
permission except in the case of brief quotations embodied
in critical articles or reviews. For information address St.
Martin's Press, 175 Fifth Avenue, New York, N.Y. 10010.

Library of Congress Cataloging-in-Publication Data

A passion for golf : the best of golf writing / edited by Schuyler
    Bishop ; foreword by Arnold Palmer ; introduction by John
Garrity.—
    —1st U.S. ed.
        p.   cm.
    "A Thomas Dunne book"—T.p. verso.
    ISBN 0-312-19027-1
    1. Golf.   2. Golf—Social aspects.   I. Bishop, Schuyler.
GV965.P37   1998
796.352—dc21   98-10263
                                                          CIP

FIRST U.S. EDITION: JUNE 1998

10 9 8 7 6 5 4 3 2 1

ACKNOWLEDGMENTS

Acknowledgment is made for permission to print the following material:

Walter Bingham, copyright © 1970. Used by permission of *Sports Illustrated.*

Thomas Boswell, from *Strokes of Genius,* copyright © 1987 by Washington Post Writers Group. Used by permission of Doubleday, a division of BantamDouble-dayDell Publishing Group, Inc.

Robert H. Boyle, copyright © 1962 by *Sports Illustrated.* Used by permission.

Christopher Bram, from *Almost History,* copyright © 1992. Used by permission of Penguin Books USA, Inc.

Elmer Osgood Cappers, from *A Centennial History of the Country Club,* copyright © 1981 by Brookline Publishing. Used by permission.

Marcia Chambers, from *The Unplayable Lie.* Copyright © 1995 by Pocket Books. Used by permission.

Alistair Cooke, from *The Americans.* Copyright © 1979 by Alistair Cooke. Used by permission of Alfred A. Knopf, Inc.

James Ellroy, from *Brown's Requiem.* Copyright © 1981 by James Ellroy. Used by permission of Avon.

John Garrity, copyright © 1997 by *Sports Illustrated.* Used by permission.

Rhonda Glenn, copyright © 1991 by *Sports Illustrated.* Used by permission.

Arnold Haultain, from *The Mystery of Golf,* copyright © by Ailsa, Inc. Used by permission of Ailsa Publishing (London).

Edwin Bancroft Henderson, from *The Negro in Sports,* copyright © 1949 by The Associated Publishers, Inc. Used by permission of The Associated Publishers, Inc.

Richard Hooker, from *M*A*S*H.* Copyright © 1968 by Richard Hooker. Used by permission of William Morrow, Inc.

Bob Hope, from *Confessions of a Hooker.* Copyright © 1987. Used by permission of Doubleday, a division of BantamDoubleday Dell Publishing Group, Inc.

Bobby Jones, from *Golf Is My Game,* copyright © 1960 by Robert Tyre Jones. Used by permission of Doubleday, a division of BantamDoubledayDell Publishing Group, Inc.

J. P. Marquand, from *Life at Happy Knoll,* copyright © 1957. Used by permission of Little, Brown.

Alex J. Morrison, from *Better Golf Without Practice,* copyright © 1940. Used by permission of Simon & Schuster.

Michael Murphy, from *Golf in the Kingdom,* copyright © 1972. Used by permission of Viking, a division of Penguin/Putnam.

Francis Ouimet, from *The Children's Hour,* copyright © 1916. Used by permission of Houghton Mifflin Co.

Arnold Palmer from *Go for Broke—My Philosophy of Winning Golf,* copyright © 1973 by Arnold Palmer (with Barry Furlong). Used by permission.

Harvey Penick, from *The Game for a Lifetime,* copyright © 1996 by Bud Shrake, Helen Penick and the Estate of Harvey Penick. Used by permission of Simon & Schuster.

Betsy Rawls, from *Gettin' to the Dance Floor,* copyright © 1986. Used by permission of Atheneum Press.

Rick Reilly, from *The Missing Links,* copyright © 1997 by *Sports Illustrated.* Reprinted by permission; and from *Tiger Woods at the Masters,* copyright © 1997 by *Sports Illustrated.* Reprinted by permission.

Gene Sarazen, from *Thirty Years of Championship Golf,* copyright © 1950 by Prentice Hall Inc. Used by permission; and from *Gettin' to the Dance Floor,* copyright © 1986. Used by permission of Atheneum Press.

Jeanne Schinto, from *Perfect Lies,* copyright © 1989 by William Hallberg. Used by permission.

Sam Snead, from *Education of a Golfer.* Copyright © 1962 by Sam Snead and Al Stump. Used by permission of Simon & Schuster.

A. W. Tillinghast, copyright © 1933. Used by permission of *Golf Illustrated.*

John Updike, from *Hugging the Shore,* copyright © 1983 by John Updike. Used by permission of Random House.

Tom Watson, copyright © 1991 by *The New York Times.* Used by permission.

The editor gratefully acknowledges the assistance of the USGA—Marty Parks and librarians Nancy Stulock and Patty Moran; the Sports Illustrated *library staff; The Reference Works—Harold Rabinowitz, Ross Mandel, David Crifendon, and Samantha Greene; my agent, Alex Hoyt; my colleagues at SI—John Garrity, Rick Lipsey, and Jim Herre; and my brother, Christopher Bishop.*

CONTENTS

What I Look For on the Golf Course

ARNOLD PALMER

I REALLY MEAN it this time," I told my family and friends last spring. "I'm going to slow down. I'm going to go to the movies when I want to. I'm going to play golf every day."

"But Arnold," interrupted my good friend and Florida neighbor, Carolyn Giles. "You *already* play golf every day."

She was right, of course. It's a rare day that I don't hit balls on a range, practice my putting, tinker with clubs, and play at least nine holes. The difference this time was that I was sixty-four years old and recovering from prostate cancer surgery. Still and all, I couldn't wait to get back on the green fairways of the Bay Hill Club.

Obviously, I have a passion for golf. But even I was surprised at how intensely I longed to play during the few weeks I was under doctors' orders to rest. Part of it, I'm sure, was my love of the outdoors. During my first rounds after surgery, I often found myself staring at the way sunlight hit the leaves of a tree. I watched the water turkeys paddling in the lake by the sixth hole. When an interesting aircraft flew over, I followed it until it dwindled to a speck. These were not the heightened perceptions of a man suddenly facing his own mortality. I've always been one who stopped and smelt the roses—if I can borrow Walter Hagen's memorable line.

There were other reasons I had to get back to golf. I've always said that when you play a round with someone, you can tell just about everything you want to know about him. I now recognize that the golf course is also where I learn about myself. All the qualities we define as "character"—discipline, concentration, honesty, humor, composure—get exercised over eighteen holes of golf, even if it's only a casual round. And the golf course is where I feel most comfortable with people I know casually. An instant camaraderie develops when you tee it up with someone, and it doesn't matter if that person is a banker or a bricklayer.

People I know well? Let's just say that I couldn't wait to trade insults again with my buddies in the daily Bay Hill Shootout.

Somebody once described a golf course as God's waiting room. I don't know about that, but I can tell you that my father played twenty-seven holes on the day he died, and he enjoyed every one of them. Generation after generation, golf provides challenge and fun to people of all ages and walks of life. Yes, many of us become passionate about the game, and I guess I'm more passionate than most because I owe everything I have to golf. But I see the same enthusiasm in the eyes of the golfers I play with.

We think we're indestructible, but we're not. It's the game that goes on.

Latrobe, Pennsylvania

Charm and Challenge

JOHN GARRITY

THIS IS NOT your father's golf anthology. In fact, if it were not for the reassuring "click" of the occasional iron shot described in these pages—and the belly laughs produced by the likes of Bob Hope and Rick Reilly—*A Passion for Golf* could easily join the more earnest tomes in the history or sociology sections of the bookstore. I plan to place my copy on the shelf between *Speed Tribes,* a study of contemporary youth culture in Japan, and *A Year in Provence,* a memoir of expatriate life in France's wine country. The selections in this collection take golf's role in American society and recent history as seriously as, well, as golfers take golf.

On another level, this volume reflects the life journey of its editor, Schuyler Bishop. I'm tempted to introduce Schuyler with the words of Groucho Marx, who once called his brother Zeppo the "brains of the organization"—adding, "which will give you some idea of the organization." Schuyler is, if not the brains, at least the superego of the outfit I work for, *Sports Illustrated.* An energetic, bespectacled New Yorker with a dazzling smile, Schuyler is our "late reader," an editorial specialist who checks virtually every line in the magazine before it goes to the printer. The job demands intense concentration and has sent lesser talents screaming into the night. No wonder the staff regards him as the steady rock in the magazine's editorial maelstrom.

It surprised me, therefore, to run into Schuyler at the 1990 Masters. I thought he had no outdoor life at all, but there he was, scrambling up and down Augusta National's hills, dining with the swells on the veranda, and generally soaking up sunshine like a plant. It was at Augusta that I learned of his own longtime passion for golf, and it was there that I discovered how much he knew about the game (he had read nearly every golf article *SI* had published in the previous ten years).

And now, with this anthology, Schuyler surprises me again. The selections, arranged by decade, destroy the stereotype of the American golfer as a middle-aged white male Republican whose last musical purchase was "Glen Campbell's Greatest Hits." In these pages, I find the complex weave of class, income, region, race, and gender that I encounter in my own golf travels; in the prose styles, I observe a rhetorical range to excite lexicographers and folklorists alike; and in Schuyler's confessional intros, I discern a timeline of self-discovery familiar to those born since the end of World War II. "Golf is the mirror of the best and the worst of our lives," Schuyler writes, and as his selections prove, that mirror need not be pocket-sized.

So at the risk of sounding like a coffee-stirring professor at the podium, I offer a reading tip. Consume this anthology as you would play a round of golf—that is, from the first hole to the eighteenth. Your father's golf anthology was assembled more or less at random and could be read that way, but Schuyler has clumped his selections to make some larger points.

Chapter One, for instance, covers "Before 1949," which I take to mean before Schuyler and before Garrity—that is to say, pre-history. However, the self-critical voices of Francis Ouimet, Bobby Jones, and Gene Sarazen will strike you as strangely contemporary. Their appreciation for the game's frustrations is prototypical and links them, despite their many titles and accomplishments, to those of us who slice and chili-dip. (Jones suffered, too!) Sarazen got so fed up with his sand play that he invented a club to make the shot easier. Is that so different from our own hunt for the titanium driver or the beryllium putter that will stop the bleeding?

Chapter Two carries us into the Fifties, but the selections by

Edwin Bancroft Henderson and J. P. Marquand take us down divergent cart paths. Henderson's "The Negro in Sports" restores the once invisible world of the black golf club and introduces us to forgotten stars like John Shippen and "Pat" Bull. Marquand, the great chronicler of the Eastern Establishment, then sneaks us inside the gates of Happy Knoll Country Club, where Shippen and Bull could have caddied, but could never have played. Schuyler's ironic twist is to join these studies of social division with Sarazen's "It Takes Brains to Play Golf." For black and white golfers alike, the Fifties was the decade when the concept of the "mental game" took hold.

Chapter Three picks up the story in 1958, which invites us to speculate that we're venturing into Palmer country. (Arnold won his first Masters in 1957, exciting television viewers and launching a ship that would dock four decades later in the form of The Golf Channel.) But our editor challenges that notion by throwing in passages by Sam Snead, a legend since the Thirties, while omitting Ben Hogan and Gary Player. His point, however, is clear: golf was becoming a game of stars. Palmer, in particular, was admired by men and women who might otherwise drive by a golf course without turning their heads. (My mother joined the women's auxiliary of Arnie's army after reading a profile of Palmer in the *New Yorker*.) Schuyler's selections also inform us that golf had become the chosen subject of star writers—most of whom worked for a young magazine called *Sports Illustrated.*

Chapters Four and Five, like Dickens's ghosts in *A Christmas Carol,* fly us over time and terrain. First, we see how golf has become the game of presidents and kings, and then Michael Murphy, in "Singing the Praises of Golf," conjures up the realm of philosopher-kings. The graceful and wry Alistair Cooke takes us behind the Iron Curtain, and Schuyler then hands us over to two eminent men of letters, John Updike and James Ellroy, fellows who are big hitters, novelistically speaking.

If the mid-Seventies were "dark days," as our guide asserts, then the Eighties must have been better, because he bookends Chapter Six with gag-strewn gems by Bob Hope and Rick Reilly. The other two selections, by Thomas Boswell and LPGA Hall-of-Famer Betsy Rawls, examine the unglamorous side of life on the professional tours.

Finally, Chapter Seven brings us to the brink of the millennium, showing golf to be a flawed but compelling institution. Rhonda Glenn and Marcia Chambers remind us that racial and gender prejudice continue to hamper the game's growth. Selections from two Kansas City natives—Tom Watson and myself—help to explain how golf can transcend societal frailties and lead us to a keener understanding of life. Schuyler's clever counterpoint is to end the book with both a poignant piece about a father and son (1946 Masters champion Herman Keiser and Herm Jr.), and his own golf memoir with its equally poignant anecdote about a *mother* and son.

So you see, *A Passion for Golf* is considerably more than the sum of its putts—er, parts. There is a tendency—mistaken, I think—to look at the current enthusiasm for Tiger Woods and to assume that his popularity drives the game. To the contrary, golf's enduring charm and challenge are what make Tiger's accomplishments so compelling. He is simply the freshest and boldest brushstroke on an already appealing canvas.

Well done, Schuyler. You have captured the big picture.

Chapter One

BEFORE 1949

I N ONE OF her great books, historian Barbara Tuchman referred
to the fourteenth century as the "distant mirror" to our time, and
from what I've seen in my sporting life and in the fifteen years I've
worked as the late reader for *Sports Illustrated,* it seems to me that
golf more accurately mirrors American life than any other sport.
Baseball, football, basketball, and the like are team games that are
won or lost; there is an immediate joy and camaraderie in winning,
a sudden and fleeting agony in losing. Golf, on the other hand, is,
like the American spirit, built on the individual quest, the continuing struggle to improve—and sometimes just to survive. I've never
seen a baseball player take himself off the mound or disgustedly
stomp off the field because of his bad play the way, say, John Daly

does. And Daly is not alone among golfers; everyone who has ever played the game has either himself picked up or had a partner quit in disgust and either walk or ride the rest of the course, refusing to lose another ball. Golf is a game for life. In fact, it *is* life, especially because, as every golfer knows, the final score isn't nearly as important as the way traveled, the swings taken, the stories told. While golf is an individual struggle, it is also the most social of games. We celebrate a terrific shot or putt; we envy a good game; we swear we'll never play again.

Golf is a mirror of the best and the worst of our lives. Tiger Woods, for all his great glory, is the *first* African American to reach the heights in golf, though certainly not the first to reach the upper echelons of play. From what I've seen, this is much more indicative of American life than is the number of blacks who have risen to success in baseball, football, or basketball. Time Warner, the corporation I work for, is considered to be enlightened in terms of racial hiring, but except for the president, who was brought over from another company, from what I can see, black employees are given low-level jobs with little chance of advancement. Until a couple of years ago, *Sports Illustrated* had only one black senior editor and one black writer, though we had plenty of black copy clerks. This seems to be the way it is in most corporations. Those who think the struggle is over are just fooling themselves; those who think it's won are living in a fantasy world.

When my friend Floran's son Brian was eleven, he delineated the world events his father and I talked about by asking if they happened before or after Babe Ruth died. The Catholic Church has wrangled a similar calendar on the western world, and similarly, because I'm gathering these stories for my generation, I'm using immediately recognizable epochs—those of my life—for the chapters of this book. To start, everything that happened before I was born in 1949 is lumped under B.S., which, as I'm sure everyone knows, means Before Schuyler.

In the attic of the house I grew up in, in the corner just past the steamer trunks and bizarrely ornate furniture that came from God-knows-where, there was an old golf bag filled with hickory-shafted clubs and gutta-percha balls. One day when we were kids, one of my brothers and I took the bag out into the front yard, dug a hole, and started smacking around the balls, trying to get them into the hole. While we were playing, my father drove into the driveway, saw we were playing golf, and came over to us. He didn't care at all that we'd dug a hole in the middle of the lawn, but when he saw the clubs we were using, he hit the roof, demanding to know where we'd gotten them and whether we'd asked if we could use them. Fearing his wrath, we cowered, but as quickly as his anger rose, it passed, and he told us they had been his father's clubs and that we could use them if we were careful, but to please return them to the attic when we were finished. He even took one of the more lofted irons and pitched a ball to the far end of the yard.

My parents loved golf, nay (to use a vaguely Scottish-sounding word) they had a passion for it. My father grew up playing at Winged Foot. My mother didn't take up the game until after she married my father, but my grandmother had been taught the game by Little Harvey Penick ("PEA-nick" is how he pronounced it), as she referred to him before his fame spread worldwide. My parents were married a month after World War II ended and honeymooned at Pinehurst, where, as my mother told it, my father got up at six to go to Mass to thank God he made it back from the war, was on one of the golf courses by seven, played thirty-six holes, had dinner with my mother—and then kept her up all night with his war-induced screaming nightmares. After four days of crying into her breakfast, lunch, and tea on the veranda, my mother took up the game. She broke 90 before their honeymoon was over.

Bobby Jones was a name I'd always known but never gave much thought to. The reading I'd done about him had him chiseled in granite, and not very well chiseled. But in his own words in *Golf Is My Game,* he came alive. Another great, Francis Ouimet, who cad-died in his youth at The Country Club in Brookline, Massachusetts (and, as he reveals in "How I Began to Play Golf," snuck onto the course as well), was, as we see in the look back at the rarefied life at The Country Club, hailed by the club as its own, though its greenskeeper did his damnedest to keep Ouimet off the grounds.

Gene Sarazen, in "Yes, I Had a Reputation," says he had to be tough because he was Italian, but as we see in "The Birth of the Birdie" by A. W. Tillinghast, the noted golf-course architect, golfers were never far from making pathetic little racist jokes at the expense of their caddies. And putting them in print no less! Jones's and Ouimet's pieces are golf at its greatest, while Tillinghast's and Rhonda Glenn's little gems let us peek into the world around golf, the way it was played Before Schuyler.

From *The Mystery of Golf*

ARNOLD HAULTAIN

Canadian author Arnold Haultain published The Mystery of Golf *in 1908. His articulate, and often poetic, reasoning regarding man's (and women's) fascination with golf makes it an ageless classic.*

What is there in the game of golf which so differentiates it from all others that in it these trifling minutiae become magnified to matters of great moment? I take it it is because in golf the *mind* plays a highly curious and important part. . . .

VIII

As a matter of fact most of the difficulties in golf are mental, not physical; are subjective, not objective; are the created phantasms of the mind, not the veritable realities of the course. Bad lies, on good links, are the exception, not the rule; and bunkers are avowedly where they are in order to catch the unworthy and the unwary. That wood to the right is no real obstacle to your drive; why then are you so fearful of a slice? Were you blindfold and could not see it, it would be as if it were not, and the so-called "difficulty" would vanish. And yet the number of balls that do go into that wood—or are pulled off to the left to avoid it—is astonishing. The mere test of strength or of skill is one of the most subordinate of the elements of golf; much more important is the test of what goes by the name of "nerve," that quiet self-confidence which no ghostly phantasms can shake, in howsoever questionable shape they come. So many golfers forget this. "If I had not done this, that, or the other stupid thing," they say, "my score would have been so-and-so." My dear sir, it is just those stupid things that make the game. Eliminate the liability of the frail and peccant human mind to do stupid things, and you might as well play pitch and toss. It is this very frailty and peccability of the human mind that golf calls in question, and it is this that differentiates golf from all other games, because in golf this frailty is shown in its utter nudity, not hidden away under cover of agility or excitement or concerted action, as it is in cricket or football or tennis or polo or what-not. The simplicity of the thing to be done strips the soul of all cloak of excuse for not doing it. You may place your ball how or where you like, you may hit it with any sort of implement you like; all you have to do is to hit it into a hole. Could simpler conditions be devised? Could an easier task be essayed ? . . .

XII

Golf seems to bring the man, the very inmost man, into contact with the man, the very inmost man. In football and hockey you come into intimate—and often forcible enough—contact with the outer man; chess is a clash of intellects; but in golf character is laid bare to character. This is why so many friendships—and some enmities—are formed on the links. In spite of the ceremony with which the game is played: the elaborate etiquette, the punctilious adhesion to the honour, the enforced silence during the address, the rigid observance of rules, few if any games so strip a man of the conventional and the artificial. In a single round you can sum up a man, can say whether he be truthful, courageous, honest, upright, generous, sincere, slow to anger—or the reverse. . . .

XXXIV

How comes it about, then, that, if the conditions are so simple, success is so difficult? The fact is, there is enormous Chance in golf. There must be, when you propel a cubic inch of gutta-percha over acres of soil. Were the links a gigantic billiard table, chance might to a certain extent be eliminated, as no doubt in billiards it actually is. But the links being what they are, namely, some two or three square miles of open country, variegated in its every square inch, in any one square inch of which you may lie, and each square inch of which may affect differently the character of your stroke or the roll of your ball, chance, to the beginner in golf, we may safely compute as infinite. But, as one improves, the conditions being fixed and determined, skill directly eliminates chance. In no other game is the equipoise between chance and skill so exact, since in all other games a third and variable factor enters into the problem, the skill, namely, of your opponent. . . .

XXXVII

John Stuart Mill once anxiously debated whether there would not come a time when all the tunes possible with the five tones and two semi-tones of the octave would be exhausted. So, many a non-golfing wife and unsympathizing onlooker think there surely must come a time when the erring husband and friend will tire of trudging over the country trying to put half-crown balls into four-and-a-half-inch holes. The outsider does not know that at every hole is enacted every time a small but intensely interesting three-act drama. There is Act I, the Drive, with its appropriate mise-en-scène: the gallery, the attendant caddies, the toss for the honor. At long holes it is a long act if we include the brassey shots. There is Act II, the Approach. This is what the French call "the *nœud* of the plot": much depends on the Approach. And the mise-en-scène is correspondingly enhanced in interest: the lie, the hazard, the wind, the character of the ground—all become of increasing importance. There is Act III, the Putt. It also has its background, its "business" and its "properties": the caddie at the flag, the irregularities of the green, the peculiarities of the turf, the possibilities of a stymie. Eighteen dramas, some tragical, some farcical, in every round; and in every round protagonist and deuteragonist constantly interchanging parts. No wonder the ardent golfer does not tire of his links, any more than the ardent musician tires of his notes. What theatergoer enjoys such plays? And what staged plays have such a human interest in them? And, best of all, they are acted in the open air, amid delightful scenery, with the assurance of healthy exercise and pleasant companionship. What theatergoer enjoys such plays? And when the curtain is rung down and the eighteenth flag replaced, instead of a cigar in a hansom, or a whisky-and-soda at a crowded bar, or a snack at a noisy grill-room, there is the amicable persiflage in the dressing-room or the long quiet talk on the veranda.

Nor does the golfer ever tire of the stage upon which these his outdoor dramas are played—I have been promising myself time and again to go round some day, unarmed with clubs and carrying no balls, for the express purpose of seeing and enjoying in detail the beauties of my links. There are some woods fringing portions of the course most tempting to explore, woods in which I get glimpses of lovable things, and a wealth of color which for its very loveliness I forgive for hiding my sliced ball. There are deep ravines—alack! I know them well—where, between lush grass edges trickles a tiny hill, by the quiet banks of which, but for the time limit, I should loiter long. There is a great breezy hill, bespattered with humble plants, to traverse the broad back of which almost tempts to slice and to pull. A thick boscage, too, whereon the four seasons play a quartet on the theme of green, and every sun-lit day composes a symphony beautiful to behold. And there are nooks, and corners, and knolls, and sloping lawns on which the elfish shadows dance. Smells too, curious smells, from noonday pines, and evening mists, from turf, and fallen leaves. . . . What is it these things say? Whither do they beckon? What do they reveal? I seem to be listening to some cosmic obligato the while I play; a great and unheard melody swelling from the great heart of Nature. Every golfer knows something of this. But, as Herodotus says, these be holy things whereof I speak not. *Favete linguis*. . . .

XXXVIII

Lastly, let us not omit to include amongst the elements of the fascination which golf yields over its votaries that *gaudium certaminis,* that joy of contest, which always the game evokes. It is one of the chief ingredients of the game, and it is evoked and re-evoked at every point of the game, from the initial drive to the ultimate putt. It is an ingredient of every manly sport, this "warrior's stern joy," but in golf it is paramount and overt. Every stroke arouses it, for the exact value of every stroke is patent to both player and opponent. Few other games keep the inborn masculine delight in sheer struggle at so high a pitch. No wonder the stakes in golf are merely nominal; no wonder that often there are no stakes at all; the keenness of the rivalry is stimulus enough. And this, surely, is one of the chief beauties of the game. It will never be spoiled by the intrusion of professionalism; at least it will never be played by highly-paid professionals for the delectation of a howling and betting mob; nor, thank heavens, will rooters ever sit on fences and screech at its results. At present it is uncontaminated by either "bookies" or "bleachers"; nay, it has not yet reached that stage in its history when it asks for gate-money. . . .

XXXIX

But the ultimate analysis of the mystery of golf is hopeless—as hopeless as the ultimate analysis of that of metaphysics or of that of the feminine heart. Fortunately the hopelessness as little troubles the golfer as it does the philosopher or the lover. The *summum bonum* of the philosopher, I suppose, is to evolve a nice little system of metaphysics of his own. The *summum bonum* of the lover is of course to get him a nice little feminine heart of his own. Well, the *summum bonum* of the golfer is to have a nice little private links of his own (and, nowadays, perhaps, a private manufactory of rubber-cored balls into the bargain), and to be able to go round his private links daily, accompanied by a professional and a caddie. It would be an interesting experiment to add to these a psychologist, a leech, a chirurgeon, a psychiater, an apothecary, and a parson.

The Birth of the Birdie

A. W. TILLINGHAST

In addition to being a noted golf architect of the first half of the twentieth century, A. W. Tillinghast was also a prolific writer. His work was collected in a book entitled The Course Beautiful: A Collection of Original Articles and Photographs on Golf Course Design. *This piece originally ran in* Golf Illustrated *in 1933.*

You may search the records of golf but there will be found no mention of the term "Bird" or "Birdie" prior to the year 1903 for that was the year of its birth. Probably the first appearance of the term in public print will date three or four years later for, at the start, it was the private property of a dozen golfing pilgrims. Today it is used universally to indicate the scoring of one less than par figures on any hole. The "Eagle," symbolic of two strokes under par, came into use very soon after the "Bird."

Thirty or more years ago, it was the habit of a few Philadelphia golfers to spend their winter weekends, playing the original eighteen holes at Northfield, the course of the Country Club of Atlantic City. There, they found winter golf conditions very different from those of the Quaker City, only sixty miles distant. Every Saturday morning this coterie of enthusiasts boarded the train, possibly leaving inches of snow at home, knowing well that the seaside course would be free of it and that the temperature would be four or five degrees higher. The regulars included the late George Crump, Howard Perrin, Cameron Buxton, Robert Large, and William Poultney Smith, A. H. Smith, Frank Bohlen, Wirt Thompson and myself. Others joined our group from time to time and usually anywhere from nine to fifteen turned out at the first teeing ground to face the wind, and there was wind and plenty of it coming in over the meadows from the sea. Those varying winds were the real hazards of the course. I recall playing the short eleventh hole one day, as an illustration. In the morning, with a following wind, it was all one could do to keep the ball on the green with a mashie-niblick. But, in the afternoon it took a full brassie to clear the front pit.

Now, instead of playing the conventional two or four ball encounters, we had drifted to the habit of all playing together if we were less than a dozen and perhaps splitting into two companies if we were more. Thus was originated a sort of mob golf, which became known about the country as a Philadelphia Ballsome, for the stakes were usually a ball or two, a corner for each hole. These sweepstakes could be quite lucrative or distressingly expensive, depending entirely upon the condition of one's game, but they did spur us on to play hard. It came to pass that one day we were playing the long twelfth hole (in the order of that time) with a keen following wind. The hole usually played as a three-shorter, but on this occasion someone got away two screamers and got home in two. As the second shot found the green either Bill Smith or his brother Ab exclaimed: "That's a bird!" Immediately the other remarked that such an effort, that resulted in cutting par by a stroke, should be rewarded doubly and there on the spot it was agreed that thereafter this should be done. And so it was, the exclamation of Smith, giving it the name, Bird, which gradually was to become a term of the game, used wherever it is played today. Hence the "Bird" is about thirty years of age and was born in South Jersey.

It was but natural that the high winds at Northfield frequently brought birds and often scores of two less than par, which were designated as "Eagles," with twice the collecting value of the "Bird." We had another term, too, but it was not original with us—the "Bob."

When any player found and held the green with his tee shot, he collected an additional ball from everyone who did not. But the payment of a Bob, or shilling, originated in England long ago, when this bonus was paid for a like performance. It can be imagined very readily that all these bonus credits and debits after each hole might become a rather involved matter with, let us say seven players, each paying balls to everyone ahead of him, but curiously enough our books always balanced and we became so expert in quick calculations in plus and minus, that strangers marveled.

I recall a very amusing incident of an unusually cold and blustery day when there were seven of us at it. At least it amused all save one, whose identity will not be revealed here. We were playing the third hole, immediately along the meadows across which a chill wind was blowing. The player in question had been fortunate enough to stick his second iron within four feet of the pin but he was equally unfortunate in having a little Negro caddie whose raiment was not suited to the rawness of the day. It was likewise unfortunate that it was this particular boy's turn to hold the tin. Everybody else was down in par 4. The putt for the "bird" would yield twelve balls. Just as he started his putt, his caddie shivered and shook the tin to rattling, a circumstance which resulted in the ball missing the cup by a good margin and slipping by for another three feet. The unhappy man glared at the shaking offender and exclaimed: "You vagabond!" And then as this seemed to fall a bit short of its purpose, he added with greater emphasis: "You black vagabond!" Then he turned to putt again. He had just missed collecting from all and if he failed again he would be forced to pay out six balls. All this while the boy had been turning things over in his mind. Without a doubt the thrust was direct for all the other caddies were white, and then, too, it evidently was uncomplimentary. Suddenly his valorous self rebelled and through chatter teeth he suddenly yelped: "No suh, I ain't." No doubt the defense was properly intended but it came at a most unfortunate instant, just as his employer was endeavoring to hole a three-footer for a half, which he did not register.

A small Negro saw fire in the eye of the stricken man and immediately he dropped the bag and started to leg it for the remote clubhouse. Soon, hard in his wake, followed his man, bellowing for him to stop. The boy, convinced that murder would attend any tarrying on his part, clutched into high and was last seen disappearing down the Pleasantville Road. And, all that our hero wanted was his return to duty. He did not fancy carrying his own kit for the remainder of the day, and that black vagabond was the last caddie at Northfield.

How I Began to Play Golf

FRANCIS OUIMET

An American golf legend born in Brookline, Massachusetts, Francis Ouimet won the 1913 U.S. Open in a classic three-way playoff and captured two U.S. Amateur Championships in 1914 and 1931. He was also a member of the Walker Cup team as a player from 1922 to 1936, and a captain from 1936 to 1949. Ouimet is considered one of the key figures in the popularizing of golf in the U.S.

"Big brothers" have a lot of responsibility in life, more than most of them realize. "Little brother" is reasonably certain to follow their example, to a greater or lesser degree, hence the better the example set, the better for all concerned. My own case is just one illustration. Whether I was destined to become a golfer anyway, I cannot say; but my first desire to hit a golf ball, as I recall, arose from the fact that my older brother, Wilfred, became the proud possessor of a couple of golf clubs when I was five years old, and at the same time I acquired the idea that the thing I wanted most in the world was to have the privilege of using those clubs.

Thus it was that, at the age of five, my acquaintance with the game of golf began. To say that the game has been a wonderful source of pleasure to me might lead the reader to think that the greatest pleasure of all has been derived from winning tournaments and prizes. I can truthfully say that nothing is further from the truth. Of course, I am pleased to have won my fair share of tournaments; I appreciate the honor of having won the national open championship; but the winning is absolutely secondary. It is the game itself that I love. Of all the games that I have played and like to see played, including baseball, football, hockey, and tennis, no other, to my mind, has quite so many charms as golf—a clean and wholesome pastime, requiring the highest order of skill to be played successfully, and a game suitable alike for the young, the middle-aged, and the old.

The first "golf course" that I played over was laid out by my brother and Richard Kimball in the street in front of our home on Clyde Street, Brookline, Massachusetts, a street which forms the boundary of one side of the Country Club property. This golf course, as I call it, was provided by the town of Brookline, without the knowledge of the town's officials. In other words, my brother and Kimball simply played between two given points in the street. With the heels of their shoes they made holes in the dirt at the base of two lampposts about one hundred and twenty yards apart, and that was their "course."

Nearly every afternoon they played, and I looked on enviously. Once in a while they let me take a club and try my hand, and then was I not delighted! It made no difference that the clubs were nearly as long as I was and too heavy for me to swing, or that the ball would only go a few yards, if it went at all. After all, as I look back, the older boys were only dealing me scanty justice when they occasionally allowed me to take a club, for when they lost a ball, I used to go searching for it, and, if successful, they always demanded its return. In the case of such a demand from two older boys, it is not always wise to refuse.

"Big brother" was responsible for getting me interested in golf; "big brother" likewise was in great measure responsible for keeping me interested. On my seventh birthday, he made me a birthday present of a club—a short brassy. Here was joy indeed! Not only had I now a club all my own with which to practice, but I already had amassed a private stock of seven or eight golf balls. The way this came about was that the journey from my house to school (this school, by the way, had only eight pupils in it, and the schoolhouse was built in Revolutionary days) took me past the present sixth hole of the Country Club course, and I generally managed to get a little spare time to look for lost golf balls.

Some boys do not like to get up early in the morning. Any boy or girl who becomes as interested in golf as I was at the age of seven, will have no difficulty on that score. It was my custom to go to bed at eight o'clock, and then get up by six o'clock the next morning, and go out for some golf play before time to get ready for school. The one hole in the street where my brother and Richard Kimball first played had now been superseded by a more exacting golf layout in a bit of pasture land in back of our house.

Here the older boys had established a hole of about one hundred and thirty yards that was a real test for them, and, at first, a little too much for me. On the left, going one way, the ground was soft and marshy, an easy place to lose a ball. If the ball went on a straight line from the tee, it generally went into a gravel pit, which had an arm extending out to the right. There also was a brook about a hundred yards from the tee, when the play was in this same direction. Here, then, was a hole requiring accuracy; and I cannot but think that a measure of what accuracy my game now possesses had its foundation back in those days when I was so young and just taking up the game. I believe, moreover, that any boy or girl who becomes interested in golf should not pick out the easy places to play at the start, simply because they like the fun of seeing the ball go farther.

What bothered me most, in those days, was the fact that I could not drive over that brook going one way. The best I could do was to play short of the brook, and then try to get the second on the improvised green. Every now and then, I became bold enough to have another try to carry the brook, though each time it was with the knowledge that failure possibly meant the loss of the ball in the brook, in a time when one ball represented a small fortune. At last came the memorable morning when I did manage to hit one over the brook.

If ever in my life a shot gave me satisfaction, it was that one. It did more—it created ambition. I can remember thinking that if I could get over the brook once, I could do it again. And I did do it again—got so I could do it a fair proportion of my tries. Then the shot over the brook, coming back, began to seem too easy, for the carry one way was considerably longer than the other. Consequently I decided that for the return I would tee up on a small mound twenty-five to thirty yards in back of the spot from which we usually played, making a much harder shot. Success brought increased confidence, and confidence brought desired results, so that, in course of time, it did not seem so difficult to carry the brook playing either way.

This was done with the old hard ball then generally known as the "gutty," made from gutta-percha. About this time I picked up, one morning, a ball which bounced in a much more lively fashion than the kind I had found previously. Now, of course, I know that it was one of the early makes of rubber-cored balls, but at that time, I simply knew that it would go much farther than the others, and that, above all things, I must not lose it. That ball was my greatest treasure. Day after day I played with it, until all the paint was worn off, and it was only after long searching that I managed always to find it after a drive.

Realizing that something must be done to retain the ball, I decided to repaint it, and did so with white lead. Next, I did something that was almost a calamity in my young life. To dry the white lead, I put the ball into a hot oven and left it there for about an hour. I went back thinking to find a nice new ball, and found what do you suppose? Nothing but a soft mass of gutta-percha and elastic. The whole thing simply had melted. The loss of a brand-new sled or a new pair of skates could not have made me grieve more, and I vowed that in the future, no matter how dirty a ball became, I would never put another into a hot oven to dry after repainting.

All this time I had been playing with the brassy that Brother gave me, and all my energies were devoted to trying to see how far I could hit the ball. My next educational step in play came when Wilfred made me a present of a mashy, whereupon I realized that there are other points to the game than merely getting distance. Previous practice with the brassy had taught me how to hit the ball with fair accuracy, so that learning something about mashy play came naturally. Being now possessed of two clubs, my ambitions likewise grew proportionately. The cow pasture in back of our house was all right enough, as far as it went, but why be so limited in my surroundings? There was the beautiful course of the Country Club across the street, with lots of room and smoother ground; nothing would do but that I should play at the Country Club. I began going over there mornings to play, but soon discovered that the groundskeeper and I did not hold exactly the same views concerning my right to play there. Whatever argument there was in the matter was all in favor of the groundskeeper. Of course I know now that he only did his duty when he chased me off the course.

While my brother's interest in golf began to wane, because football and baseball became greater hobbies with him, other boys in our neighborhood began to evince an interest in it, until it became a regular thing for three or four of us to play in the cow pasture after school hours and most of the day Saturday. We even had our matches, six holes in length, by playing back and forth over the one-hundred-and-thirty-yard hole three times, each using the same clubs. We even got to the point where we thought it would add excitement by playing for balls, and one day I found myself the richer by ten balls. But let me add that it is a bad practice for boys. There is too much hard feeling engendered.

As we became more proficient in play, we began to look over the ground with an eye to greater distance and more variety, until finally we lengthened out the original hole to what was a good drive and pitch for us, about two hundred and thirty yards; likewise we created a new hole of about ninety yards, to play with the mashy. From the new green, back to the starting point, under an old chestnut tree, was about two hundred yards, which gave us a triangle course of three holes. In this way we not only began gradually to increase the length of our game, but also to get in a great variety of shots.

As I look back now, I become more and more convinced that the manner in which I first took up the game was to my subsequent advantage. With the old brassy I learned the elementary lesson of swinging a club and hitting the ball squarely, so as to get all the distance possible for one of my age and physical make-up. Then, with the mashy, I learned how to hit the ball into the air, and how to drop it at a given point. I really think I could not have taken up the clubs in more satisfactory order. Even to this day, I have a feeling of confidence that I shall be sure to hit the ball cleanly when using a brassy, which feeling probably is a legacy from those old days.

And a word of caution right here to the boy or girl, man or woman, taking up the game: do not attempt at the start to try to hit the ball as far as you have seen some experienced player send it. Distance does not come all at once, and accuracy is the first thing to be acquired.

The first time that I had the pleasure of walking over a golf course without the feeling that, at any moment, I should have to take to my heels to escape an irate greenskeeper was when I was about eleven years old. I was on the Country Club links, looking for lost golf balls, when a member who had no caddy came along and asked me if I would carry his clubs. Nothing could have suited me better. As this member was coming to the first tee, I happened to be swinging a club, and he was kind enough to hand me a ball, at the same time asking me to tee up and hit it.

That was one occasion in my golfing career when I really felt nervous, though by this time I had come to the point where I felt reasonably confident of hitting the ball. But to stand up there and do it with an elderly person looking on was a different matter. It is a feeling which almost any golfer will have the first time he tries to hit a ball before some person or persons with whom he had not been in contact previously. I can remember doubting that I should hit the ball at all, hence my agreeable surprise in getting away what, for me, was a good ball.

Evidently the gentleman, who was not an especially good player himself, was satisfied with the shot, for he was kind enough to invite me to play with him, instead of merely carrying his clubs. He let me play with his clubs, too. That was the beginning of my caddying career. Some of the other members, for whom I carried clubs occasionally, made me a present of some clubs, so that it was not long before my equipment contained not only the original brassy and mashy, but also a cleik, mid-iron, and putter.

Needless to say, they were not all exactly suited to my size and style of play; yet to me each one of them was precious. I took great pride in polishing them up after every usage. The second time I played with the gentleman who first employed me as caddy, I had my own clubs. I had the pleasure of playing with him two years later, after he came home from abroad, in which round I made an eighty-four, despite a nine at one hole.

All this time, my enthusiasm for the game increased, rather than diminished, so that, during the summer of 1906, I was on the links every moment that I could be there until school opened in September; after which I caddied or played afternoons and Saturdays until the close of the playing season.

The Education of a Competitor

BOBBY JONES

Considered by many as the greatest golfer of all time, Bobby Jones collected thirteen major championships in his brief eight-year career—all while remaining an amateur. His dominance reached its peak in his final year of competition when he won the U.S. Open, British Open, U.S. Amateur, and British Amateur, then known as the Grand Slam of Golf. Upon his retirement at age twenty-eight, Jones remained active in golf, making several instructional films and was a key figure in the creation of the Masters in 1934. The following piece is from Jones' classic, Golf Is My Game.

Many times I have been asked why I retired from competition in golf, but no one has ever asked how I got into the thing in the first place. Perhaps this is just as well, for there were reasons for quitting and none for starting. The beginning just began, as it often does.

In my view, competitive golf has never been a term to be extended to sectional and local tournaments. These are fun affairs, pure and simple, and take place in an atmosphere relatively free of strain. To me, competition means the National Championships, Open and Amateur, both in America and in Great Britain. Yet the tournament which set me off into National competition was the Georgia State Championship of 1916, and I think this tournament marked the beginning of my taste for and appreciation of real competition in golf.

I think it may be said that I was of the second generation in this country, having the opportunity to grow up in the game. Francis Ouimet perhaps belonged to the first. I do not mean to imply that Francis is old enough to have been my father. Actually, our ages are only eight years apart. But he was born about the time the first golf clubs were brought to America and the game began to take root there and I was born in the exact year marking the advent of the rubber-cored ball.

When I was playing around the East Lake course as a child, there were only two or three golf courses in Atlanta, where now the number is nearer twenty, and there were only half a dozen or so kids our age interested in the game at all.

Almost as soon as I was to be trusted to play a round of golf on the course under my own responsibility, I began playing regularly with Perry Adair, the son of one of my father's good friends, who was about three or four years my senior. Perry, quite naturally, came along faster than I did; and by the time he was fifteen he was one of the best amateur golfers in the South. But I grew up a little faster physically than did Perry; and by the time I was thirteen I could hold my own with him quite well. At that time, in the invitation tournaments around the South he and I were among the most favored competitors.

The first tournament I played in away from home was the Montgomery, Alabama, Invitation in the year 1915, when I was thirteen years of age. Perry won this tournament, and I lost in the finals of the second flight to a left-handed player, which I considered at the time the ultimate disgrace. Later that year, however, Perry and I met in the second round of the invitation tournament in Birmingham, and I beat him and went on to win the tournament.

In the following year—1916—Perry beat me in Montgomery, but I won from him in the final of the Invitation at East Lake, and won a couple more tournaments in which Perry had been beaten by other players. At the end of this season we found ourselves again opposed to one another in the final of the Georgia State at the Capital City Club in Atlanta.

Up to this moment, despite the fact that I had won two out of the three matches in which Perry and I had met, I still considered that he was the better golfer. I looked up to him and thought that I had managed to win from him a couple of times mainly by accident. It was in this match at Brookhaven over thirty-six holes that I finally gained confidence in myself and in my game.

In the morning round I think I must have been tense, over-anxious, and perhaps a little bit resigned. At any rate I played some pretty sloppy golf and came in for lunch three down. While I was having a few practice putts prior to the start of the afternoon round, the tournament chairman came up to me and asked that I play out the bye holes, with the obvious inference that Perry would beat me several holes before the finish, and he wanted the gallery to have the privilege of seeing a full eighteen holes of play. I replied that I would, without calling his attention to what I considered to be a rather obvious and unpleasant implication. Nevertheless, it appeared that he was right when I began the afternoon round by hooking my tee shot out of bounds and losing the first hole with a scrambling six, thus becoming four down.

But at this point I remember to this day that my whole attitude changed completely. Instead of being on the defensive and uncertain, I began to play hard, aggressive golf, hitting the ball with all the force at my command and striving to win hole after hole, rather than to avoid mistakes.

After halving the short second hole in three, I drove to the edge of the green on the third hole—something I had never done before—and from then on hit the ball as hard as I had ever hit it in my life. Perry played reasonably well, but he missed a couple of putts, notably on the eighth and tenth greens and I finally won the match on the last green two up. I had played the eighteen holes in seventy, with a six at the first.

This was the match which gained for me my first opportunity to play in a National Championship, and also gave me what assurance I needed to enjoy taking advantage of it. I think what did most for me was Perry's remark as he put my ball into my hand on the last green. With understandable disregard for grammar, he had muttered, "Bob, you are just the best."

A few days later my father told me that Mr. Adair had come to him to say that he had planned to take Perry to the National Amateur Championship at Philadelphia, and would like to have me go along with them. Thus was I started into National competition.

Until that very moment, however, I am sure that I had never given even one thought to ever playing in a National Championship. I remember waiting on the front steps of our home at East Lake for my father to bring back the afternoon paper, so that I could find out how Francis Ouimet had fared in his play-off for the National Open with Vardon and Ray. And I had read with much interest of Bob Gardner's winning the Amateur Championship the year before at Detroit; but somehow it had never occurred to me that I might one day be playing in tournaments of this kind.

It must be admitted that golf in those days was very little like golf today, especially in big-time competition. In 1915, when the Southern Amateur Championship had been played at East Lake, the two ultimate finalists—Nelson Whitney and Charlie Dexter—had tied for the medal with eighty-one. It is fairly revealing of the quality of golf in those days that Perry at the age of sixteen, and I at the age of thirteen should have been among the top competitors for the Southern Championship. Granting all possible precocity on the part of us both, one had to admit that we were so prominent because most other competitors had learned to play golf after reaching maturity. In the same manner most of them had perforce learned to drive automobiles after reaching maturity, and few of them ever attained the facility with a motor car easily acquired by members of my generation who more or less grew up at the wheel.

This was true not only in the South, but, as was attested by the play at Merion, throughout the rest of the country as well. My first qualifying round on the West Course at Merion was a fair seventy-four, but my second was an eighty nine, for a total of 163, and yet I qualified easily.

Since my seventy-four on the easier West Course had led all

morning play, I was thus cast in the limelight at once. My eighty-nine in the afternoon before a considerable gallery probably convinced everyone that they had seen the last of the fourteen-year-old kid from Dixie. But I won in the first round from Eben Byers, a former champion, and from Frank Dyer, the Pennsylvania champion, in the second round. Dyer had been considered by many to be a possible winner of this tournament. In this second match, moreover, I had been five down through the first six holes, but had come on to even the match in the morning and win on the sixteenth green in the afternoon. So when I met Bob Gardner, the defending champion, in the third round, the match attracted quite a bit of interest. Although I had no such thoughts at the time, I have since had emotions of sympathy for Bob Gardner on that day, and at the same time admiration for the gallant and courtly way in which he met and handled what must have been a very difficult situation.

Gardner was a tall, handsome, athletic young man who looked every bit the champion he was. He had even held the world record for the pole vault a few years before when he was at Yale. His victory in the Amateur Championship the year before had been his second, and he was now in quest of his third title.

On the other side was I, a pudgy school kid of fourteen, playing in my first National Championship. I was wearing my first pair of long pants, and I owned one pair of golf shoes, a pair of old army issue into which I myself had screwed some spikes.

Gardner was a good six feet; I a bare five feet four.

I have often thought since how little I should have relished being asked to play against such a kid in a National Championship. Truly, I realize now, as no one seemed to then, that all the advantage was on my side. What could I care about who my opponent was? I was having the time of my life, with nothing to lose, and thinking of nothing to gain except playing golf. And I was doing that about as well as anyone in the tournament.

Anyway, we had a really good match; not flawless golf exactly, but good and bad. Gardner messed up the first two holes and handed me a two-up lead; he took these back, then went ahead himself; then came my turn, and I was again two up at the seventeenth. But Bob won the eighteenth, and we went to lunch with me one up.

Of course, that was enough to bring out the crowd for the afternoon round, which I began, as Gardner had in the morning, by losing the first two holes, putting me once more a hole behind.

The fourth hole was mine, but Gardner won the fifth, so that I was again one down as we stood on the sixth tee. In the next three holes I experienced as much excitement as I can remember on a golf course. All that registered at the time was the excitement, and perhaps frustration, because I hadn't yet thought of anything such as a golfing career. But I have since looked back on that little stretch and realized how unfortunate it might have been for me had things happened differently on those three holes.

Here is the way Grantland Rice described this sequence in his column the next day:

> After the fifth, there came three holes in succession that broke the kid's heart, and that would have broken the heart of almost any golfer alive.
>
> Coming to the sixth after the drives, Jones placed an iron within twelve feet of the pin. Gardner's second was ten feet above the green with a ridge to pitch over and a fast downhill slope awaiting his shot. No one believed he had even a chance to get the ball close, but by a wonderful recovery he stopped the chip shot within four inches of the hole and got a half in four.
>
> This was the first shock. The second came at the 210-yard seventh. Jones was on the green twenty feet away, while Gardner's long iron had carried over into the rough. Once more, he had to call upon his nerve and skill for another chip shot over a ridge to a fast, downhill slope, and this time the ball stopped only a foot from the cup for another half.
>
> But the kid was still fighting. At the eighth, he was on the green ten feet from the cup in two. Gardner's second struck the back of the green and bounded well over upon a neighboring tee. He had saved two holes, but how could anyone save this situa-

tion? No one but a champion could. This time, Gardner pitched back fifteen feet beyond the cup, but he sank his putt for a par four, getting another half.

As ever, Grant's description was accurate. Even so, words simply could not describe the amazing quality of these recoveries. Because of the severity of the slopes and the speed of the shining greens, the first two at least were authentic miracles.

After all these years I remember exactly how I felt as I walked on to the ninth tee, and I remember exactly what I did. I felt that I had been badly treated by luck. I had been denied something that was rightly mine. I wanted to go off and pout and have someone sympathize with me, and I acted just like the kid I was. I didn't really try to hit the next tee shot, and I didn't really try on any shot thereafter. In short, I quit. Ten years later it might have been different, but it wasn't then.

It is the keen, poignant, and accurate recollection of this episode which has caused me so often to be thankful it happened just as it did. If I had won those three holes, or even two of them, I should probably have won the match. And, it is not inconceivable that I might even have won the tournament. I hadn't had any experience, but neither had I any fear or self-consciousness. There was no tougher competitor than Bob Gardner in the tournament. If I had beaten him, I might well have beaten the others.

Yet if I had won, what would have happened next? Not giving myself any the worst of it, I think I was a fairly normal kid of fourteen. But how many of us today can look back at ourselves at that age and be completely proud of the picture? I must admit that I had already become a bit cocky because of my golfing success in play against grown men. Had I won that championship, I should have been Amateur Champion for not only the next twelve months, but, because of the suspension of play for the period of the war, for three whole years. I shudder to think what those years might have done to me, not so much to my golf, but in a vastly more important respect, to me as a human being.

I think of some of these things today as I see fathers enraptured by precocious sports accomplishments of their offspring. To take pride in these things is normal, but let me admonish these fathers to be not too unhappy when their youngsters take a beating now and then. The chastisements are bound to come sometime. The boys will fare much better if they get some of this bitter taste early in the game.

All in the Day's Work

ELMER OSGOOD CAPPERS

Long associated with the Brookline Country Club, Elmer Cappers wrote a history of the club for its one hundredth anniversary. The details of this excerpt present a frozen-in-time snapshot of country-club life both before and after the Second World War.

Among the most inaccurate forecasts ever made to the Board of Governors was the one put forth back in 1947 when the Chairman of the Grounds Committee said, "It seems unlikely we have anything to worry about in regard to our elm trees being injured by the elm beetle." Only four years later President Jaques reported that twenty elms had been lost, owing to the ravages of Dutch elm disease. Subsequently even more elms had to be removed, most of them being taken down by the Town of Brookline Forestry Department. For years now the Club has had a tree-planting committee, and considerable sums have been spent on saving the remaining beautiful elms which give the grounds the appearance of an English estate, as once remarked by the well-traveled golfer Gary Player. The Tree Committee has supervised and continues to supervise the planting of trees and shrubs, a number having been donated as memorials to various former members. There is an interesting memorial to Dr. Langdon Parsons near one of the ponds. Several years before his death he had suggested, in his humorous way, that a willow tree should be planted near some green in memory of the many times he had wept over a missed putt. Friends have complied with his request.

By the beginning of 1951, activities at the Club were in full swing again and the effects of the war were rapidly diminishing. The membership rolls were fully restored. The totals at the end of 1951 were:

> Active   895
> Associate   132
> Junior   37
> Life   15
> Exempt   42
> Nonresident   68
> Army, Navy, Consular   5

There was a good waiting list.

The swimming pool was a great success. In its first year the Swimming Committee reported "the amazing total of 9565 individual swims and the house account shows an excellent increase." There has never been occasion since to doubt the great popularity of the swimming pool. A minor item of construction in 1951, the gift of forty-five members, a gift that has long given comfort and solace to weary golfers, curlers, and tennis players, was the creation of a bar and lounge in the locker building.

In February of the same year "Mr. Richard Button, World Championship Figure Skater, and Miss Tenley Albright, National Junior Ladies' Champion, skated before an appreciative audience" at the Club ponds. Many prominent figure skaters had developed their art on the Club ponds, but Miss Albright was probably the most famous. Between 1950 and 1956 she spent many hours skating at the ponds, often skating at night with her brother, Nile. In the course of her career she won five U.S. Singles Championships as well as other competitions at home and abroad. Her greatest achievement came in 1956 when she won the Olympic gold medal.

The year 1951 brought further fame to Francis Ouimet. *Golf*

World reported that on September 19th "the citizens of the historic golfing city of St. Andrew's, Scotland, were up early and off to the links. They did not wish to miss the ceremony at 8 A.M. when a cannon boomed as Francis Ouimet, the American, played himself in as the first foreigner to be elected Captain of the Royal & Ancient Golf Club of St. Andrew's. They witnessed a ceremony first enacted 197 years ago." As part of the proceedings the Captain has to drive a ball off the first tee before the gathered throng. "Ouimet's drive flew over Grannie Clark's wynd about 225 yards. It was retrieved by Arthur Speight, a bus driver. He was rewarded with a United States $5 gold piece instead of the traditional sovereign." The record does not say how an American obtained the five-dollar gold piece at a time when the United States banned ownership of gold by its citizens! The ball was of U.S. specifications. That night Ouimet wore his tail coat of red with the Queen Adelaide medal pinned on it. The medal was presented in 1838 by Her Majesty the Queen Dowager, Duchess of St. Andrew's, "to be worn by the Captain as president on all public occasions." A portrait of the new Captain with the medal showing prominently was painted in 1952 by Thomas E. Stephenson. Copies of it are to be found in many an American golf club or golf museum. The fine copy that hangs in the Club's grill room was presented by Mr. William H. Danforth of Wellesley.

The series of honors given Francis Ouimet would have turned the head of a lesser man, but he remained as always the splendid, modest, friendly gentleman who did not look upon himself as being different from anyone else. In 1949 the Massachusetts Golf Association further honored him by starting the Ouimet Caddie Scholarship Fund; it still carries on in his name. On the evening of April 18, 1952, the Club gave a dinner in celebration of his election to the Captaincy of the Royal and Ancient and presented to him The Country Club gold medal "in friendship and admiration." At the same time he was made an honorary member of the Club.

In the century of the Club's existence only four individuals have been elected honorary members. They were J. Murray Forbes, William Cardinal O'Connell, G. Herbert Windeler (for one year), and finally Francis D. Ouimet. It should be recorded that beginning in World War I and continuing until 1955 the Commanding General of the First Corps Area and the Admiral of the First Naval District were invited to become honorary members if they so desired, but this was primarily in recognition of the offices they held.

On December 1, 1952, Herbert Jaques retired as President, and Henry K. White was elected to succeed him. Mr. Jaques did not live to enjoy his retirement long as he died the following April 30th at the age of sixty-four. His obituary stated that his death was caused by a sudden heart attack. It described him as a prominent industrialist and a former track star at Harvard. He had competed in the famous meets between the Harvard-Yale team and the Oxford-Cambridge team. The resolution passed by the Board of Governors spoke of the days when he had come as a boy with his father to practice on the track "which had been his training ground for the running at which he had been so preeminent." By a general subscription among the members a sizable sum was raised to construct in his memory the outdoor dining terrace where pleasant summer meals are served.

The first United States Golf Association event to be held at The Country Club after World War II was the National Junior Girls Championship. It was held between August 17th and 21st, 1952. After watching some of the girls at practice, Russ Hale, the Club pro, told one reporter, "I'm amazed at the way these girls [all under seventeen] can play golf." He had further cause for amazement when three of the young ladies brought in identical scores of seventy-seven in the qualifying round. From then on it was match play, and very shortly all three medalists were eliminated. In the final, Miss Millie Myerson, a sixteen-year-old Los Angeles player, won the title by defeating Holly Jean Roth of Milwaukee 4 and 2. Once the match started she was never headed or tied. It was only the fifth annual tournament for girls.

At the Club's annual meeting in December of 1953 President White referred to the death of Herbert Jaques and of Richard Floyd, the Club Secretary for many years. He referred to another great loss to the Club in the resignation of Harold Pierce after twenty-seven years as Chairman of the Golf Committee, remarking that "he has brought prestige to the Club not only in this country but also in England and Scotland." It would not have been proper for him to mention at that time the iron hand with which "Hal" Pierce ruled the Club's golf course. Two years before his resignation he had been given a silver tray engraved with an outline of the entire Club property showing all buildings and athletic areas and the golf course in detail. When he died in 1958 it was found that his will left the tray to the Club, and it is still among the Club's trophies. The will had another and rather touching clause: all his golf clubs were to be distributed among the caddies.

Rising costs continued to force increases in dues, although they were small ones. At a special meeting in June of 1954 dues went up thirty dollars, and a small assessment was voted. That fall further expenses were caused by two hurricanes, "Carol" and "Edna." All utilities were completely interrupted for a total of eleven days.

A minor problem of the next year (1955) arose in connection with the Jaques Room. Many of the members wanted to have an entrance made from that room to the main parlor and rearrange things so that it might be possible for men and women in sports clothes to use the Jaques Room as a cocktail lounge. It took a special meeting to get the change approved. The vote was one hundred and thirty-two in favor and thirty-seven against. Some of the men did not want women so near the men's grill, some were allergic to change, and some did not approve the six-thousand-dollar expenditure required by the innovation. As late as 1958 the Board carried out the wishes of the Old Guard by refusing to accede to the request that ladies in shorts be allowed to use the living room or main dining room. The rule is still in effect for ladies and men as well.

And now the matter of how best to celebrate the forthcoming seventy-fifth anniversary of the Club in 1957 came up for discussion. Someone suggested that a book be published bringing the fifty-year history up to date, but the idea was voted down on the ground that it would be too expensive and moreover "the lack of new material since 1932 would not make the effort worthwhile." Instead it was voted to arrange with the United States Golf Association to hold the National Amateur Championship Tournament in September of 1957 in recognition of the anniversary. A further reason for holding the tournament at The Country Club was that it had not been held in New England since it was held at The Country Club in 1934.

With the National Amateur less than two years away, the Club suddenly was faced with two problems that might affect the golf course. The first was an announcement by six members of the ground personnel that they had voted to join a union. Subsequent steps resulted in the formation of such a union and the signing of a contract running through September 30, 1957, by which time the Amateur Tournament would be over. Actually the union did not have a long life; when its membership dropped to three it was dissolved. The other problem was that a notice had been received from Norfolk County and the Town of Brookline that there would be a land taking of twenty-nine thousand square feet near the 17th green and 18th tee in order to widen Clyde Street. After a visitation by members of the Club, the town fathers kindly agreed to postpone the taking until after the tournament. In the spring of 1958 the taking became effective, the green and tee were relocated, and the town paid $21,000 in damages.

In February of 1956 a potential problem which turned out to be not a problem came with the resignation of Luther Grimes, manager for sixteen years. He was replaced by Harold T. Hueber who capably managed the clubhouse affairs during the tournament. He held the position of manager for twenty-three years.

Two 1956 items of interest were, first, the donation of several beautiful pieces of English china with golfing scenes painted on them; the china had once been owned by Harry Vardon and was given by him to Mr. John Hylan who in turn donated it to the Club's trophy cabinet where it is on display today. The other item was the adoption of the present Country Club green coat with its primrose squirrel emblem. Members could buy the jackets then for fifty-five dollars.

On October 22, 1956, the Board of Governors entered in its

records a resolution noting the death of A. Winsor Weld. Born on July 12, 1869, he had joined the Club in 1902. He became Secretary in 1909 and served in that capacity under four Presidents until he himself was elected the Club's eighth President in 1933, which office he filled until 1944. "His thirty-five years of service as an officer of the Club were the longest in its history."

The great event of 1957 at the Club was, of course, the United States Golf Association Amateur Tournament. Charles Devens was appointed Chairman, and serving as Honorary Chairmen were Francis Ouimet and Harold Pierce. Newspaper cartoonists had great fun with the Devens straw boater, which he sported whenever he walked about the course in connection with his duties. Much was made of Ouimet's record in prior National Amateur Tournaments. Many remembered his great victory in the 1934 Open, but not everyone recalled that he had also been National Amateur Champion in 1914 and 1931, one of the few to have won twice and the only one to have achieved a second victory seventeen years after the first.

A newspaper item stated a week before the tournament that "several members of The Country Club are threatening to sue the Club for the loss of privileges for two weeks while the course will be closed to members." John English of the United States Golf Association when told of the contemplated action commented, "This often happens but when the championship has come and gone, everybody relaxes and the air clears nicely." He was an accurate prophet.

To achieve greater length, important changes were made in the course layout. Three of the holes on the old course were dropped and three new ones were added from the Primrose course. For those who are interested, it is recorded here that holes number 1, 2, and 4 were eliminated. The holes were played in the following order, beginning at number 10 (the Maiden): 10, 9, 3, 5, 6, 7, 8, 11, 12 and 13; then the 1st and 2nd Primrose were combined to make one hole followed by 8 and 9 Primrose; then back to the old course to conclude with 14 through 18.

There were two hundred entrants who teed off on September 9th for the championship, which was contested entirely at match play beginning with a blind draw. All matches were to be for eighteen holes except that the semifinal and final rounds would be for thirty-six holes. The winner would receive a gold medal and the runner-up a silver medal.

Billy Joe Patton was picked by many as the favorite, but he was defeated early along with three other outstanding players: Jesse Guilford, Ted Bishop, and Chick Evans. Evans was sixty-seven years old. In the fourth round a former Junior Champion, Jack Nicklaus, lost to Richard Yost, 3 up and 2 to play. Looking back from Nicklaus's present preeminent position in the world of golf, it almost seems that one reporter was quite disrespectful in speaking of him with the diminutive sobriquet of "Jackie." The writers in describing the fourth round match between Yost and Nicklaus said that "birdies were flying in all directions."

The four semifinalists were all members of the American Walker Cup team: Dr. Frank Taylor, E. Mason Rudolph, Hillman Robbins, Jr., and Rex Baxter, Jr. The finalists were Taylor and Robbins. Dr. Taylor, a dentist in Pomona, California, was forty years old. One of his claims to fame was that he had done a fair amount of work on General Eisenhower's teeth just before the Normandy invasion. Hillman Robbins, Jr., twenty-five years old and an Air Force lieutenant, came from Memphis, Tennessee. A very slight figure, he weighed only one hundred and thirty-five pounds when the tournament ended, having lost almost a pound a day, with the biggest loss coming on the last day when the temperature was in the nineties.

Before a crowd of five thousand Robbins defeated Taylor 5 up and 4 to play. On the completion of the morning eighteen holes, Taylor had an advantage of one hole, but he could not keep it in the afternoon round. Taylor had bad luck at the 31st hole (9th Primrose). He would have done well to memorize the description of the hole in the program which contained this sentence: "A straight drive is important here for woods on the left and a pond on the right await any shot off line." His drive landed in the mud on the rim of the pond; a diligent and lengthy search failed to discover it, and Dr. Taylor was teetering on the edge of defeat. It came at the next hole, the par five 32nd (the old 14th) where Hillman Robbins rolled a fifteen-foot putt downhill for a birdie. The roar of the crowd told that the tournament was over.

President Henry White in speaking of the tournament said, "There was some question as to the adequacy of such an old course for the modern golfer even though lengthened by the use of three Primrose holes and whether the Boston area would support an amateur golf championship. As to the latter the crowds were the largest since the Bob Jones era." *Golf World* said, "Financially and socially the event was a great success. The Club which has furnished six United States Golf Association presidents, which scrutinizes applicants for membership closely, and does not worry over the fact that two score weekend golfers are a large number, did its utmost to make things pleasant for freight-payers and others." The final accolade came from Herbert Warren Wind and it answered President White's comment about the adequacy of the course: "The Amateur has been held on several excellent courses since the war, but it's really doubtful if any of them are as ideal for match play as the honored old holes of The Country Club which with their rugged fairways and their amazing variety of perched, canted and contoured greens demand shot-making that is both full-blooded and tidy every step of the way." Many, many players agree thoroughly with that description. The Board of Governors were well pleased with the net profit of thirty-four hundred dollars, instead of the loss they had been prepared to accept.

At the end of 1957 President White resigned, and Samuel H. Wolcott, Jr., who had been Secretary, was elected to succeed him. He was faced with the many continuing problems which never seemed to get solved. Members would on occasion take pictures at the Club and publish them without permission. This was always frowned on by the Board and reprimands were forthcoming. The fence on Clyde Street was a long fence and it seemed to be a constant target of speeding automobiles; the President had to ask for appropriations to mend it. The old difficulty with water standing after heavy rainfall at certain areas within the racetrack oval bothered the management but never troubled the seagulls who appeared to think it was arranged for their benefit. At this remove of time it may seem slightly amusing that nonmembers were crossing the Primrose fence to shoot ducks on the ponds, but President Wolcott could say with Queen Victoria, "We are not amused," as he brought up the matter of policing to stop the trespassing Nimrods. The ever-present problem of dues engaged the President's attention, and at the end of his first year in office he had to ask for an increase of thirty-five dollars in the basic dues of the Club. Another years-long problem, that of insufficient parking, was solved partially by blacktopping the old and unused tennis court area between the driveway and the swimming pool. The Golf Committee repeatedly brought up the question of allowing electric carts on the golf course, and at last in 1959 a member who could furnish a doctor's certificate to the effect that a cart was necessary for him to play golf was permitted to buy and use his own cart.

A more pleasant subject was the rental of curling ice to ambitious curlers from neighboring curling clubs and not just because of the income. For many years The Country Club curlers had fostered the introduction of curling at other clubs. The Country Club was by no means the founder of the game in New England, for even prior to the Civil War there were curling matches where "the Boston Public Garden pond now ripples." But in the matter of indoor curling on artificial ice The Country Club took precedence and was instrumental in "spreading the gospel" in the Northeast. A newspaper article by A. Linde Fowler, himself a curler, stated, "It was under the stimulus of Alex S. Porter of The Country Club that the old St. Andrew's Club of New York became interested enough to erect the first artificial ice rink in that state." Cuyler Stevens of the Ardsley Club wrote, "We consider ourselves as distantly related to curling at The Country Club since Bill Kimbel who founded our club was son-in-law of your distinguished member, Herbert Windeler." Nashua

Country Club's Don Ramsey made similar acknowledgment: "Here in your neighboring State of New Hampshire you have a curling family connection reared, educated and encouraged by The Country Club."

None of the clubs mentioned had rented the ice at Clyde Park. Beginning in 1950 Winchester Country Club curlers began to rent ice and continued to do so until 1954 when they built their own facility. Brae Burn later followed the same procedure, as did Wellesley and Weston after them. A happy result of this proliferation was the establishment of regular curling competitions between The Country Club and the neighboring clubs, such as the annual Angier and Wikstrom matches, although these newer clubs seem to take the measure of The Country Club curlers rather frequently.

In curling as in golf The Country Club has given leaders of importance to the national picture, having furnished five Presidents of the Grand National Curling Club of America: Alexander S. Porter, C. Campbell Patterson, Jr., Franklin King, Lucius T. Hill, and Henry K. Cushing.

The latest changes in the boundaries of the Club property were made by exchange of land with Melville P. Merritt near the 4th green and the 5th fairway and by purchase of land next to the Primrose course from Edward Dane. From a survey instigated by the Treasurer, Alfred S. Woodworth, it was discovered that The Country Club golfers had been trespassing for years on a strip of the Dane property. Both Mr. Merritt and Mr. Dane were members of the Club and completed the transactions on terms very favorable to the Club.

On December 5, 1960, President Wolcott announced to the Board of Governors that it was possible the United States Golf Association might be receptive to an invitation to hold the National Open Tournament at The Country Club in 1963 on the fiftieth anniversary of Francis Ouimet's famous victory. If such an invitation were to be accepted, The Country Club would become involved in its most extensive undertaking in the field of sport since the Club was founded.

Yes, I Had a Reputation

GENE SARAZEN

Rising up from the caddie yard to become the first professional to win all four majors, Gene Sarazen is one of golf's all-time greats. His on-the-course heroics have been well documented—most notably his immortal double-eagle on the par-5 15th in the 1935 Masters. Off the course, his contributions have been almost as impressive. He invented the sand wedge, was the first to use the interlocking grip, and has written much about the game he helped usher into its modern era.

I sometimes think I was born a pro. I was a caddie when I was ten. Ed Sullivan and myself were caddie mates at Apawamis (Golf Club, Rye, New York). Ed became a newspaper columnist and was on television. He was number 98. I was 99. We stayed up on the hill until we were needed, then the caddie master, George Hoose, would yell up, "Nuuumber ninety-eight, nuuumber ninety-nine."

I always remember a time with Sullivan. You know, we went by the bag. If a guy had a new bag and a set of new clubs, you figured he had the dough, he's gonna give a good tip. So one time, up come these two bags. One had a brand new set of irons and woods, and the other one was a little Sunday bag with rusty clubs. The caddie master yelled out, "Next twooo." Sullivan could run like Nurmi in those days, and he outran me to get the good bag. When the players came up, one of them was a very attractive fellow—he had on white flannels and was wearing a gold key chain—and the other guy was a big, fat palooka. He was the police commissioner of New York, Enright; he had the new bag and clubs. I got hooked with this little Sunday bag and I said, "I'll get no tip here." Well, that bag belonged to Grantland Rice, and he and I became very intimate friends from that day until the day he died. Oh yes, he gave me a substantial tip that day.

You could say my caddie days were fun. I had great experiences, because the people you caddied for in those days were entirely different than today. You didn't hear the language you hear today. They were very high-class people. All college graduates. I learned a lot from them, from listening to them. I learned a lot about life. And I learned my golf in the caddie yard. We walked from Harrison to Rye to caddie, and had nine holes between which we made ourselves in empty lots along the way. There was nothing but big open fields then, between Harrison and Rye. But nobody gave me lessons. I used to watch the players, I'd go miles and miles to watch players in tournaments. My favorite golfer was Walter Hagen. I used to admire his ways, his technique, the way he would slash at the ball. And the way he dressed. He was my hero. He was still a great star when I began my playing career, and, yes, it was a great kick when I beat him in matches and tournaments.

In 1922, after I won the Open championship, the PGA championship came along and Hagen wouldn't play in it because he was up in Buffalo playing an exhibition. I won that PGA, but Hagen hadn't been there, so somebody started up the World Championship Match between us. We played seventy-two holes, Hagen and I. He was five up on me at one time, but I managed to beat him three and two. We played Oakmont thirty-six holes, and Westchester-Biltmore thirty-six holes. That was the most grueling seventy-two holes I ever played in my life, because I had appendicitis and I took it for just a pain in the stomach. Well, when I got through playing at Westchester-Biltmore the pain got worse. I went up to my room and threw up, and I called one of these Park Avenue doctors and he said, "Oh, that's just nervous indigestion." So, finally, about three o'clock in the morning it got very serious and I called my friend Dr. Frank Landolfi, from Portchester, to come and see me. He examined me and first thing you know I'm on my way to the hospital in Yonkers. They got Joe Kirkwood, who was living at the Westchester-Biltmore, to help carry me down. When I got to the hospital Frank got a surgeon to operate on me right away. The appendix hadn't burst, but it was on the verge. That was a very dangerous event. In those days, a lot of people died from appendicitis, because they thought it was an upset stomach and would take a physical and that would burst it. Nobody knew then. So I won the World Championship by beating Hagen, but I couldn't play any exhibitions because I was recuperating. I couldn't take advantage of it.

But I had a more serious illness when I was younger. In 1916, when I was fourteen, I had empyema. That's pus in the pleural cavity—in your lungs. It was during the war, when I was working at Remington Arms in Bridgeport (Connecticut). I was the first case recorded where they sawed the rib, put in a tube, and blew a gallon of water in there to push that stuff out. Every morning. It was cleaned out, and then it started to heal. But it didn't look like I was going to make it at first. I was on the deathbed for four or five days. There was no such thing as sulfa drugs or anything then. I remember lying in the Bridgeport Hospital and these priests would come in and pull the curtain around. They figured I was going to go. That was in 1916, and in 1920, I could hardly break 80.

Two years later I won the U.S. Open and the PGA championship. How do I account for that? Well, I was young and could get my strength back quickly. Otherwise, I think it was because I had a lot of spirit and fight in me. I was fearless. It might have been because I had been so close to death as a boy. What could scare me on a golf course? Nothing. I'll never forget playing the last hole at Skokie in the '22 Open. I hit a good drive, and for my second there was water to the left and out on bounds to the right. My caddie wanted me to play safe, but I heard somebody say Jones and Mehlhorn were right back of me and I said, "Oh, hell, give me that brassie." I shot right for the green and put it about 12 feet from the hole. On the seventeenth Jones hit it out of bounds, and I won by a stroke.

Of course, I was a great chipper and putter at that time. That helped. I was a bold putter, and when I practiced putting, I hit just three-footers, not ten- or twelve-footers, because I didn't expect to hole them. But I was not a great hitter of the ball, I had a bad grip. My right hand was way underneath, and once or twice in every seventy-two holes I would hook one out of bounds. That's why after I won those two championships I sort of went to pieces. I had that bad grip, and it caught up with me.

Well, I decided I had to do something about the right hand. Instead of having it underneath, I had to put it up like Jones and Hagen had it. One day I was playing golf with Ty Cobb, and I asked him what he did to exercise his hands and arms. He said he had a heavy bat loaded with lead that he kept in his room and would swing. He gave me an idea. I took a golf club and made it into seventy-two ounces, and took it up to my farm in Germantown (New York). I would swing that club all the time. Finally, one day, I found myself playing in a tournament with the same grip Hagen and Jones had. You see, I couldn't hold on to that heavy club the other way, because my hand would twist when I swung it. But when I put the hand up on top, it didn't move. I swung that heavy club religiously. I had half a dozen of them made at Wilson's, and I would put them all over the farm and pick one up and swing it thirty or forty times, back and forth.

Another problem I had was the shot out of the bunker. That was one of my weakest shots. I lost several Opens because of it. So when I invented the sand iron I licked the sand, and I had licked the hook. In 1932 I knew I had it all. I was ready, and that year I won the U.S. and British Opens.

The idea for the sand iron came when I was taking flying lessons while I was living in Florida. I used to pal around with Howard Hughes, we played a lot of golf together. Hughes was a good golfer, by the way, about a three handicapper. Anyway, when I took off in the plane I pulled the stick back and the tail went down and the nose of the plane went up. Something flashed in my mind, that my niblick should be lowered in the back. So I had Wilson send me seven or eight niblicks. I went downtown in New Port Richey and bought all the solder I could get my hands on and put it on the clubs. What I did was put a flange on the back of the club and angled it so the flange hit the sand first, not the front edge, which was now raised. It was just like the airplane when it took off. Now I could hit behind the ball and explode it out. See, in those days we played out of the sand with a regular niblick, which didn't have a flange, and you had to chip the ball. You couldn't explode it, because the front edge of the club was sharp and would dig too much. Hagen was a terrible exploder. So was Jones . . . and Sarazen. Everybody was. When I first tried my new club I said, "My God . . ."

I spent hundreds of hours practicing that shot and getting the flange just right, and it got so I would bet even money I could go down in two out of the sand. When I went to the British Open in 1932 I practiced and played with the club and then put it under my coat and took it back to my room at night, because if the British had seen it before the tournament they would have barred it. Oh yes. In the tournament I went down in two from most of the bunkers.

There was a sand iron before mine, one with a concave face. That's the one Bob Jones used when he made his Grand Slam, won those four big tournaments in 1930. But in 1931 it was barred. At that time Horton Smith was connected with the Hagen Company, which made the club, and before you could get one of them you had to buy a whole set of Hagen irons. That's the demand it was in. When they found out you hit the ball twice with it, because of the concave face, they barred it. But I didn't get my idea from that club. Oh no. I couldn't hit the damn thing. It had a rounded back. In 1931 I invented the real sand iron. They couldn't bar it, because they'd have to bar all the irons. You see, everybody then came out with irons with a flange on all the irons, not just the sand iron. So they didn't do anything about it.

I learned to work on golf clubs in the first place at the Brooklawn Country Club in Bridgeport, Connecticut. I was a boy in the

shop. There were a couple of people at the club, the Wheeler brothers, and they took a fancy to me. When they came over in the spring
of the year looking at clubs, they'd always pick out the ones I worked
on. "Oh, I like that one there George," they'd say, and George, the
pro, would say, "Ahh no." George wasn't for the Italian boys.

Yes, it was tough for a little Italian. The Scots and the English
pros didn't much like us. I remember in 1922 at Skokie, Francis
Ouimet asked me to join him, Chick Evans and Jim Barnes for a
practice round. Barnes said he didn't want to play with me—"that
little guy," as he put it. Well, after I won that Open, there was a special match arranged to be played in New Jersey between the current
Open champion, me, and the previous one, which was Barnes. The
night before the match, Barnes asked me if I wanted to split the
purse, and I told him no, it's winner take all. I beat him six and five.

Yes, I had a reputation for being tough when I was young. You
had to be when you were Italian. When I was about sixteen years old
I used to look at my name—Saraceni—and it sounded and looked
like it should be on a violin, not a golf club. So I changed it around
a few different ways and came up with Sarazen. Then I looked in the
phone book and there was no Sarazen and I said, "Geez, that's
good." There's nobody in the world by the name S A R A Z E N. If
there is, now he copied it from me. Yeah, Saraceni was a violin
player.

My father was a carpenter. He became a contractor in this
country, but went broke two or three times because he got caught by
the First World War, then the Depression. He saw me play golf once,
when we lived in Pelham, New York, and the PGA championship
was being played there. I bought a house for my parents there. He
took a trolley car to the golf club and stayed outside the fence at the
tenth hole, which was near the road. He didn't come onto the
course, because he felt Italians weren't welcome and he would be uncomfortable. I was playing a fellow named Willie Campbell, and
had a forty-foot putt that I missed by about six inches. My father
said, "Can you imagine him being paid for missing things like that?"
He wanted me to be a carpenter. He kept all his old tools so they'd

be ready for me to take over. Like we do now with our grandchildren, we save our golf clubs for them and they don't want them. But I was a carpenter during the war, in 1914. I was building barracks in Yaphank, Long Island. The carpenters didn't like hammering nails, so they'd put the boards in place and say to me, "Hammer that, kid."

My first professional job was in Titusville, Pennsylvania. I was nineteen years old, and it really was my first time away from home. I remember I lived in the clubhouse and there was nobody there at night—just me—and when there was a thunder-and-lightning storm it was a scary place. There were two women there that cooked for the club, and they would cook all my meals. I have very, very pleasant memories of that place. But what happened. I used to go down to Pittsburgh and play in some of the tournaments and I met a man by the name of Emil Loeffler. He was the greenskeeper and pro at Oakmont Country Club. He thought I was a comer, and was instrumental in getting me a job at the Highland Country Club in Pittsburgh. So I left Titusville to go there. Well, my course wasn't ready so they let me play Oakmont and one day I played with Bill Fownes, who owned the course. This is in 1922, early in the year. After we played he said to Emil, "I want you to take this boy out to Skokie (Country Club) and let him practice." This was a month before the U.S. Open was going to be played there.

So we got to Chicago on a Saturday night and Sunday we went out to play, but the pro wouldn't allow us. Emil was very disturbed and called Mr. Fownes, who told him to stand by, he'd call right back. So Mr. Fownes called up Bob Gardner, who was a U.S. Amateur champion and a businessman in Chicago, and said to him, "See that this kid plays that course just once." So it was arranged. Oh, the pro was sore as hell. We went out, I looked the course over, and I knew what I had to do. I went back to Pittsburgh and wrote a card to Tom Kerrigan, the pro at Siwanoy, who was a good friend, saying that the course is built right around my game.

So I went to Skokie. I was staying out at the Edgewater Apartments. Bob Jones and Stewart Maiden were there too, and I was rooming with Leo Diegel. Well, after shooting two good rounds I went down into Chicago and had dinner with a guy by the name of Pietzcker. He was a photographer. He kept me out until twelve o'clock at night. I didn't even know how to find this apartment going back at night. Finally I got back and Diegel says, "You idiot, here you are almost in striking distance of the Open, and you're staying out this late." So I go to bed, get up the next morning and take a good shower and go out and shoot a 75. And I was lucky to be at 75. Then the next round that afternoon, I shot 68. So 145 and 143 made it 288 and I won.

I guess the sand iron would have to be one of the most important contributions I've made to golf. That was a big one. I think the club saves everybody six shots a round. But I also think the reminder grip was a great contribution, although it wasn't my idea. In 1931 I had trouble with my left hand, keeping it in the same position all the time. My grip would change and my thumb would go straight down the center of the shaft. So one day I was in Mr. Icely's office at the Wilson company and I saw this plug. I asked him what it was, and he said some fellow from Canada wanted Wilson to put it on their clubs. It was a wooden plug with a flat side that hit you on the pad of the left hand. It put the hand in the correct position, turned to the right. You couldn't hold it any other way. I said it looked like a pretty good thing and asked Mr. Icely if he would make me up a couple of sets with it. He was the president of the company. He did, and at first it was uncomfortable and I said it would never go. Then I began to see the fruit ripen. The ball would draw the same way every time. That meant my left hand was in the same position every time. By 1932 I had it perfected and they came out with it and, oh, it went wild. I remember after it was out for a while I was up in Canada and a fellow pulls up in a Rolls-Royce and comes over to me and says in an English accent, "Sarazen, I want to buy you a drink. You made me rich. I invented the reminder grip. I got a penny a grip."

Mind you, I didn't get a cent out of it, no more than I did with the sand iron, because in fine print in my contract with Wilson it said it all belonged to the company. I got nothing for the grip and I popularized it. They had to stop making it because of the labor costs. This was a tailor-made thing. You can't make it by machine. See, they had to stick it in the steel, line it up just right and put a rivet through it. If it didn't line up, it was bad.

My most satisfying achievement as a player? Winning all four of the modern major championships—the Masters, the U.S. Open, the PGA, and the British Open. I was the first one to do that. Ben Hogan was next to do it when he won the British Open in 1953. I won my only British Open in 1932 and I almost didn't get there. See, I was wiped out by the stock market crash like a lot of people were. So, no matter how much I made during the 20's, I was absolutely flat in 1930, '31. All my securities were worthless. That's why I had to work so hard on my game. I remember I had my eye on the British Open in 1932 and Mary, my wife, said I had my game just right and I ought to go over. I said, "How could I? We don't have any money to spend a thousand dollars." She said, "You're going to go. You've improved your sand shot and your grip. You should win." So she got me the tickets and I went over and won the championship. First prize was only £100, but it was the title that meant something. Then, in 1935, I won the Masters to complete the four victories. That's when I made the double-eagle which was just a lucky shot. It had to be luck.

Chapter Two

1949–1958

WHILE I WAS in the backyard doing a snake dance in my playpen—and trying to figure how to keep the peace with my two older brothers—Ben Hogan was coming back from the car crash that nearly killed him and was having one of the two best years of his life. But after that, golf, like the rest of America, was in transition. The euphoria of the war being over faded as the country got down to living the American Dream and found it wasn't all it was cracked up to be. Hogan, Sam Snead, and Jimmy Demaret, all moving into their forties, fought off or lost to one another or to a pack of no-names (Jack Fleck) and former dentists (Cary Middlecoff).

My mother, meanwhile, terrified by my German au pair and by the fact that she had three boys under the age of four, went from smoking ten cigarettes a day to two-and-a-half packs. Golf was not only her passion, but also her escape from the life everyone told her she was lucky to have, but about which she didn't quite feel the same way. She usually played two or three times a week, in Pelham and at different clubs around the New York metropolitan area, which she drove to in her wood-paneled station wagon. When my father turned thirty-five, he inherited a bunch of money and decided to retire to the golf course, which was where he was when he heard about the birth of his fourth child, my brother Chris. Dad was thrilled—another boy—but he'd had a good nine, so he decided to play in before going to the hospital.

Over the next years, we children were busy digging holes, playing cowboys and Indians, and watching *Davy Crockett* on television. I have a picture of my grandfather and me holding hands as we stand before the Alamo. I'm dressed in a tie and jacket and look like the saddest child in the world, because I'd just come to the awful realization that what I saw on television wasn't necessarily real. In Disney's *Davy Crockett,* the Mexicans needed ladders to climb the Alamo's high walls, when in fact my eight-year-old body could have easily climbed into the fort with a boost. It was one of my first disappointments. But golf on television was something else. The Open was first televised in 1954, nearly to the day my mother realized she was pregnant again.

Like many people who grew up with maids, I had and still have a strong attachment to black women. Our parents were disciplinarians, and we children were to be seen and not heard, but the black women who took care of us were our life. They taught us that no one was better than anyone else, that life was tough, and most important, how to express love. I knew nothing of their other lives until we began to spend Augusts in Virginia Beach. The club pro at Pelham had been the only adult we'd been allowed to call by his first name, but at the Princess Ann Country Club, the pro, Leo Kernan, was Mr. Kernan, hopefully said with a Southern drawl. Mr. Kernan was a robust man with straight white hair and patrician plantation looks. Problem for me was that he called all the black caddies "boy," no matter how old they were. Now, I knew from Pelham that caddies were from a different economic strata than we were, but other than that, there was no difference, except that they could, as my mother often said, be extremely vulgar. But Mr. Kernan's calling them "boy" separated them, made them lesser. And you could see the pain in their eyes. When I came across Edwin Bancroft Henderson's *The Negro in Sports* at the USGA's great library, I was surprised to learn that there actually were golf clubs for blacks, just as in Westchester there were golf courses for the Jews who weren't allowed in the WASP clubs.

My father spent the mid-Fifties at the country club, playing golf or gin rummy and drinking martinis. It didn't please my mother, but other than complain, there wasn't much she could do; the men's grill was off-limits to women and children, and it was my father's money they were spending. The goings-on in the men's grill and in the men's locker room, where many men seemed to spend their whole day, were as mysterious to me as my father himself. In J. P. Marquand's *Life at Happy Knoll,* pretty much the only old chestnut of golf I actually found interesting and amusing, I see into my father's world in a way I never had. Finally, perhaps worn down by my mother's harping, my father decided to work again. With grand ambitions, he bought up a lot of the land around Winged Foot country club and built high-end houses, figuring golfers would love to live around a golf course (good idea, bad timing). The best part for us was that whenever Hank, a strong black man who was my father's foreman on the project, came to our house, he picked us up and put us on his shoulders, two at a time, and gave us rides in the mud-caked Jeep they used on the construction site. Unfortunately, something I was too young to understand happened (the Eisenhower recession was the given excuse, though I'm sure it had something to do with my father's martini habit as well), and my father lost a good chunk of his cash.

Still, we kept living the good life, tarnished only by our very real dread of the Red Menace. After my father decided not to build a bomb shelter in the backyard—better dead than Red—I took it upon myself to write Nikita Khrushchev to let him know that I, in fact, would be happy to be his friend and that, if he took over America, he should look me up. One of the many golf books I found in the sunporch off my parents' bedroom and devoured was *Better Golf Without Practice,* which seemed to suit my ideas on life just fine. This step-by-step instruction classic by Alex J. Morrison tells how you can improve your game while sitting in your living room. It's not only informative and funny—it works.

My happy childhood ended when Arnold Palmer won his first Masters, not because Arnie won, but because I was taken out of Siwanoy, the public school I loved, and was sent kicking and screaming to the local Catholic school, which had been built in great part with my father's money.

The Negro in Sports: Golf

EDWIN BANCROFT HENDERSON

Edwin Bancroft Henderson has pioneered as an author and as a participant in the field of athletics. A native of Washington, D.C., he taught in that city's school system and also served on the board of directors for the Washington, D.C., NAACP. In 1939, he authored The Negro in Sports—*one of the first serious efforts to tell the story of the black athlete.*

NEGRO GOLFERS IN ACTION

Shortly after golf was introduced to America, a few Negroes began to play the game. The use of colored boys as caddies quickened the interest of younger men in golf. Not only did these boys pick up the fine points by apt imitation of the masters of the sport but learned much when many of the exclusive clubs would occasionally hold "caddy" matches. Some of the greatest of golfers today were the "caddy" boys of yesteryear.

Negro golfers find their best opportunity today largely on public courses. Golf courses were for many years almost exclusively private. The golf courses and accompanying club houses are expensive to own and maintain. In the last decade there has been a great growth in municipally owned golf courses. Colored golfers in the North and West have taken their turns on the courses with other Americans. In Baltimore and in Washington there are nine-hole courses for colored golfers. The first golf courses for Negroes were probably Mapledale at

Stowe in Massachusetts, the Asbury Park course, and the Sunset Hills at Kankakee, Illinois. There are a few country clubs operated or owned by Negroes that have nine-hole courses. Among them should be mentioned the Shady Rest Country Club of Westfield, New Jersey; the Sunset Hills Country Club of Kankakee, Illinois; and the Lincoln Country Club of Atlanta, Georgia.

Golf among Negroes is flourishing chiefly in the cities of New York, Philadelphia, Baltimore, Washington, Harrisburg, Atlanta, Jacksonville, Chicago, Cleveland, Detroit, St. Louis, Kansas City, Indianapolis and Los Angeles. Among the prominent clubs should be noted the St. Nicholas of New York City; the New Amsterdam of Palisades, New York; the Wolverine of Detroit; the Fairview of the City of Philadelphia; the Douglas Club of Lancaster; the Yorkshire Club of Pittsburgh; the Monumental of Baltimore; the Royal of Washington, D.C.; the Lincoln of Atlanta; the Trophy Club of Chicago; the Douglas Park of Indianapolis; the Apex Club of Atlantic City; the Keystone Club of Harrisburg; the Shady Rest Club of Westfield, New Jersey; the Cosmopolitan Club of Baltimore; the Forest City Golf Club of Cleveland; the Sunset Hills Club of Chicago; the West Coast Golf Club of Los Angeles. Most of these clubs are affiliated with the United Golfers' Association, the national organization.

UNITED GOLFERS' ASSOCIATION

The fourteenth annual tournament of the United Golfers' Association was held from August 22–25, 1939, at Griffith Park under the auspices of the West Coast Golf Club. The use of this park was donated by the Los Angeles Board of Park Commissioners in a precedent-smashing action. The West Coast Golfers' Club was offering, as an added attraction, $800 in cash prizes for professional golfers, along with a variety of cups and trophies for the amateurs. About 150 or more Negro golfers entered the National Open and Amateur, and the Southern Open and Amateur each year.

Negro professional golfers have had little opportunity to match their skill with those of other races in the United States. John Ship-pen, reputed Indian, from Shinnecock, Long Island, entered the national championships in 1913 and finished fourth.

JOHN SHIPPEN

John Shippen was an instructor on some of the finest courses in the East. He and his brother, Cyrus Shippen, had been associated with golf as players or instructors since around 1900. Both of these gentlemen had professional privileges at many of the clubs in New Jersey. John Shippen played rounds of golf with many famous golfers, particularly with the famous Vardon. For a while, John was credited with the longest American drive record. He was an instructor on such courses as those of the East Hampton Club in New York, the Merion at Philadelphia, the Spring Lake Golf and Country Club and others.

PROFESSIONAL GOLFERS

"Pat" Ball of Chicago, ex-champion among colored golfers, always made a good showing in the open competitions in and around Chicago. The 1938 professional champion was Howard Wheeler of Atlanta, Georgia. John Dendy of Asheville, North Carolina, in 1936 and 1937, and Solomon Hughes of Gadsden, Alabama, in 1935, became the earlier day's professional champions. The first professional to win a national championship was Harry Jackson of Washington, D.C. Other outstanding "pros" were Porter Washington of Boston, Massachusetts; "Zeke" Hartsfield and Howard Smith of Atlanta, Georgia; E. Marshall, Green, and Rhu of New Orleans.

THE AMATEURS PRIOR TO 1939

Among the amateurs, Frank Gaskins of Philadelphia won three times. George Roddy of the Agricultural and Mechanical College at Greensboro was once a captain of the Iowa State College golf team, and twice winner of the Negro amateur championship. Frank Radcliffe of New York, James McCoy of the same city, Beltran Barker, George Adams, and Albert Harris of Washington, were enthusiastic golfers and did much to promote the game. In the effort to secure a national organization, several golfers deserve high commendation. Chief among these was Walther Speedy of the former Windy City Golf Club, which was functioning for golf many years before the United Golfers' Association was formed.

National tournaments were held nearly every year after 1926. Some years they were held on golf courses operated by clubs and at other times on public courses. In 1934, it was voted to hold tournaments on public links where 18 holes were available. Since then the golfers have been afforded a first class test of their abilities and skill. The leading figure in conduct of the first national meeting was Robert Hawkins of the Mapledale Club in Boston. He had operated clubs for colored and white groups, and placed large sums in prize money for the professional contenders. Among the leading golfers of later years were Albert Harris, George Adams, Robert Ball, Edison Marshall, Howard Wheeler, John Dendy, Robert Seymour, Solomon Hughes, Frank Gaskin, George Roddy, Harold Hunter, James McCoy, Lawrence Frierson, Percy Jones, Elmer Brent, Clifford Taylor, John Roux, Hugh Smith, Zeke Hartsfield, E. Jenkins, A. D. V. Crosby, Ben Greene, Clarence Chandler, O. R. Jackson, John Buchanan, and Oscar Clisby. Of the ladies who showed prominence in golf were Marie Thompson Jones, Lucy Williams, Melnee Moyce, Ella Able, Julia Siler, Aileere Davis, Cleo Ball, Sarah Smith, and Ethel Webb Terrell. In Washington, D.C., there has existed a women's golf club, the Wake Robin Club of which about twenty members play regularly.

COLLEGE GOLF

Tuskegee Institute, Alabama, fostered the first inter-collegiate golf championship in 1938. It was played on the Tuskegee Course and was won by Alfred Holmes. Much interest was manifested.

For the first time in the history of the University of Michigan, in 1930, two Negroes entered the All-Campus Golf Tournament. These two Negroes met in the final round and A. D. V. Crosby was the winner; R. G. Robinson was runner-up.

In 1933, the Asheville Country Club of North Carolina had four Negro golfers to play an exhibition match on its course and invited them to stay over and play an exhibition golf match on the Asheville Municipal Course on Sunday afternoon. Three of the four Negroes who played were Howard Wheeler, A. D. V. Crosby, and John Dendy.

GOLF CHAMPIONSHIP

The 1939 National Negro Open golf championship was played during the last week in August at Los Angeles, California. The winner was Clifford Strickland of Riverside, California. Leading from the start, Strickland added a 75 to a 71, 77, 73 score and finished nine strokes in front of Edison Marshall of Indianapolis; Erroll Strickland of Riverside, a cousin, was third with a score of 305. Hugh Smith, Atlanta, Georgia, with 306; John Roux, New Orleans, 307; Howard Wheeler, Atlanta, 1938 Open champion, 308; A. D. V. Crosby, Columbus, Ohio, with 309; and William Haze and Pat Ball, Chicago, with 310, were leading contenders. Par for the Griffith Park municipal course is 71. In the East, at Atlantic City in the week of August 14, 1939, the Royal Golf Club of Washington, D.C., won the Eastern Golf Association team competition, and won also the Maryland Open championship at Baltimore.

LATER DEVELOPMENTS

During the Second World War many golf tournaments were passed. In recent years the most important advance in the golf picture has been the increase in the number of clubs and greater interest in golf all over the nation. Another notable sign of progress lies in the willingness of some tournaments of national repute to accept the entry of Negro golfers in national and sectional meets. Some of these have been the Los Angeles Open, the Tam O'Shanter, the Philadelphia Open and the United States Golf Association Open. Also encouraging has been the fight in many southern cities to insist upon the opening of tax-supported golf links to all citizens. Much progress has been made in Washington, D.C., and Baltimore.

Colored golfers are able to match strokes with some of the best ranking golfers in America, and have won many friends for the Negro golfer. One of the regrettable occurrences in 1947 was the refusal of the Richmond, California, Open Tournament to admit Bill Spiller and Ted Rhodes to this tournament although by their showing in the Los Angeles Open they had qualified. They were among the first 60 in this event. Spiller was 25th and Rhodes 23rd. The suit filed by these men because of the humiliation and denial was settled out of court with the promise of the tournament promoters to eliminate racial discrimination in the future.

Right Thinking

ALEX J. MORRISON

Alex J. Morrison began his career as an engineer, but then began to write a col-
umn on golf that remained widely syndicated twenty-eight years later. A firm
believer in the importance of the mental aspect of the game, Morrison wrote
Better Golf Without Practice, *considered the golf bible of its time. The fol-*
lowing selection originally appeared in that witty and instructional book,
which shows how to take strokes off your game without ever lifting a club.

"Mr. Morrison, I come to you for personal instruction. For years I
have been trying many things without getting any real or lasting
benefit from them. But I believe you can help me."

Well, I'm glad you have confidence in me, but I warn you, I'm
not a miracle worker. I can help you only if I receive your full coop-
eration. You see, you have all the mental and physical equipment
needed to play good golf. And I will give you positively the best way
of using your equipment to the greatest advantage. But, with all this,
you cannot be consistently successful without doing some head
work. However, I'm sure you will supply this head work after I've told
you how simple it is and what rewards it will bring. While I tell you
about these rewards, just make yourself comfortable in an easy chair.

Naturally, you and everyone who plays golf would like to make
lower scores, for improvement in this great game brings a personal
satisfaction and a tremendous boost to individual ego. Unfortu-

nately, instead of lower scores, most players finish with lower spirits and higher figures. And for their failures they invariably resort to that old alibi—"lack of practice." This seems logical, for very few players have the time or the inclination for long hours of practice.

Let me assure you that this excuse will no longer hold. That "no practice" alibi is through, finished.

Now I guarantee you can make lower scores without practice!

Skeptical? Well, this is exactly what I mean. You do not have to spend weeks swinging a club, hitting balls indoors or on the practice ground. You can play better golf without making even one practice swing! You can go directly to the course and make better shots with every club in your bag, take fewer strokes per round and eliminate most of your worries about the game.

Right Thinking

How can this be done? It can be done, if you have had some experience at the game simply by Right Thinking, which in turn means giving the proper attention to the MORRISON KEYS. Let me tell you, by a few case histories, what I mean.

Lew Lehr, of newsreel and radio fame, despite years at the game, was unable to break ninety. He was discouraged to the point of quitting golf. He came to me for help because his busy days and nights gave him no time for practice, and he heard that my pupils had improved immeasurably through mental application.

In the living room of his home at Great Neck, Long Island, sitting in an arm chair, as you are now, Lew received his first instructions about giving attention to the Morrison Keys. It was strictly a mental session for him, with only a demonstration on my part of the correct swing and a lecture on the Keys. I left him with the assurance, as well as the conviction, that five minutes in any easy chair visualizing himself attending to the Keys would be of more benefit than a week of hip-swiveling on a practice tee with a blank mind.

Several days later, with no physical preparation whatever, he joined his regular foursome from Movietone, Ed Reeke, Ed Thorgesen, and Jack Painter.

His score for the first nine holes was rather disappointing. He took exactly fifty. But this was due mainly to the fact that he had permitted the conversation and ribbing of his opponents to distract him. I happened to be standing on the tenth tee as the foursome came along. When Lew saw me, he said, "Now that the professor is watching, I'll have to give the proper attention to his Keys and show you boys a thing or two."

That round had a happy ending. By following my instructions to the letter he shot the last nine in thirty-six, even par. Winter closed that playing season for him. Nevertheless, his opponents continued to play or practice every week through the cold weather. They had a job before them when the new season opened—revenge on Mr. Lehr. In spite of his dislike for the cold, Lew was persuaded to play early in March. The weather was anything but pleasant.

Now think of this. His only preparation for this match was refreshing his memory about the Morrison Keys. Over a course partly covered with snow and with frosted, bumpy greens, he turned in a score of forty-two, forty-one, a total of eighty-three, good enough to win from the boys again. This was about three years ago. Since that time, his scores are under or very close to eighty.

The Keys Prevent Tension

Attending to the Morrison Keys will enable you to avoid nerve strain and muscular tension as well as other bugaboos so damaging to your score and disposition.

Henry Picard, the P.G.A. champion and leading money winner of 1939, told me, "Your instructions have given me, in addition to many improvements in my swing, a greatly improved mental attitude about the whole game. This has been most helpful to me when playing under extreme pressure."

When such a star uses the term "extreme pressure" in reference to the nerve strain of competitive golf, he is not exaggerating. Your own experience with pressure, even in your friendly games, should convince you that this nerve tension can be greater in golf than in any other sport.

Throughout the P.G.A. event, which pros say is the toughest of all tournaments to win, Picard maintained a scoring pace over the par seventy-two Ponionok course which found him just forty strokes under par for two hundred and five holes! This blistering pace meant an average of only three strokes and a small fraction per hole for almost eleven and a half consecutive rounds. And he wound up by defeating the National Open champion, Byron Nelson, in a match that is recorded as one of the most brilliant in golfing history.

The Morrison Keys Are Practical for Everyone

The improvement to be had through attending to the Morrison Keys should not surprise you. Making lower scores by mental application is an old story, something that has proved its worth, over a long period of time, to all kinds of players under all sorts of conditions. And the method of properly applying yourself mentally which I give you is as simple and positive as you'll find to coordinate mind and body in connection with any activity on or off the course. Its simplicity and positiveness are the direct result of the most comprehensive and scientific study ever made of golf technique.

All of the findings of my study and analysis, which I began in 1912, have continually pointed to the greater importance of the mental side of the game. In fact, these findings prove that golf is about ninety percent mental, eight percent physical, and two percent mechanical. Likewise, everything you do when you have a golf club in your hands is a true reflection of your mental state.

True, luck often determines the winner of a match or tournament, but it shouldn't be considered a deciding factor, because every player, in the long run, will benefit from good breaks as much as he suffers from bad ones. And it is obvious that clubs and other tools do not make the golfer. The same thing can be said about the physical make-up of the player. I do not know of any other activity, wherein the entire body is used, that places so small a premium on age, build, or condition as golf.

During the Open Championship at Merion in 1934, Olin Dutra suffered from a very painful stomach ailment. His suffering increased until he literally had to crawl to the last green. Yet this did not keep him from finishing ahead of a field packed with healthy athletes.

There are many indications that results are not determined by the player's physical condition. Undoubtedly, you've had some first-hand experience with links ailments. You have had days when you scored well despite annoying aches and pains. Also, when in the pink of condition, you have been beaten, much to your embarrassment, by a Rheumatic Golfer.

On occasions, you may have been amazed at the sudden and remarkable improvement in the game of a friend who had been partying the night before. You didn't realize that he came to the course with a mind too deadened or weary to house the inhibitions which bedevil him on normal days. He could relax and swing the club with abandon. Now, I'm not advocating this procedure for you; I mention it merely to point out the value of a mind unhampered by distractions. This same freedom and abandon can be had at any time by the proper mental application.

So far you may feel that you are getting a lecture instead of a lesson on golf, since you are in the habit of walking directly onto the tee to swing a club or go right out on the course. Well, be patient, for you can't be too well prepared to do either of these things.

Sam Snead's performance in the National Open at Philadelphia in 1939 is a perfect illustration of the greater importance of the mental side. Among the present-day money players Swingin' Sam is supposed to have the best physical equipment—the ideal golf physique. The average observer, in watching his smooth muscular co-ordination, gets the impression that it would be impossible for him to make an awkward or wild swing. Bobby Jones told me, "Sam Snead has the only swing I've seen for which I would be willing to trade mine."

Yet, as you know, Snead played like a duffer on the last two holes, where easy pars would have won the title for him. "What happened to Snead?" everyone asked. It was plain to see that his swing had gone haywire, but nobody seemed to gather that the upset was more mental than physical. His followers would not believe that he could blow up under pressure, for previously on many occasions he had demonstrated his superiority as a money player. But in the locker room, immediately after the round, he admitted to me that his difficulty was due to mental confusion. He said, "Alex, I just didn't use my head."

Snead became annoyed at himself for missing an easy chip shot just off the edge of the seventeenth green. This annoyance led to the mental confusion which caused him to make mistake after mistake on the eighteenth hole. Now there is a moral for you in Sam's debacle. Don't get mad at yourself for mistakes! When you do, your mind gives way to the physical and you strive with anger-driven force to rectify errors that are more mental than physical. Remember the times you stood on a tee and sent two or three consecutive shots out of bounds or into a water hazard?

Most of the upsets in your game as well as the kinks in your swing are traceable to one thing: fear of the unknown. You become petrified when you realize that you do not know beforehand what mistakes you are liable to make, or how much you may be penalized for even the smallest of them. I can honestly say that this burden of confusion and worry you have been carrying around the course will be set aside the minute you begin to use the Keys.

An Application of the Morrison Keys

No doubt you are anxious to learn how these Keys will afford you success in some part of your game, so I will give you a sample of their application to your swing. Just take off your coat and pick up a club. Any wood or iron club will do. Yes, even a putter will answer the purpose. Take your regular grip on the club and stand where you can make a full swing without striking any person or object. Now start easily and make a number of swings without trying to hit a ball or any spot on the ground. There now, rest a bit—that is enough for me to see that your swing lacks such fundamentals as the proper foot action, a firm grip with the left hand and the correct head position. (These and other fundamentals are fully illustrated in the Key section.) You will never play good golf until these things are a part of your regular swing. And it is best to learn the proper foot action first. Naturally you must have a clear mental picture of the correct thing before you can do it consistently. So that you can form this picture, I'll stand before you and go through a slow-motion demonstration of the proper foot action. While doing this I will try to direct your attention to the fact that, in turn, each foot rolls over toward the inside before the heel of that foot leaves the ground. It looks simple and it is.

Now you try it. Hold on—you're not doing anything like it. You may have the most vivid mental picture of the correct golf swing, but that doesn't mean you will automatically execute it. Getting a mental picture of the proper movements is only part of the job. Not realizing this, many players are mystified by their failures to carry out their mental pictures.

Rex Beach, when experiencing just what you are going through, said, "I have a perfect picture of the correct swing in my mind, but very often as I go to make it, something goes wrong. I don't know what it can be unless it is a failure of the old telegraph system between brain and muscle." If you had a glimpse of the famous author swimming, diving, hunting, fishing, or performing in any one of a dozen sports at which he is expert, you would agree that there is nothing wrong with his telegraph system. And I am reasonably sure there is nothing wrong with yours.

Where a golfer has a clear mental picture of what is correct and doesn't at least approximate it in his movements, the trouble lies not with his telegraph system, but with the operator who fails to send the right message to the right place. In other words, in addition to having a mental picture of the proper foot action, your attention must be centered on the right Key.

This time, before you attempt to produce this foot action, set aside your club. Now stand fully erect, head and eyes up, with your hands clasped behind your back. The purpose of this is to place most of your weight back on your heels and enable you to give all of your attention to the right Key, namely, the contact of your heels with the ground. I explained that in learning the proper foot action your heels must remain touching the ground. Again you try to roll your feet. Stop! Instead of rolling your feet, you are letting your heels jump up and down as though you are doing a toe dance.

Your difficulty is due solely to the fact that you are not attending to the Key to proper foot action. I will prove this if you will just stand upright again. That's it, head and eyes up. Now, the instant your left heel starts to come off the ground I reach out and tap it with my club. Presto! The heel remains touching the ground and the left foot rolls over nicely. If necessary I will do the same thing for your right foot. After this prompting your heels stay down and your feet roll as though they have been doing it for years.

This light tap on your heel served to accomplish what you failed to do, namely, to make yourself properly conscious of the Key. Rest assured that before resorting to this procedure I always give my pupils every chance to focus their own attention properly. I know this is done most efficiently when you do it through your own mental application.

There is no limit to the practical knowledge to be gained from this demonstration. Among the more important things you should learn from it are: how immediate improvement is had by attending to the Morrison Keys, the simplicity and positiveness of the Keys covering the rest of your swing and everything else about the game, also the vital importance of giving the proper attention to the right Key.

No doubt this sample makes you curious about the Keys for the various shots to be played on the course. So I must tell you that if you let curiosity dominate you, your mental application will be anything but proper. This means that in reading these instructions you should not jump from item A to item L or try to digest too many points at one sitting. By doing so you are encouraging old faults, both mental and physical.

Make sure of real and lasting improvement in your game by considering each subject in the order presented and according to the importance I give it. Let us begin by considering the all-important matter of attention.

ALL THE equipment needed to play good golf is the normal use of your hands and feet and the intelligence to attend to the Morrison Keys. Use your intelligence to give the proper attention to the Keys I will supply, and you have a combination which will afford you unlimited success on the course. This combination is truly a magic power, virtually an Aladdin's Lamp which is always ready to serve you.

The kind of attention required to play consistently well is similar to that you give to things you MUST do, whether or not you like to do them. It finds your mind so filled with thought about ONE THING AT A TIME that you are not influenced by anything else. It is the sort of centered mental direction which makes you impervious to heat, cold, and other distractions.

Ralph Guldahl, winner of the National Open in 1937 and 1938, the Masters in 1939, the Western Open in 1936, 1937, and 1938, as well as many other tournaments, owes most of his success to his ability to give this singleness of attention to his game. And he realizes this, for after winning the Open in 1938, he told of being in a trance-like state from directing his mind so steadfastly to shot making. This is not unusual with most successful players for they do nothing but play, talk, and think golf.

Yes, you can call it concentration. I haven't used the word for a number of reasons. To many players it is misleading. It conveys a picture of bulging muscles and furrowed brow, the outward indications of tension. And, even if you know how to concentrate perfectly in connection with other activities, it doesn't mean you will do so in golf. The very mention of the word suggests the kind of work most people labor to avoid, especially when it comes to recreation.

My experience in getting many players properly to apply themselves mentally proves that the smallest amount of effort is needed and the best results are obtained simply by supplying the necessary attention to the right Keys. In golf, mistakes are made, they just don't happen. And most of them are caused by failure to give attention to the job at hand. Unfortunately, there are many ways of failing to attend to the right thing on the course. It is very easy to be mistaken about the things which afford success. You may try to attend to more than one thing at a time. And you can think that you are giving attention to the right thing when actually you give none. This happens when you mistake intention for attention.

In the summer of 1935, Joseph Clark Grew, United States Ambassador to Japan, in this country for a short vacation, asked me to help him improve his game as much as possible in a few days' time.

During his first lesson he was given the same instructions I've just given to you. After he had learned to roll his feet, we dealt with the head position. First, in my own swing, I demonstrated that the proper position found my head neither raising, lowering, nor turning in relation to the ball. Also that it remained in this position until well after the club head struck the ball. Then I told him that he could keep his head in this position simply by holding his head up and keeping his chin pointed back of the ball during his downswing. He promised to give all of his attention to this Key.

His first attempts were unsuccessful. When it occurred to him that he was taking too long to point his chin properly, he turned to me and said, in his most serious tone, "Have patience with me, young man, for I have much more character than you suspect." I was amused, not by his remark, but by the fact that he was mistaking intention for attention. As soon as I explained his difficulty, he supplied the necessary attention, kept his chin back, and sent his shots down the middle of the fairway. I am willing to concede that you always have the best of intentions, but this is not enough.

You must realize that your attention is not always under control. Many of us are troubled with Grasshopper minds. And whether or not we desire to have our attention shifting about, it is bound to heed the loudest call from any source. This source can be within or outside of your own mind and body. For example, your attention will automatically go to an aching tooth, the brightest object appearing before your eyes or the sharpest sound reaching your ears. Through these and other senses you are continually subject to distractions. There is no possible way of eliminating all distractions, but you can avoid being handicapped by them with a little mental application.

How to Supply the Proper Attention

Naturally, some mental effort is needed to direct and hold your attention on one thing. However, the amount of effort is determined by your familiarity with the procedure and the nature of the distraction to be overcome. Now you may have better ways of centering your attention on the Keys, but I strongly urge you to follow my suggestions in this matter.

First, to direct your attention to a Key you must be convinced that it will afford you success. Then you must center your thoughts on the Key much as you tune in a certain station on your radio. At times you may have considerable static in the form of distractions to eliminate before you can give your full attention to the Key. But there is a very simple way of making yourself properly conscious of it. Let us say that you are faced with the necessity of driving down a narrow fairway, lined on both sides with trees. You know you must keep your chin back in order to hit a straight shot. Yet you will invariably look up. Worry over the outcome of the shot makes you forget the Key. Now you can keep the Key uppermost in your mind by saying "CHIN" audibly at the start of your backswing and again at the start of your downswing.

You may hesitate to follow this suggestion about saying "Chin" aloud during a regular game. If so, do your reciting on the practice ground. If you mean what you say, you'll soon be keeping your chin back. Also, if you remind yourself before every swing that by pointing your chin properly you are bound to stay on the fairway, your success will be heightened. As a further incentive to use this method I add that Henry Picard attributes most of his accuracy and consistency to the practice of saying "Chin" to himself during his downswing.

Once you have directed your attention to a Key, you can hold it there by showing a keen interest in its particular characteristics. And every Key has certain points which should be of interest to you. A case in point is the procedure of making the ball the main object of your attention. When you first look at the ball, it appears as a small blurred sphere on the ground. Careful study should reveal such things as the manufacturer's stamp, a smudge or a bruise on the cover. Generally you'll find one of these marks close to the spot where your club head should strike. By noting the relative positions of these marks you can attach your mind to the ball with an imaginary ribbon. And this ribbon should be strong enough to hold your attention on the ball until after your club head strikes it.

Giving the proper attention to the Morrison Keys is indeed like directing your muscles by radio. When your mental beam is focused on the right Key at the right time you are bound to perform properly. And, for reasons I will give when explaining the foundation of the Keys, you need not be in doubt at any time about the kind of attention given to a Key. Your performance always tells the story. By performance I mean your positions and movements as a movie camera would record them. Truly, as your attention goes, so goes your whole game.

The Way To Look at a Golf Ball

The sight of a golf ball is definitely harmful to your game if it appears as an object that is hard to hit and control or, worse yet, if it arouses fear and causes tension.

On the other hand, the sight of it can be an excellent means of reading your mental state before making a shot.

For example, if in looking at the ball, with normal eyesight, you see it only as a tiny blurred sphere resting on the turf, you can be sure that you are in a confused mental state.

But, if you can distinguish some of its individual characteristics such as the manufacturer's stamp, smudges or bruises on the cover, you are ready to supply the proper attention to the essentials of your swing.

By magnifying the markings on the ball and noting their positions in relation to the spot where the club face should strike, you can fasten your attention on the ball with an imaginary ribbon. Magnifying the characteristics of each Morrison Key will enable you to give the proper attention to the Key.

The Way the Ball Bounces

J. P. MARQUAND

Born in Delaware, but known as a Massachusetts author, J.P. Marquand wrote on a variety of subjects, most of which revolved around life in New England and the people who comprised its unique character. His portrayal of the country club and its problems is depicted in the letters that make up Life at Happy Knoll, *published in 1957.*

Dear Albert:

The Board of Governors at the Happy Knoll Country Club faces a crisis right at the height of our golfing season. It suddenly looks as though we may lose our golf professional on a two weeks' notice. I know what you are going to say. You are going to say that the Board voted another thousand dollars for Benny Muldoon at one of their recent meetings, and you are also going to say that we should at least have tied Benny up on a season's contract. Well, I suppose you are right on both scores, but still, facts are facts. We have never signed Benny up on a contract because Benny has always said he loved the Club and he has always seemed to us like one of our members. Actually, one cannot help being touched by Benny's reaction because he seems more upset, if possible, by the prospect of impending change than any of his host of admirers.

You know as well as I do that Benny is a sentimentalist at heart.

There is a genuine quaver in his voice when he speaks about the possibility of leaving Happy Knoll, which he says very frankly is his second home. But, as Benny says, you have got to face facts. It is like, he said when I interviewed him yesterday, the time when he was playing his second 18 at Rough Briar in the State Open. He had belted out a 300-yard drive right down the middle of the fairway. There was quite a gallery following because, frankly, he was hot as a pistol right up to the 7th. There was the green, 80 yards away, heavily trapped, but a cinch for a roll to the cup, if you aimed for the upper slope. Would he use an eight-, a nine-iron or a wedge? He had to make up his mind. He must have been thinking about all his responsibilities there because he called for the wrong club, landed in the trap and blasted out for a measly four. So you have to make up your mind, and either in match play or in life, making up your mind is a pretty tough proposition. Come to think of it, as Benny told me, and you know how philosophical Benny can get when he has the golf house to himself, life from his experience is a good deal like a game of golf. You get yourself into the rough in life just the way you do when you slice off the tee and you've got to take a wedge and some religion to get yourself squared away. Just like in life, in golf you start out with nothing but you have to come home with something.

I took the liberty of interrupting Benny at this point, telling him that in golf the less strokes you came back with the better, and that in life, too, a large income is often a source of worry.

Benny said that at the same time you had to come back with something. And these days when he came back to Patricia (that's Mrs. Muldoon), Patricia didn't feel he was bringing home enough, even if life wasn't exactly like golf. It seems that Patricia has been needling Benny Muldoon ever since he won that State Open. I told you at the time, Albert, you never should have offered to pay Benny's expenses for that occasion, and if you hadn't, I don't believe that Patricia (that's Mrs. Muldoon) would have allowed Benny to take the money out of what he calls "the kitty" for any such long shot. After all, Benny always said, previous to the State Open, that he was a teacher and not a tournament player. Well, now it's different. Benny now wants to go out to California to Pebble Beach or somewhere so that he can slug it out with "the circuit," and Patricia (that's Mrs. Muldoon) has begun reading the sports columns, and if an unknown like Fleck could beat Hogan, why couldn't Benny beat Fleck?

It seems that Patricia is now making notes on the annual incomes of Hogan and a few others, and these figures prove that Benny is not coming home with enough. It seems that he is not thinking of the future of their two children and of the other that is on the way. Instead he only thinks about analyzing the golf swings of a lot of stingy though rich old loafers at the Happy Knoll Country Club. These are my words, not Benny's. These people, Patricia says, could never win the State Open and she could give any of them a-stroke-a-hole and beat them herself if she weren't expecting. That's the way she is, pugnacious (I'm referring to Mrs. Muldoon). It seems that she keeps needling Benny. Only yesterday she asked him, now that he has won the State Open, why he can't go to a sporting goods store and get his name inscribed on a set of matched irons, like Mr. MacGregor? Ambition, it seems, is Patricia's middle name. It seems to me that Lady Macbeth displayed many of the same attributes on the evening that King Duncan dropped in for the night.

Well, as Benny said yesterday, that's the way the ball bounces and he is a family and not a single man and now there has come a crisis. Hard Hollow first made a bid for him and now comes Rocky River. Rocky River is willing to guarantee Benny two thousand dollars more than we are after we have met the Hard Hollow offer. Benny has been most honorable about it and is holding nothing up his sleeve because he loves Happy Knoll and everybody in it, but that's the way the ball bounces. Besides, if he turns Rocky River down, how can he tell Mrs. Muldoon? In addition, Rocky River has a golf house twice the size of ours and everybody at Rocky River loyally buys all their equipment from it. Benny doesn't mean to say anything tough about Happy Knoll members because he loves them all, but sometimes, just to save a buck, they do go to some cut-rate store in the city and come back to the Happy Knoll course with a lot of junk that he would be ashamed to handle, but that's the way the ball bounces. He has an ironclad guarantee that they never will do that at Rocky River, and they have a display room that can even handle slacks and tweeds besides caps and windbreakers. So here we have the question. What are we going to do about Benny Muldoon? I know what our deficit is, but Benny has been here for 10 years. A lot of people, including you, Albert, have to go to him regularly. How would you like it if you had to start with someone else? A golf pro, after all, is like a priest in a parish or a headmaster at school.

There are of course people who shop around among golf teachers, but these are hypochondriacs who can never cure themselves by advice from several sources. We both know this, Albert. You may recollect that some years ago I caught you sneaking out to the Hard Hollow Country Club to see whether their Jerry Scalponi could do more about your basic game than Benny Muldoon. I met you there because, frankly, I had come out for the same purpose and we were both agreed that all that results from promiscuous golf advice is unhealthy cynicism. Most professionals after diagnosing your golf ailments ask who taught you. When you tell them, they say it is too bad and all that can be done now is to start all over again and, by the way, your set of laminated woods are too heavy in the head and disturb your back swing.

I cannot bear at my time of life to face anyone else except Benny Muldoon, because he has a beautiful gift of sympathy and on the practice tee he suffers with me always. I admit it has been true lately, perhaps because Mrs. Muldoon has been suggesting that he underrates himself, that Benny seems to be cultivating a Scottish accent. The other day I thought I heard him say "Verra guid," but if Benny wants to be Sir Harry Lauder he still comforts me and leads me safely over the water hazards because his good words are with me; and I certainly ought to remember what Benny Muldoon has told me, because he says the same things over and over but then, what else is there for him to say?

You have got to be calm and collected, he says. Golf, if you will excuse his using a long word, is a psychological game. Have a mental picture in your mind, he says, of the right way of hitting through the ball and you can do it. Golf, if you will excuse his saying so, is a wee bit like religion, and a while ago a gentleman whom he doesn't think I ever knew, because Benny met him years ago at Hot Springs (but he was very important in the coal business and had a Rolls Royce and two lovely daughters) told him about a French doctor called M. Cooey or something like that. You'll have to excuse his French, but seriously, this Doctor Cooey or however you say it stated that you simply had to say a couple of thousand times every morning, "Every day in every way I am getting better and better" and, believe it or not, you did. What Benny wants you to say is simply that every day in every way your golf is getting better. Say it two thousand times and then go out and see what happens. Only recently he made this suggestion to Mrs. Falconhurst. Benny was worried so sick about Mrs. Falconhurst that when he came home at night he couldn't eat. Frankly, Mrs. Falconhurst was a lovely lady, but he couldn't teach her to hit a balloon. But then he told her about this Frenchman and you ought to see her now. Confidence is what you need in golf. If you want it in two words, confidence and Cooey is all there is. Now of course, Benny says, golf isn't like trying to bat a baseball or anything so easy, but in the end, like batting a baseball, it's confidence. Benny says he almost lost his confidence on the long 13th in the Open up at Rocky River. It was the afternoon round and something he ate wasn't sitting well on his stomach. He was using the two-wood on the fairway, giving it everything he had, and he might have even pressed but it was probably the frankfurter he had for lunch. Anyway, instead of making the green he hooked over the third bunker. Frankly, his knees sagged and he burst into a cold sweat, but he said to himself, "I can do it, I can do it," and he came across with the sweetest wedge shot of the day. It wasn't Benny who did it. It was Doctor Cooey and that's the way the ball bounces. As Benny says, there's some other things to golf. Sweep your club head low back on the ground, make a nice pivot, hit from the inside out clean, crisp and smooth. That's another little motto: be crisp and smooth, and let the club head do the work. Don't worry where the ball goes. Just do it and Benny will be happy. Just be crisp and easy and relaxed.

Well, I have been going to Benny more often I am afraid than I go to church. I have heard everything, and in fact I now know exactly what he will say next. In spite of Doctor Cooey, my reason tells me that my golf never will greatly improve and yet I do keep going back to Benny and so does everyone else at Happy Knoll. Why? I don't know any direct answer except that Benny can always make you feel that you're going to do better sometime in the foreseeable future. After all, as Benny said when I was speaking to him yesterday, golf teaching is like being a shill in a crap game. You've got to keep the customers coming, you've got to make them feel good and if you don't—no bottle for Buster.

Yet there is another, more cogent reason, I believe, that Benny is able to hold the large and captious public that he has at Happy Knoll. It is because he universally commands a deep respect. Somehow whenever I see Benny Muldoon I know I am in the presence of greatness. In a way he is more of a doctor than a teacher, but he does not need signed certificates nor garbled language to make his point. The tee-side is different from the bedside manner. The truth is, Benny always comes across. He can invariably chip to six inches of the cup. With his left arm alone he can send the ball two hundred yards. He can slice or hook at will and can parody the play of any of his pupils, but always in a genial manner. He can also drive a ball from the top of a gold watch without damaging its mechanism and once he was prepared to drive a ball off the head of our fellow member, Mr. Featherstone, who was in one of his customarily genial moods, but the Greens Committee intervened. I have always been sorry for this because it might have been that Benny would have hit below the ball for once in his career. Somehow when Benny Muldoon wears the golf accessories that are on sale in the golf shop they always fit him; they never look ridiculous as they do on some of the rest of us—not the loudest shirts, not even tam-o'-shanters. But it is not dress, not exposition, but his unfailing kindness that I most admire. Benny knows very well that we could all be as good as he if we had had his chance to be a caddie at a New Jersey country club whose name I can never pronounce. He has a special niche in his heart for everyone, and a very long memory, too. It is true that he asked me the other day how my water on the knee was getting on, but he corrected himself immediately. He had been thinking of Mrs. Falconhurst. He meant the bursitis in my right shoulder, the same complaint from which President Eisenhower suffers, and Ike is a pretty hot golfer, considering. It is inconceivable to think of telling any more intimate golfing troubles or the more disgraceful things I have done on the Happy Knoll links to anyone except Benny Muldoon. There is a personal rapport in these matters which cannot be overlooked.

Frankly, Albert, I have not had a good year in a business sense, but the stock market has been rising in spite of the Fulbright Committee. I can, if necessary, sell something. There has been so much hat passing lately that any more might cause repercussions. I think that you and I have got to take it upon ourselves to fix this thing about Benny Muldoon. In fact, I have done so already. I have told him that I would pay half and you would pay the rest, and just remember, that's the way the ball bounces.

It Takes Brains to Play Golf

GENE SARAZEN

Originally published in 1950, this selection is from Sarazen's Thirty Years of Championship Golf.

As I near the age when fans are beginning to regard me as a sort of elder statesman of golf, I find that I am expected to sit on a bench by a tee and give advice. Along with overcomplicated instruction, the average golfer's greatest handicap, as I see it, is his own impatience to run before he can walk, to score before he understands the fundamentals of the golf swing. The inevitable result, of course, is that he will never be a regular low scorer. The multifold compensations he resorts to in order to remedy a swing that is basically faulty do about as much good as anchoring a shaky house with yards of velvet. I think the Japanese clubs have something when they rule that novices will not be allowed on to the golf course until they have reached a certain degree of proficiency. The novices practice their shots on a large field, something like a polo field, until a committee passes on them as ready to play on the course itself. While the idea of having a committee dictate to a golfer what he is allowed to do and what he isn't allowed to do is a practice we would not want to copy in letter or in spirit, the new players in our country would benefit immeasurably if they voluntarily set aside a period of time in which they learned to hit their shots with some correctness before invading the course in search of scores. All players, not just the beginners, would do well to think of winter as the ideal season for disciplined indoor practice that will reward them with many summers of pleasure.

In my tours throughout the country I have observed that less than 1 percent of our golfers know how to practice correctly. At every club there is a group of over-eager beavers who bang hundreds of balls down the practice fairway and are muscularly tired before they actually tee off. You've got to be fresh to play good golf. Ben Hogan is the one player I know who has the physical and mental stamina to play his best golf after expending maximum power and concentration on the practice field. It exhausts me, and most of the other professionals, just to watch Ben practice, and there are occasions on which I think that even the super-disciplined Hogan leaves his finest strokes on the practice grounds. Before a round a player should warm up, not practice. At my age, preferring as I do to conserve my energy, my warm-up consists of fifteen or twenty shots with my No. 6 or 7 iron on which I can check my timing; four or five drives to unlimber my other muscles; and then five minutes or so on the practice green.

It does you no good to practice after a round when you are feeling tired, or at any time when your coordination is worn down. You should not practice all the clubs in the bag indiscriminately. You should concentrate on the one club you were playing the poorest on your preceding round. If your irons need attention, do not succumb to the lure of practicing your woods, your best shots, just because there are a few friends watching on the porch of the clubhouse. I know some pros, who are old enough to know better, who are 70-golfers with their woods and 78-golfers with their irons and will always remain so since they apparently cannot resist impressing the spectators on the practice ground with their exceptional length with the woods.

But the cardinal error which players commit today when they practice is to nudge each shot on to a perfect lie. You can never develop the proper hand action if you sweep the ball rather than strike it. You must practice hitting balls out of fair, poor, and downright bad lies. If you just want to go out and kid yourself, you would do your game as much good by staying in the clubhouse and playing a few hands of pinochle. I think it follows that I am against playing preferred lies on the course itself unless conditions truly warrant this. Our national infatuation with scores and record breaking lies behind this deplorable trend. One year the directors of the Miami Springs tournament allowed preferred lies on perfectly healthy fairways, and also put the markers on the ladies' tees and set the pins in the easiest position on the greens, all this to encourage a barrage or 61's and 62's. Well, they got a few 64's by such measures, and these 'sensational scores' were a travesty on the honest 67's that golfers had played.

I can sympathize with the millions of golfers who read that the sand-iron shot is really a cinch but who encounter paralysis every time they step into a bunker. Few clubs provide facilities for practicing trap shots. After the golfer finishes a lesson on how to get out of traps, the pro admonishes him to be sure and practice that stroke. The next day the zealous pupil takes his wedge and a few balls out to a trap, but before he has played five shots some emissary from the pro shop dashes out to ask him what he thinks he's doing—doesn't he know that he's spattering the green with sand, and didn't he ever read the green committee's regulation that under no conditions will any member practice in a trap? The common sense solution is for clubs to build practice traps. While they are at it, it wouldn't be a bad idea if golf clubs made provision for practice grounds which can accommodate more than three players at a time. They might think about erecting an inexpensive canvas awning, so that the industrious members are able to practice in all kinds of weather; lessons would not have to be canceled because of rain. I have expressed myself earlier as favoring practice greens which bear a vague resemblance to the eighteen greens the player meets on the course.

One last criticism of practice habits. When most golfers practice their putting, they start out with the thirty-footers and then work in. I think it is much more advisable to start a foot or so from the hole and gradually work back to fifteen feet or so. You are more likely to develop a smooth stroke. Golfers think too much about holing their practice putts. Great putters like Horton Smith concentrate on their stroke when they practice. They know that if they are stroking the ball correctly, they will get their share of putts.

A golf type that I run into with irritating regularity is the person who weeps in the locker-room, "But I wasn't putting." Anybody can hit the ball. It takes a golfer to put his shots together, and a three-foot putt is every bit as much of a golf shot as a 250-yard drive. The putter is the dipper. It separates the cream from the milk. The great champions have all been beautiful putters—Walter Travis, Jerry Travers, Hagen, Jones, Nelson, and Hogan. Harry Vardon is the one exception to this rule, and when Vardon was winning, he wasn't a bad putter. A champion cannot remain a champion if his putting falls off. In the 1946 Open, Byron Nelson played immaculate golf from tee to green, the best in the field, I thought. Nelson failed to win not simply because he three-putted the seventy-first and made a miserable putt on the seventy-second, but because on his full rounds his putting was not coordinated with the pitch of the rest of his game.

I have never seen a consistently able putter who used a club with a rounded edge to the sole. For that matter, you must be sensible about all of your equipment. Get on intimate terms with your clubs so that none of them are strangers to you. Maybe you're carrying too many. I think a principal reason why we developed such solid shot-makers in the early days was that golfers played with only eight or nine clubs and got to know them all. When I won my third P.G.A. title, I had five or six irons in my bag, no more. Any club that cut into my confidence, I threw out. Whenever I pulled a club out during that tournament, I knew I was working with an old friend. "Here's a fellow I know," I would feel as I gripped my mashie, for example. "I've had a lot of dealings with him. I can depend on this fellow."

One club that the average golfer does not need is the No. 1 iron. Only players of the caliber of Nelson, Snead, and Hogan can play the temperamental No. 1, and they have to practice it assiduously. Hogan and Nelson, who are the finest long-iron players golf has known, realize that the No. 1 iron must be played with a swing that's a bit on the upright side. Snead is not quite as effective with the long irons as Hogan and Nelson. Sam has a tendency to flatten them out and hook them. He plays them with his wooden club swing, and I would much rather see him hit a wood. Instead of playing his No. 1 iron, the average golfer is far better off playing his No. 4 wood.

Another club I cannot endorse for the average golfer is the straight-faced driver. I believe it throws a man off to see the heel of his club. He is much better off with a driver that has a slight hook face. Then, when he addresses his tee-shot, he will see the face of the club and this creates the necessary feeling in a golfer that he will pick the ball up and get through it. He will hit that shot with confidence. You can help yourself to get this feeling—that you are going to get through the ball easily—by taking a little time on each tee to select a level spot, or if anything, a slightly uphill lie. The experts all do this. You will never see them making the error common among weekend golfers of teeing up on a low spot and struggling from a downhill lie.

I am an outspoken advocate of shallow-face fairway woods. I like to see the top of the ball over the top of the club. That ball is going to get up with no effort, I know, and there are no bunkers in the air. I have yet to see the occasion when I needed a deep-faced brassie to keep the ball low. My match against Henry Picard in the 1940 P.G.A. was played after a torrential downpour, and the thick clover fairways of the Hershey Country Club were soggy, almost morassy. I managed to pull that match out because Henry couldn't get his brassie and spoon shots off the ground. The other players marveled at my wood shots off the fairway until they saw that my clubs had extremely shallow faces, and then they realized that the woods they were using were faulty for those particular conditions.

For a similar reason, the jigger is a club that has an enormous appeal for me. The ball always rides well over the top of the shallow blade at address. I hit my first golf shot with a jigger, and from that day on I never forgot how easily I got that ball off the ground; I have always had a definite partiality for that club. In my opinion it was the finest golf club that was ever in a duffer's bag. The jigger passed out of the picture when the clubs began to be numbered. The week-end golfer wanted to use numbered clubs like the pros he read about, and he felt he was being old-fashioned in relying on his jigger when none of the stars were reported to be playing jigger shots. The jigger has a very strong personality which overpowers the dull personalities of the No. 3 iron and the No. 4, and it would make sense to me if the jigger were given a number and incorporated in the modern set, possibly as an alternate for the No. 3 and the No. 4. My old jigger was the most responsive club I ever owned. I used to play it for everything from a No. 2 to a heavy 4. I could instinctively get just the height I wanted, lofting it over trees and banging it low beneath the limbs. I liked to chip with it. Every time Bobby Locke sees me, the first question he asks is, "Where are your jiggers, Gene?" He is as fond of the club as I am.

There would be a much larger percentage of confident iron players if golfers today weren't so hungry for distance, at the wrong time. A golfer gains nothing by trying to reach a green with a No. 8 iron from 165 yards out when the No. 5 iron is the club—nothing but the vain satisfaction of telling the boys about the tremendous distance he gets. He doesn't add that the ball rolled half the way, and he never narrates the gloomy tales of what happens twenty-four out of twenty-five times when he tries to impress himself with his own strength. You never hear of the wide hook, the fast slice, the lookup, and the fluff. When Babe Didrikson was first turning to golf, her desire to be a sensationally long hitter retarded her development. Babe would close the face of the seven and toe it in and belly the ball 170 yards. When Babe stopped kidding herself and began playing a seven like a seven and not like a two, she started to develop a grooved swing and a glorious golf game.

If I were asked which clubs are the most important for scoring, I would say the pitching staff—Nos. 7, 8, 9, and the sand-iron. These are the weapons that can set up a one-putt green. The leading players today use the sand-iron or wedge not only in traps but in the rough and on the fairway for playing shots 100 yards and under from the green. I see no reason why the average golfer should not do likewise, for the manufacturers have modified the sand-iron so that it can be played from rough grass and fairway lies. These modifications, narrowing the sole of the club, have, however, made the present models less efficient in traps than their wide-soled ancestors which came out in the thirties.

The sand-iron stroke remains the same on the fairway as in the trap. The club is picked up rather than swung, and picked up quite vertically, well on the outside of the normal line. You then come down on the same line as the backswing, cutting across the ball with an open face—hitting two inches or so behind the ball on the average explosion shot. Naturally, the longer the shot, the less sand you take. The most common fault among poor trap players is that they take the club back on the inside. They have two chances of getting out—slim and none.

The sand-iron is a club that demands many hours of practice, but once mastered it is the greatest stroke saver in the game. I'm proud to have invented it.

It takes some intelligence to play good golf. An ambitious player must think clearly about his practice habits and his equipment. On the course he must know his limitations and not expect to hit eighteen perfect tee-shots. Middlecoff and Mangrum don't. He mustn't destroy his concentration before a shot by wondering if thirty-three anatomical parts are going to perform their appointed functions. If he falls into an error which he does not understand, that's what qualified professionals are for. He must remember that a good grip is the foundation of a good golf swing. If your foundation is right, your house will stand firmly down through the years. If the foundation is faulty, it doesn't matter how well you have decorated the rooms, the house will collapse anyway. I am sincerely convinced that if the average player approaches the game sensibly, he will soon discover that he is well above average.

Chapter Three

1958–1965

F ROM THE FIRST time I was on a golf course with my father, I realized the way to my parents' hearts was through golf. They basically lived, breathed and slept it from the middle of March, when
they went to Sea Island, Georgia, for two weeks of golf, until the end
of October, when the putters came out in the living room. Even
with my young eyes, I could see that my parents had it pretty good.
In addition to the golfing they did together, my father and a bunch
of friends who called themselves the Bogey Club would go off for
days at a time to play one terrific golf course or another.

Though my golf awareness grew as the age of Arnie and Jack
was adorning, as heroes they were, with all apologies, too easy—
plus, my friend and golfing mate Wingdale idolized Arnie, and Jack

was, well, Jack. Gary Player was my man, in part because he wore black. In my family, we weren't allowed to wear black because that's what hoodlums wore. Then Gary Player put black on the golf course. For my birthday, I asked for and received my first black shirt—a LaCoste, of course—which, though cool as could be, was hot as hell in the blazing sun.

Wingdale was a major soldier in Arnie's army. Foreshadowing by many years the age of labels we live in, Wingdale played with the clubs Palmer used and wore Arnie's shirts and gloves and belts and pants. Wingdale was a better golfer than I was, but on any given day I could beat him. Unfortunately, often when I was ahead, I'd get to feeling bad—he took losing hard—and I'd give up holes I shouldn't have. Would that I'd had the killer instinct Arnie writes about in *Go for Broke: My Philosophy of Winning Golf.* I would have whupped Wingdale, as another sports figure of the time used to say.

I also played with my brother Peter, who was much more interested in girls than in golf. Playing with Peter was always fun, because he had a temper like no other I've seen on a golf course (and curiously, only on a golf course does his temper ever erupt). I still smile when I think of Peter burying the head of his putter in the middle of a green after missing an easy putt or flinging his five iron into the pond on the eighteenth hole after splashing his third ball into the drink. I hope Peter reads what Sam Snead had to say about anger in *The Education of a Golfer.* Now that Peter's on the eve of his fifties, golf seems to hold more interest for him than it did then. Nevertheless, water holes still psych him out, and he buys only the clubhouse's retrieved balls, which, knowing he'll buy the same balls back another day, he says he's only renting.

I pored over every *Sports Illustrated* delivered to our house but somehow missed Jack Nicklaus's "I Changed My Game to Win the Masters." My game never seemed to change. Wingdale chopped ten strokes off his game, and I still worried about how he felt when he lost. Still, I knew what I wanted. Under my graduation picture in the Iona Grammar School yearbook, my stated goal was to be a golf professional, high ambitions for a kid whose schoolmates included Claude Harmon's kids Butch and Billy.

When adolescence hit, I stopped being so serious. I played golf, but ceased caring whether I won or lost, and so, zenlike, I began to win more. Happiness followed, and fun, but then at the end of ninth grade, just as the golf season was coming into full bloom, I got caught by the police doing ninety miles per hour in our Corvair Monza convertible at four in the morning. My friend Dennis was riding shotgun, and the three most beautiful girls in town were in the back. When the cop shined his flashlight into the backseat and asked why the girls had done this, in unison they cried, "We didn't know." I was grounded for the entire summer and forbidden to see Dennis ever again. But three weeks later, one of my mother's friends called to ask if I could possibly play in a tournament our club would have to forfeit if I didn't show up. My mother grudgingly said all right.

I was thrilled to get out of the house. The kid I played, the son of a famous architect, was cheating like a bastard, but after eight holes, he was barely beating me. On the ninth, after a lousy drive, his second shot hooked into a tree and bounced back onto the fairway five feet behind him. I'd walked up the rough on the left, and as I stepped into the fairway to cross to where my ball was, I called back to my opponent and asked where he'd hit his. Indicating the hill ahead, between us and the green, he said, "Over the hill." I nonchalantly crossed the fairway, wanting to catch his cheating in action. Out of the corner of my eye, I saw him sneak back to his ball, set up, and hit what was probably his best fairway wood of the day. The ball shot straight at my head and, before I could move, hit me just above my right temple. And then an amazing thing happened. As stars came into view, a clear voice in my head said, "Omigod, I've been hit in the head with a golf ball. What do I do?" Another voice answered, "Fall down." And I did. My opponent ran up, asking if I was all right. I had a golf-ball–sized lump, but I was conscious. I asked, "What do you lie?" He said two. I started screaming, accused him of cheating, and said, "You lie three." I played out the hole, beat his ass on the nine, and then, because my vision was blurring and my head hurting, I walked in. The pro told me to put ice on the egg on my head and said I'd be fine, but then a friend of my mother's came by, said I had to go to the doctor, and took me there. To make a long story short, emerging from ten days of semicoma after a spinal tap, I was released from the hospital.

The sun now gave me headaches, so golf was out for me. Besides which, I was still grounded. I read all the books on my summer reading list, but friendless and miserable as I was, what I needed was something to cheer me up. On my father's bookshelf by his bed, I found an old copy of Richard Hooker's *M*A*S*H*. Hawkeye and the gang cheered me just fine, for a while. Still confined and usually alone, with everyone else in the family enjoying the summer fun, I took to watching the eight-millimeter movies my father had taken through the fifties. My favorites were of the parties my parents had and the things they did at the club. And I loved the one where my father and several of his friends, wearing grass skirts, danced the hula on stage. But *Sports Illustrated* writer Bob Boyle's article on country club life says it better than I ever could.

During my sophomore year in high school, the life had gone out of me. Then I was allowed to play golf again, and my hopes for a career stayed alive until the summer of 1965, when in Virginia Beach I played a willowy twelve-year-old who had learned golf on a municipal course and didn't seem to have a muscle in his body. He was allowed to play at Princess Anne because he was the Virginia junior champion, which I had a hard time believing—until he teed off. He had the slowest, easiest swing I've ever seen, and after the second hole it was clear to me that this kid played a different golf game than I did. Every time he struck the ball, I heard that click I strived for. He shot a 72. Without a gimme or a mulligan. Some got it, and some don't.

To top off a bad year, a close friend of my parents, on his young deathbed, asked my mother if she knew that Dad had lost his money, sold everything but the house, and as a result would have an income for ten years. Of course, she'd had no idea. She spread the bad news to us kids, who figured we'd be moving to a little house or maybe even to an apartment. We obviously knew nothing about the human capacity for self-delusion. Not only did nothing change in the financial life of our household, but to quote a minor poet, we sang in our chains like the sea.

Keeping the Shirt On: Golfer, Cure Thyself

SAM SNEAD

Sam Snead was golf's biggest drawing card in the 1930s and had what many called the finest swing in golf. "Slammin' Sam" won over 100 tournaments in his illustrious career, including three PGA Championships and three Masters, and was elected to the PGA Hall of Fame in 1953. This piece is from Snead's classic, Education of a Golfer.

Each man's boiling point differs, and different types of aggravations touch us off. Bob Rosburg, a current star, can't stand a partner who dawdles around the course, examining every shot. Poor chipping made Byron Nelson blow up. Dutch Harrison couldn't stand a crackling popcorn bag in a fan's hand. Whirring movie cameras could make Ben Hogan swear out loud—and me, too, until I formed the habit of just dropping my club to the grass and staring holes through the movie fan: this is much easier on your nerves and game than calling him a loggerhead, illegitimate S.O.B. On the green, I always have to remind myself to keep my head no matter what happens.

What drove this home was a round at St. Andrews, Scotland, where the fifth and fourteenth greens coincide into one huge rolling carpet. My approach wound up on the wrong green, leaving a 160-foot putt. The lag was 40 feet short.

"Dirty —!" I swore, whacking my putter against the sole of my shoe and then swinging it again. This time it was such a wallop that I bashed in the cap of my alligator-hide shoe. The pain as that toe began to swell made me want to bust out crying. I could barely see, for the tears in my eyes, but wouldn't admit it to the gallery and forced myself not to limp.

At the next hole, the agony got so bad that I had to sit down, remove my shoe, and poke out the cap with the shaft of my club. While I blew on my toe, about 10,000 people stood around snickering.

Ten days later my toenail fell off, and I couldn't play at all until a new one grew in.

Other times I've paid through the nose for having the physical sort of blowup where you try to hurt yourself as punishment for a missed shot.

In the last round of the Augusta Masters, after a short putt rimmed out, I leaned on the putter, almost to the breaking point. A few holes later, on No. 16, I angrily bent the putter again. This time it was weakened enough to snap off at mid-shaft. An official tapped my shoulder. "Under the rules, you cannot replace that club."

From then on I had to putt with my driver, and on No. 17 and No. 18, I found myself putting for birdies and missed both. The money difference between making and missing them was the difference between $2,500 and the $700 I collected.

The lesson you never want to forget is that you can't stay mad in golf without it hurting you.

In the case above I got off easy; in another blowup, when the shaft of my putter snapped, the sharp end punctured my palm and put me out of action for a while.

In private matches I threw dozens of clubs before cooling off on this after meeting a caddie in Philadelphia who carries a silver plate in his skull from a club thrown by a mad golfer. Another kid who once carried clubs for the pros was killed when struck by an iron hurled by a country-club member. This member was exonerated, after an investigation, then threw another stick and was kicked out of his club for life.

In tournaments, I go by Mark Twain's advice, which was to

count four when angry and when very angry to swear. Once in a while I'll step into the woods, out of sight, and beat the leaves off a bush. There's no club-throwing, though, nor abusing of officials, opponents, or the gallery. My practical side tells me that by blaming others, or your sticks, you show yourself to be a damned fool to people who might be valuable friends. A few years ago, the head of a sporting-goods firm asked me about a certain pro who was always picking up, wrecking clubs, and blasting officials.

"This boy has so much talent," he said, "that I'm thinking of paying him $50,000 to sign with us. What's your recommendation?" "I don't have one. Do what you like," I replied.

In the next few weeks, the player created scenes in two tournaments, and when I saw the manufacturer again, he said, "I've dropped so-and-so from consideration. I wouldn't have him at any price."

Sam Snead's Comment:
A Few Clues to Keeping Calm

What can a man do to curb his temper?

If you're talking about a young golfer, I'd say that Jack Burke, Sr., the late, great Texas pro and teacher, and Claude Harmon, the former Masters champion, had the proper slant. Burke's son, Jack, Jr., was eighteen years old when he appeared in a junior tournament in Houston, where he blew a payoff putt. Jack hauled off and banged his ball a mile off the green. Just then, his old man stepped from the gallery and, with fire shooting from both eyes, read the kid off in front of the spectators. "If you can't play without losing your head," he wound up, "give up the game."

Since then I've seen Jack, Jr., in spots where he'd love to bury his club in some noisy fan's skull. He has a tough disposition, having taught bayonet fighting and judo to combat Marines during World War II. But he walks away from blowups far more than he gives in to them. Jack keeps a lot of time and space between his moments of anger. With a temperament like that, he's won both the Masters and P.G.A. championships.

Claude Harmon's son is another fine player who once had temper trouble. "I just locked his clubs in the trunk of my car for a month," Claude tells me, "and from then on he took a grip on himself."

Youngsters around a course imitate their bad-acting elders. They think club throwing is the thing to do, having seen so much of it from the start. Professional fathers catch the kid early and knock it out of him, where many fathers just go on setting a terrible example.

For the older man who snarls like a tiger if somebody just jingles the change in his pocket, there are two facts I learned the hard way:

The minute you blow, a charge seems to go through your opponent and he begins to play better golf; you've shown him a weakness and practically asked him to take advantage of it.

And, by blowing, you bleed off your own energy from the job of making shots. Getting sore and staying that way is hard work. I have a saying about my own game—"all the wheels ran off the track." What that really means is that whenever I took an 80, as I once did in the Masters after leading the 1951 field into the final round, my temper got out of hand. I fought myself out of the money. It cost me a drop from first place to tenth at Augusta, 11 strokes off the pace I'd set for fifty-four holes.

Any time a wild spell is coming on, I try to switch my thoughts to something else. Doug Ford showed me how well this works when we were battling it out in the '54 Miami Open, a tournament I'd won five times previously. During the second round a kid of about eight in a baseball cap began to tag after Ford, asking to see his clubs and jabbering away. Between holes, the kid never got off his back. I thought Ford would throw him to the marshals on one bounce. A pro needs that absolute concentration.

Instead, Ford talked to the kid and laughed with him all around the course. Meanwhile, he fired a 67 and a 70 at me. The kid was still sticking like a burr to Ford the next day when he holed out an 80-yard wedge for an eagle 3 to beat me in the Open.

"What is this?" I asked Ford later.

"If I couldn't get mad at that pesky kid," answered Ford, "I couldn't get mad at *anything*."

Another thing: at all times you should definitely know what you're doing on the links, which isn't possible with your eyes bulging out. There are many rules in golf, and the angry player costs himself an edge here. In the 1958 Masters last round, Arnie Palmer's iron shot on the par-3 twelfth hole was embedded in spongy ground off the green. The rains had brought a local ruling that a buried ball could be dropped without penalty. Just to pin it down, Palmer checked with an official, who said, "No—you have to play it as it lies."

In Palmer's place, I'd have wanted to explode. Palmer *knew* the man was wrong, and yet, there he stood, shaking his head and shutting the door in Arnie's face. You could see Palmer struggling with himself. Then he said, "You're wrong, but I'll play it where it lies." He needed 4 shots to get down from the mud.

And then, very cool, Palmer went back to where his ball had been buried, dropped a provisional ball, chipped up, and was down in par 3. "I'll want a ruling on this," he warned the officials.

He got it three holes later—in his favor.

Palmer won the Masters by 1 shot—284 to Fred Hawkins' and Doug Ford's 285s.

I don't say Palmer wasn't plenty riled. It was the fact that he stayed cool-mad that won him $11,250.

Not so long ago I was playing a round with Vic Ghezzi, the old scrambler and automatic-machine tycoon, and with whom I've blown many a fuse. When I missed a shot, I twisted myself into a full-body turn in order to throw my club for a new Snead distance record.

"Save it, Sam," said Vic. "You set a record long ago you'll never top."

"When was that?" I asked.

"In the Western Open at Canterbury, the time you disqualified yourself."

Then it all came back from fifteen years before—how Vic and I had teed off and after I'd gone sixteen holes in 3 under par he'd asked me, "Do you have all your clubs with you?"

Looking into my bag, I said, "Yep—all sixteen of them."

"Well, it's a long hike to the clubhouse and you might as well start walking in now," said Vic. "They put a new limit on clubs the other day. It's fourteen now. Or didn't you hear?"

Before leaving to be disqualified, I got down to the legal limit. Some of these days, I'll bet, one of those extra clubs will be picked up by the satellite-tracking stations.

The Maddening First Hole

ARNOLD PALMER

The most popular player in the history of golf, and the man responsible for the "golf explosion" of the 1960s, Arnold Palmer needs little introduction. In 1967, he became the first to win a million dollars in prize money, much of which he won with long drives and gutsy late tournament charges. This bold style of play endeared him to his fans who follow him religiously and became known as "Arnie's Army." They have been there to witness his seven major championships, including four Masters, and continue their allegiance to this day.

There was a sharp bite and sparkle in the mountain air. The Rockies loomed clearly in the distance—immense, clean, barren. I remember on the first hole at Denver, the sun was so bright that it hurt your eyes to look down the fairway. Standing on the tee, it was difficult to see the green without a pair of dark glasses. It took me four rounds to find it—but when I did, the whole thrust of my life was altered.

The time was 1960. The place was Cherry Hills Country Club. The event was the U. S. Open.

On the fourth round of that tournament, I tried a shot that I'd missed three times in three rounds. I tried it again not because I'd failed—or because I like failure—but because I was convinced that it was the shot necessary to win the tournament.

A bold shot?

Yes.

But you must play boldly to win. My whole philosophy has been based on winning golf tournaments, not on finishing a careful fifth, or seventh, or tenth.

A reckless shot?

No.

In eighteen years of tournament golf I feel that I've never tried a shot that I couldn't make.

On that summer day in 1960, I was young in what the world calls fame, but I was ripe in golfing experience. I'd been a professional golfer for five years, and up to then I'd won twenty tournaments. In those years, I'd learned something about the strategy of the game and its psychology and rewards. If there was any reward I treasured most, it was the way that the game responded to my inner drives, to the feeling we all have that—in those moments that are so profoundly a challenge to man himself—he has done his best. That—win or lose—nothing more could have been done.

My own needs were deeply driven ones: I could not retreat from a challenge. If the chance was there and if—no matter how difficult it appeared—it meant winning, I was going to take it. It was the "sweetness" of risk that I remembered, and not its dangers.

In looking back, I feel that in these years I was learning something of the subtle dimensions of all this—I was learning the *meaning* of boldness as well as its feeling.

For boldness does not mean "recklessness" to me. Rather it involves a considered confidence: I know I'm going to make the shot that seems reckless to others. I also know the value of the risk involved: A bold shot has to have its own rewards winning or losing the match, winning or losing the tournament.

But perhaps it was not until the U.S. Open at Cherry Hills that I put it all together, philosophically as well as physically. For not until that summer day in 1960 did it become apparent to me how boldness might influence not just a hole but an entire round, an entire tournament, and even an entire golfing career.

It began, really, on the first tee of the last round at Cherry Hills. On the face of it, there was nothing terribly subtle about this hole:

You could see every mistake you made. It was downhill to the green; the tee was elevated perhaps 150 feet above the green. It was only 346 yards long, not a terribly long par 4—and a terribly tempting birdie 3 . . . to me. It was guarded on the left by an irregular line of poplars and pines and on the right by a ditch that the membership had practically paved with golf balls. A nice direct hole for the strong driver, somebody who could—in that thin, mile-high air—get the ball out there 300 yards or so.

But there *was* one nasty little afterthought that had been provided for the U.S. Open: The grass was allowed to grow very long and become a "rough" right in the fairway, about 50 or 60 yards in front of the green. Moreover, the hazard was heightened by a treacherous bunker guarding the gateway to the green. It had grass in it that looked like it was three feet deep. If you got in there, you might never be found again. I mean it was the kind of place where you hunted buffalo—not par.

The idea, of course, was to penalize the strong driver, to threaten him with capture by the rough—and a difficult second shot—if he played to his own best game (a powerful drive) on his first shot.

The safe way to play that hole, for most golfers, was not to invite trouble—not to challenge the rough or the bunker in the first place. In that sense, the first hole was an authentic mirror of the entire course. For Cherry Hills was long in yardage (7004) but not in reality: The thin air gave most tee shots a much longer carry than on a sea-level course. But its greens were small and well guarded by bunkers and water hazards; there was an added danger that under the hot, direct sun and the afternoon winds they would become so dried out that it would be all but impossible to get the ball to stop on them. If you hit those greens with power, the ball would roll right over and off them on the far side. So it was a course that took accuracy, touch, and an unflagging concentration. It *looked* to many like a course whose yardage beckoned to power—Mike Souchak, a powerful golfer, led at the halfway mark of the 1960 Open with a remarkable 68-67 for a thirty-six-hole score of 135. But it was, in reality, a course that catered to placement more than to power—in that opening round of 68, Souchak had only twenty-six putts, nine or ten short of normal for an eighteen-hole round. So he wasn't up there scattering power shots; he was getting good placement with everything he did.

To focus on the first hole: It was the kind of hole that shaped your entire approach to the course in that it could reward you for power or for placement.

To the pretty good amateur golfer, it was an opportunity for a par 4. He might put the ball out in the fairway pretty much where he could—far short of the rough—and then hope to get close to, or onto, the green with his second shot.

To the venturesome pro, it was an opportunity for a birdie. He'd use an iron to hit his shot off the tee, expecting to get enough accuracy from it (which he would less likely get from a driver) to drop the ball precisely in the fairway, where he'd have the ideal second shot. In short, he intended to place his first shot so that he could hit his second shot precisely to the cup—not just any old place on the green but *specifically* to the cup. For this was the kind of shot where the pro prefers—where he *intends*—to get his second shot so close to the cup that he'll need only one putt to "get down." So if he emphasized placement over power, he hoped to wind up with a birdie 3, not a par 4.

From my angle of vision—somewhat singular, I'll admit this was an eagle hole, not a birdie hole. I figured that, with boldness, I could get down in two strokes, not three or four.

That meant being on the green in one shot, not two.

That meant getting into the cup in one putt, not two.

That meant emphasizing power over placement.

That meant using my driver, not my iron.

My intention was simply to drive the ball hard enough and far enough so that it would bound through the rough in front of the green and run up on the putting surface to a good position near the cup. To get a ball to stop precisely on a green, you must give it backspin, so that it bites into the grass when it hits and then stops short, or even hops backward. That's fairly easy to do when you're using an iron from the fairway that is fairly close to the green; you merely strike straight downward at the ball, taking a divot after making contact with the ball, and take a normal follow-through. But it is difficult to do while driving off the tee and ramming the ball through the rough. For one thing, on tee shots you may be hitting the ground a microsecond before you make contact with the ball. At least that's what I was doing with my driver back in 1960 (though since then I've changed my style somewhat). Then you normally give the ball a considerable overspin when you hit the ball dead center (or thereabouts) and make the big follow-through. Normally you want to give the ball some overspin when hitting off the tee with a driver. Overspin will cause the ball to roll a little farther after it hits the ground. So my tee shot would, I expected, be hitting those small greens without backspin. And if the greens were dry and hard, as I expected, the ball might never stop rolling this side of the Continental Divide.

So I was proposing to use a power club—the driver—rather than a placement club—the iron—on a hole that demanded placement as well as power. And I was accepting overspin, not backspin, on a green that threatened to be faster than the Indianapolis Speedway on Memorial Day.

"Boldness" is what my friends called it. "Insanity" is what they meant.

But I figured to have two things going for me when the ball hit the green:

If the ball went through the rough, not over it, the thick grass would cut down significantly on the ball's momentum, and very likely on how far it would roll, once it hit the green. Also, I'd be playing this hole relatively early in the morning on the first three rounds. (On the fourth and last round—because of the way the U.S. Open was run in those days—I'd be playing it in the early afternoon.) I knew that every green was being heavily watered at night, simply because the tournament officials were afraid that otherwise the greens would be hard and dry by the afternoon. So in the morning, the first green—obviously the first to be played—would likely be heavily laden with the water from the all-night sprinkling, and the water residue would slow down any ball hit onto it. That's another reason why the roll of the ball would be reduced.

(You didn't *really* think that I just went out there and hit the ball hard, without giving any thought to what would happen to it once it came down—now did you?)

The way I looked at it, all I had to do was pound the ball bouncingly through the rough and onto the heavily watered green. Then I'd one-putt and have an eagle. I'd have that course by the throat, and—as my fellow pro, Jerry Barber, once said—"shake it to death."

Only it didn't happen. Not on the first three rounds. That green was tough to reach with a rifle, much less a driver. In my first round I sent my tee shot into the ditch on the right. I didn't get an eagle or a birdie or a par on the hole. I didn't even get a bogey, for that matter. I got a double bogey 6—two over par, instead of the two under par that I'd aimed for. After that, things got better—but not much. I got a bogey 5 on the second round and a par 4 on the third round. So in the first three rounds, I'd taken fifteen strokes on that hole, instead of the twelve strokes that playing it safe might have given me. And instead of the six strokes that—in wild flights of genius—my boldness might have given me.

More than that, starting off every round with a deep disappointment damaged my whole pattern of play. After three rounds, I had a total of thirteen birdies in the tournament, but they were so scattered that I'd never gotten any momentum out of them—no "charge," so to speak. The result was that I was in fifteenth place with a 215 after three rounds.

Just before lunch, and the start of my last round, I paused outside the vast white scoreboard outside the rambling, neo-Tudor clubhouse at Cherry Hills. There in the elaborate black and red numerals of golf, written in a manner as highly stylized as medieval script, I saw how the field lay. I was seven strokes behind the leader, Mike Souchak. But Mike wasn't the only hurdle. Between me and the leadership lay such great golfers as Ben Hogan and Sam Snead, Julius Boros and Dow Finsterwald, Dave Marr and Bob Goalby, and a twenty-one-year-old amateur named Jack Nicklaus.

By the time I sat down to a sandwich in the clubhouse, my mood was about as black as a witch's heart. Ken Venturi and Bob Rosburg, who also seemed to be out of contention, joined me, and a couple of newsmen stopped by our table to offer solace to the newly bereaved.

One of them was an old friend, Bob Drum, then of the Pittsburgh *Press*. He knew of my tribulations with that first hole and of my conviction that it was an eagle hole that would unlock the entire course to the player bold enough to attack it. He also knew that my failure in a daring power approach had—in an era of golf when meticulous precision was most admired—given a certain satisfaction to a few older hands around professional golf. "There are some guys out there who think you're just an upstart, a flash in the pan," he'd told me. So when he began to console me, and hint that maybe it was time to play it safe and try to pick up some good also-ran money in the U.S. Open—since it was obvious I couldn't go from fifteenth place to first place in one round—the chemistry began working in me. Explosively.

"What would happen if I shot a 65 on this last round?" I asked, perhaps more aggressively than in the thirst for pure knowledge.

"Nothing," said Bob. "You're out of it." He was an old friend but a realistic one. Only one man had *ever* shot a 65 in the final round of the U.S. Open: Walter Burkema in 1957.

But that got to me. And to my pride. Realism—and pessimism—I did not need.

"Well," I said, my voice lowering into my don't-tread-on-me tone, "the way I read it is that a 65 would give me 280 for the tournament. And 280 is the kind of score that usually wins the U.S. Open."

Bob gave me a startled look, as if he just noticed I had two heads.

"Sure," he said, "but you won't do it by taking another double-bogey on the first hole."

So there it was: I still looked at the first hole as a chance for triumph; Bob—and a great many others—looked at it as a place for patent disaster. I suppose they were right. If I'd played it safe on the first hole and teed off with my iron, instead of the driver, and gone for placement and par, I'd be three shots closer to the leaders after the first three rounds. If I'd picked up a birdie or two along with it, I might even be right on their necks. So the thing to do now was admit that the first hole had me beaten and go back to playing it like the other pros did—with an iron off the tee—and figure that by placing the ball and playing it safe, I might pick up enough strokes in the standing to avoid further shame.

But that's not the way I saw it. I wasn't playing golf to avoid shame. I was playing it to win championships. And the last round of a National Open is no place to start changing your whole style and philosophy of golf.

The way I looked at it, being fifteenth made it more *imperative* that I play boldly. It couldn't cost me much: The difference between being fifteenth or twenty-fifth or fifty-fifth is not terribly meaningful—at least to me. It's the difference between first and second that has meaning. And a considered boldness might—I was sure—still win me the tournament.

So when I got to the first tee, I reached for my driver. Even though it was now one-forty-five in the afternoon and the green figured to be dried out and it would take incredible accuracy to hit the green and hold it. One of my luncheon companions (not Bob Drum) had come along, and he looked as if there were nothing wrong with me that brain surgery couldn't cure. I addressed the ball as if it were my enemy—or my slave—and hit it with everything I could get into it. The ball went up and hung in the sharp, clear air as if it had been painted there. When it came down—with overspin—it leaped forward and ran through the rough and right onto the middle of the green.

Twenty feet from the hole.

Three hundred and forty-six yards and I'd not only driven the green but drilled it right in the heart!

Just like I'd been planning it all along.

Right? Right!

Okay—two putts. A birdie, not an eagle. But that didn't much depress me. For I'd show that my idea *did* work—that boldness could conquer this hole. And that if it made the first hole yield, then the whole course could be conquered with boldness.

Suddenly my whole spirit, my entire attitude changed.

I charged onto the second hole—a 410-yard par 4 with an elevated green and trees right in the fairway. In two shots I was not quite on the green. But I chipped the ball from off the green right into the cup for another birdie 3. I charged onto the 348-yard third hole and birdied it, I charged onto the fourth hole and birdied it with a twisting 40-foot putt. Four holes, four birdie 3s. A par on the fifth, a birdie on the sixth, a birdie on the seventh: six birdies on seven holes. I finished the first nine holes in 30 strokes, just one short of a record.

"Damn!" I said to Bob Drum when he finally caught up to us. "I really wanted that 29." Bob exhibited deplorable self-control: "Well," he murmured consolingly. "Maybe next time."

By the tenth hole, I was tied with Mike Souchak. By the twelfth, I was ahead of him. But it was not all over: There had been fourteen men between me and the lead. And before the afternoon was over, a half dozen or more held or challenged for the title. "This was, to put it mildly, the wildest Open ever," said *Sports Illustrated.* For me, the birdies disappeared, but the pars survived. The final five holes at Cherry Hills are a punishing finishing stretch: Ben Hogan, then forty-seven, felt it and he faded here; Nicklaus was twenty-one, and so did he. I managed to play each of those last five holes in par and to come in with a 65 for the eighteen-hole round. Boldness had paid off: That surge at the start was, in the words of golf writer Herbert Warren Wind, "the most explosive stretch of sub-par golf any golfer has ever produced in the championship. . . ." I finished the tournament with a seventy-two-hole score of 280. That was enough to give me the U.S. Open championship and, as it developed, a certain hold on history.

For the "charge" didn't stop there. It was not, in the long per-spective, to be confined solely to one round or one tournament. It became a sort of phenomenon that marked my career: In the period 1960–63, I was to win thirty-two tournaments and go on to become the first million-dollar winner in golf history.

From *M*A*S*H*

RICHARD HOOKER

*Richard Hornberger, a doctor from Maine who served in the Korean War, spent twelve years trying to publish his book detailing his experiences as a war surgeon in Korea. M*A*S*H was finally published in 1968 under his pen-name which Hornberger said came from his golf game—Richard Hooker.*

Trapper John McIntyre had grown up in a house adjacent to one of suburban Boston's finest country clubs. His parents were members, and, at the age of seventeen, he was one of the better junior golfers in Massachusetts.

Golf had not played a prominent role in Hawkeye Pierce's formative years. Ten miles from Crabapple Cove, however, there was a golf course patronized by the summer resident group. During periods when the pursuit of clams and lobsters was unprofitable, Hawkeye had found employment as a caddy. From time to time he had played with the other caddies and, one year, became the caddy champion of the Wawenock Harbor Golf Club. This meant that he was the only one of ten kids who could break ninety.

In college Hawkeye's obligation to various scholarships involved attention to other games, but during medical school, his internship and his residency he had played golf as often as possible. Joining a club had been out of the question, and even payment of green fees was economically unsound. Therefore he developed a technique which frequently allowed him the privilege of playing some public and a number of unostentatious private courses. He would walk confidently into a pro shop, smile, comment upon the nice condition of the course, explain that he was just passing through and that he was Joe, Dave or Jack Somebody, the pro from Dover. This resulted, about eight times out of ten, in an invitation to play for free. If forced into conversation, he became the pro from Dover, New Hampshire, Massachusetts, New Jersey, England, Ohio, Delaware, Tennessee, or Dover-Foxcroft, Maine, whichever seemed safest.

There was adequate room to hit golf balls at the Double Natural, and with the arrival of spring Trapper and Hawkeye had commissioned the chopper pilots to bring clubs and balls from Japan. Then they had established a practice range of sorts in the field behind the officers' latrine. The Korean house boys were excellent ball shaggers, so the golfing Swampmen spent much of their free time hitting wood and iron shots. They began to suspect that if they ever got on a real course they'd burn it up, at least from tee to green, but that possibility seemed as remote as their chances of winning the Nobel Prize for medicine.

The day after The Second Coming of Trapper John, however, a young Army private, engaged in training maneuvers near Kokura, Japan, had, when a defective grenade exploded, been struck in the chest by a fragment. X-rays revealed blood in the right pleural cavity, which contains the lung, the possible presence of blood within the pericardium, which surrounds the heart, and a metallic foreign body which seemed, to the Kokura doctors in attendance, to be within the heart itself.

Two factors complicated the case: (1) there was no chest surgeon in the area and (2) the soldier's father was a member of Congress. Had it not been for the second complication, the patient would have been sent to the Tokyo Army Hospital where the problem could have been handled promptly and capably.

When informed immediately of his son's injury, however, the Congressman consulted medical friends and was referred to a widely known Boston surgeon whose advice in this matter would be the best available. The Boston surgeon told the Congressman that, regardless of what the Army had to say, the man to take care of his son was Dr. John F. X. McIntyre, now stationed at the 4077th MASH somewhere in Korea. Congressmen make things move. Within hours a jet was flying out of Kokura and then a chopper was whirling out of Seoul, bearing X-rays, a summary of the case, and orders for Captain McIntyre and anyone else he needed to get to Kokura in a hurry.

Unaware of all this excitement, Trapper John and Hawkeye were hitting a few on the driving range when the chopper from Seoul arrived. They first heard, then saw, it approaching, but as they were off-duty and it was coming from the south anyway, they ignored it. Trapper, still taken with his new image, had not gotten around to shaving his beard or having his hair cut, and he was bending over and teeing up a ball when the pilot, directed to them, walked up.

"Captain McIntyre?" the pilot said.

"What?" Trapper John said, straightening up and turning to face his visitor.

"God!" the pilot said, stunned by his first look at the man whose importance had set a whole chain of command from generals down to clerk-typists into action.

"His son," Hawkeye said. "Would you like to buy an autographed picture for. . . ?"

"*You're* Captain McIntyre?" the pilot said.

"That's what the Army calls me," Trapper said. "Take off your shirt, stick out your tongue and tell me about the pain."

Completely bewildered now, the pilot silently handed over the white envelope containing orders and the explanatory letter from General Hamilton Hartington Hammond and with it the large brown manila envelope containing the X-rays of the chest of the Congressman's son. Trapper read the first and handed them over to Hawkeye and then, as Trapper held the X-rays up to the sunlight, the two looked at them.

"I don't think the goddam thing's in his heart," said Hawkeye, without great assurance.

"Course it isn't," affirmed Trapper John, "but let's not annoy the Congressman. Let us leave for Kokura immediately, with our clubs."

Delaying only long enough to clear it with Henry, they lugged their clubs to the chopper, boosted them in and climbed in after them. At Seoul, Kimpo airport was shrouded with fog and rain, which did not prevent the chopper from landing but which precluded the takeoff of the C-47 scheduled to take them to Kokura. To pass the time in pleasant company, the two surgeons ambled over to the Officers' Club where, after the covey of Air Force people at the bar got over the initial shock, they made the visitors welcome.

"But you guys are a disgrace," said one, after the fourth round. "You can't expect the Air Force to deliver such items to Japan."

"Our problem," Hawkeye explained, "is that right now we've got the longest winning streak in the history of military medicine going, so we don't dare get shaved or shorn. What else can you suggest?"

"Well, we might at least dress you up a little," one of the others said.

"I'm partial to English flannel," Hawkeye said.

"Imported Irish tweed," Trapper said.

The flyboys had recently staged a masquerade party in their club and they still had a couple of Papa-San suits. Papa-San suits take their name from the elderly Korean gentlemen who sport them, and they are long, flowing robes of white or black, topped off by tall hats that look like bird cages.

At 2:00 A.M., Trapper and Hawkeye climbed aboard the C-47, resplendent in their white drapery and bird cages, their clubs over their shoulders. Five hours later they disembarked at Kokura into bright sunlight, found the car with 25TH STATION HOSPITAL emblazoned on its side, crawled into the back and awakened the driver.

"Garrada there," the sergeant said.

"What?" Trapper said.

"He's from Brooklyn," Hawkeye said. "He wants us to vacate this vehicle."

"I said 'garrada there,'" the sergeant said, "or I'll . . ."

"What's the matter?" Trapper said. "You're supposed to pick up the two pros who are gonna operate on the Congressman's son, aren't you?"

"What?" the sergeant said. "You mean *you* guys are the doctors?"

"You betcher ever-lovin' A, buddy-boy," Hawkeye said.

"Poor kid," the sergeant said. "Goddam army . . ."

"Look sergeant," Trapper said, "if that spleen of yours is bothering you, we'll remove it right here. Otherwise, let's haul ass."

"Goddam army," the sergeant said.

"That's right," Hawkeye said, "and on the way fill us in on the local golfing facilities. We gotta operate this kid and then get in at least eighteen holes."

The sergeant followed the path of least resistance. On the way he informed the Swampmen that there was a good eighteen-hole course not far from the hospital but that, as the Kokura Open was starting the next day, the course was closed to the public.

"So that means we've got a big decision to make," Trapper said.

"What's that?" Hawkeye said.

"The way I see it," Trapper said, for the benefit of the sergeant, "we can operate on this kid and then qualify for this Kokura Open, or we can qualify first and then operate on this kid, if he's still alive."

"Goddam army," the sergeant said.

"Decisions, decisions, decisions," Hawkeye said. "After all, *we* didn't hit the kid in the chest with that grenade."

"Right!" Trapper said. "And it's not *our* chest."

"It's not even our kid," Hawkeye said. "He belongs to some Congressman."

"Yeah," Trapper said, "but let's operate on him first anyway. Then we'll be nice and relaxed to qualify. We wouldn't want to blow that."

"Good idea," Hawkeye said.

"Goddam, goddam army," the sergeant said.

Delivered to the front entrance of the 28th Station Hospital, Trapper and Hawkeye entered and approached the reception desk. Behind it sat a pretty WAC, whose big blue eyes opened like morning glories when she looked up and saw the apparitions before her.

"Nice club you've got here, honey," said Hawkeye. "Where's the pro shop?"

"What?" she said.

"What time's the bar open?" Trapper said.

"What?" she said.

"You got any caddies available?" Hawkeye said.

"What?" she said.

"Look, honey," Trapper said. "Don't keep saying 'what.' Just say 'yes' instead."

"That's right," Hawkeye said, "and you'll be surprised how many friends you'll make in this man's army."

"Yes," she said.

"That's better," Trapper said. "So where's the X-ray department?"

"Yes," she said.

They wandered down the main hallway, people turning to look at them as they passed, until they came to the X-ray department. They walked in, put their clubs in a corner and sat down. They put their feet on the radiologist's desk and lighted cigarettes.

"Don't set fire to your beard," Hawkeye cautioned Trapper John.

"Can't," Trapper said. "Had it fire-proofed."

"What the. . . ?" somebody in the gathering circle of interested X-ray technicians started to say.

"All right," Trapper said. "Somebody trot out the latest pictures of this kid with the shell fragment in his chest."

No one moved.

"Snap it up," yelled Hawkeye. "We're the pros from Dover, and the last pictures we saw must be forty-eight hours old by now." Without knowing why, a confused technician produced the X-rays. The pros perused them carefully.

"Just as we thought," said Trapper. "A routine problem."

"Yeah," Hawkeye said. "They must have a hair trigger on the panic button here. Where's the patient?"

"Ward Six," somebody answered.

"Take us there."

Led to Ward Six, the pros politely asked the nurse if they might see the patient. The poor girl, having embarked from the States many months before fully prepared in her mind for any tortures the enemy might inflict upon her, was unprepared for this.

"I don't know," she said. "I don't think I can allow you to see him without the permission of Major Adams."

"Adams?" Trapper said. "John Adams?"

"Adams?" Hawkeye said. "John Quincy Adams?"

"No. George Adams."

"Never heard of him," Trapper said. "Come on now, nice nurse-lady. Let's see the kid."

They followed the hapless nurse into the ward and she led them to the patient. A brief examination revealed that, although the boy did have a two-centimeter shell fragment and a lot of blood in his right chest and that removal of both was relatively urgent, he was in no immediate danger. His confidence and well-being were not particularly enhanced, however, by the bearded, robed, big-hatted character who had dumped a bag of golf clubs at the foot of his bed and had then started to listen to his chest.

"Have no fear, Trapper John is here," Hawkeye assured him in a loud voice, and then, privately, he whispered in the patient's ear: "Don't worry, son. This is Captain McIntyre, and he's the best chest surgeon in the Far East and maybe the whole U.S. Army. He's gonna fix you up easy. Your Daddy saw to that."

When they asked, the Swampmen were told by the nurse that blood had been typed and that an adequate supply had been cross-matched. They picked up their clubs and, following directions, headed for the operating area where they found their way barred by a fierce Captain of the Army Nurse Corps.

"Stop, right where you are!" she ordered.

"Don't get mad, ma'am," Hawkeye said. "All we want is our starting time."

"Get out!" she screamed.

"Look, mother," Trapper said. "I'm the pro from Dover. Me and my greenskeeper want to crack that kid's chest and get out to the course. Find the gas-passer and tell him to premedicate the patient, and find this Major Adams so he can get his spiel over with. Also, while you're at it, I need a can of beans and my greenskeeper here wants ham and eggs. It's now eight o'clock. I want to work at nine. Hop to it!"

She did, much to her own surprise. Breakfast was served, followed immediately by Major Adams who, after his initial shock, adjusted to the situation when it developed that all three had a number of mutual friends in the medical dodge.

"I don't know about the C.O., though," Major Adams said, meaning the Commanding Officer.

"Who is he?" Hawkeye said.

"Colonel Ruxton P. Merrill. Red-neck R.A. all the way."

"Don't worry about him," Trapper said. "We'll handle him."

At nine o'clock the operation started. At nine-oh-three Colonel Merrill, having heard about the unusual invasion of his premises, stormed into the operating room. He was without gown, cap or mask, so Hawkeye, deploring the break in the antiseptic techniques prescribed for OR's, turned to the circulating nurse and ordered: "Get that dirty old man out of this operating room."

"I'm Colonel Merrill!" yelled Colonel Merrill.

Hawkeye turned and impaled him on an icy stare. "Beat it, Pop. If this chest gets infected, I'll tell the Congressman on you."

After that there was no further excitement, and the operation, as the Swampmen had surmised, turned out to be routine. Within forty-five minutes the definitive work was done, and only the chest closure remained.

When the operation had started, the anesthesiologist of the 25th Station Hospital had been so busy getting the patient asleep in order to meet the deadline imposed by the pros from Dover that he had not been introduced. Furthermore, he had not seen them without their masks—nor had they seen him—but when he had a chance to settle down and relax, the shell fragment and the blood having been removed to the perceptible betterment of the patient's condition, he wrote at the top of his anesthesia record the name "Hawkeye Pierce" in the space labeled "First Assistant." He wrote it with assurance and with pleasure.

The anesthesiologist was Captain Ezekiel Bradbury (Me Lay) Marston, V, of Spruce Harbor, Maine. In Spruce Harbor, Maine, the name Marston is synonymous with romantic visions of the past—specifically clipper ships—and money. The first to bear the name captained a clipper, bought it and built three more. The second commanded the flagship of the fleet and bought four more. Number III was skipper of the *Spruce Harbor,* which went down with all hands off Hatteras some three years after number IV had been born in its Captain's cabin forty miles south of Cape Horn. Number V was Me Lay Marston, the only swain in Spruce Harbor High who could say, "Me lay, you lay?" and parlay such a simple, unimaginative approach into significant success with the young females of the area.

Hawkeye Pierce thought of it first, and last, but Me Lay Marston had also gone around for a while with the valedictorian of the Class of '41 at Port Waldo High School. In November, 1941, after Spruce Harbor beat Port Waldo 38–0, Pierce and Marston engaged in a fist fight which neither won decisively. In subsequent years they belonged to the same fraternity at Androscoggin College, played on the same football team, attended the same medical school and, during internship, they shared the same room. Me Lay was an usher when Hawkeye Pierce married the valedictorian, and Hawkeye provided a similar service when Me Lay did the same for the Broad from Eagle Head, whom Hawkeye had also dated for a while.

During his adolescence and earliest manhood, Me Lay had been proud of his name. Now, circumstances having forced him to correct his behavior, he was merely resigned to it. By 1952, however, he had not been addressed as Me Lay for three years. He had not seen Hawkeye Pierce for three years.

So on a bright, warm day in Kokura the fifth in a series of Captain Marstons looked up from his chart and asked, "May I have the surgeon's name, please?"

Hawkeye Pierce answered, "He's the pro from Dover and I'm the Ghost of Smoky Joe."

"Save that crap for someone else, you stupid clamdigger," answered Captain Marston.

The surgeons stopped. The first assistant leaned over and looked at the anesthesia chart and saw his name. He knew the writing and recognized the writer. He took it in his stride.

"Me Lay, I'd like you to meet Trapper John."

"The real Trapper John? Your cousin who threw you the pass and went on to greater fame on the Boston & Maine?"

"The one and only," affirmed Hawkeye.

"Trapper, you are in bad company," said Me Lay, "but I'll be happy to shake your hand if you'll hurry up and get that chest closed. You still workin' the trains?"

"Planes mostly. May take a crack at rickshaws. You still employing the direct approach?"

"No, not since I married the Broad from Eagle Head. I've been out of action now for four years."

"Then what the hell do you do around here?" asked Hawkeye. "It doesn't look like you're very busy. You mean to tell us you don't chase the local scrunch?"

"I don't seem to be interested in it from that angle. The first month I was here all I did was wind my watch and evacuate my bladder. Now I'm taking a course in Whorehouse Administration."

"Under the auspices of the Army's Career Management Plan?" inquired Trapper.

"No, all on my own."

"It was Yankee drive and ingenuity that built the Marston fortune," Hawkeye pointed out. "I'm proud of you, Me Lay. Where are you taking the course?"

"At Dr. Yamamoto's Finest Kind Pediatric Hospital and Whorehouse," Captain Marston informed him.

"Cut the crap, Me Lay. This sounds like too much even for you."

"I'm serious. This guy practices pediatrics, has a little hospital and runs a whorehouse, all in the same building."

"What are you? A pimp?"

"No. I keep the books, inspect the girls and take care of some of the kids in the hospital. Occasionally I tend bar and act as bouncer. A guy needs well-rounded training to embark on a career such as this."

The chest got closed, despite the conversation. In the dressing room the Swampmen got back into their Papa-San suits and continued the reunion with Me Lay Marston.

"What's with this Colonel Merrill?" asked Trapper.

"Red-neck R.A. all the way," Captain Marston said. "He'll give you a bad time if you let him."

A messenger entered and stated that Captains Pierce and McIntyre were to report to the colonel's office immediately. Me Lay gave them the address of the FKPH&W and suggested that they meet him there at seven that evening for dinner and whatnot.

"OK," Hawkeye said, and then he turned to the messenger waiting to guide them to the colonel's office. "Got any caddy carts?"

"What?" the messenger said.

Sighing, they slung their clubs over their shoulders and followed the guide. The colonel was temporarily occupied elsewhere, so rather than just sit there during his absence and read his mail, the Swampmen decided to practice putting on his carpet.

"You men are under arrest," the colonel boomed, when he stormed onto the scene.

"Quiet!" Trapper said. "Can't you see I'm putting?"

"Why, you . . ."

"Let's get down to bare facts, Colonel," Hawkeye said. "Probably even you know this case didn't demand our presence. Be that as it may, your boys blew it. We bailed it out, and a Congressman is very much interested. We figure this kid needs about five days of postop care from us, and we also figure to play in the Kokura Open. If that ain't okay with you, we'll get on the horn to a few Congressmen."

"Or one, anyway," Trapper John said.

It was mean but not too bold, and they knew it would work. They took their clubs and walked out. At the front door of the hospital they found the car which had brought them from the airport. It was the colonel's car, and the sergeant was lounging nearby, awaiting the colonel. Trapper John and Hawkeye got into the front seat.

"Hey, wait a minute," the sergeant said.

"The colonel is lending us his car," Hawkeye informed the sergeant. "We'll give it back after the Open."

"That's right," Trapper said. "He wants you to go in now, and write some letters for the Congressman's son."

"Goddam army," the sergeant said.

They drove to the golf course and parked, unloaded their clubs and walked into the pro shop. Although most of the golfers were members of the American and British armed forces, the pro was Japanese and he greeted the appearance of two Korean Papa-Sans with evident hostility.

"How do we qualify for the Open?" asked Hawkeye.

"There twenty-five dollar entry fee," the pro informed him, eyeing him coldly.

"But I'm the pro from Dover, and this here is my assistant," announced Hawkeye, handing the Japanese his Maine State Golf Association handicap card.

"Ah, so," the Japanese hissed.

"We're just in from visiting relatives in Korea," Trapper informed him. "Our clothes got burned up. We can't get any new ones until we win some dough in your tournament."

"Ah, so," hissed the pro, much relieved, and he promptly supplied them with golf shoes and two female caddies.

With the wide-eyed girls carrying the clubs, they trekked to the first tee. There, waiting to tee off, they were taking a few practice swings, to the amusement of all in their vicinity, when they observed four British officers, one of them a colonel, approaching. In a matter of minutes two things became evident. Judged by his own practice swings the British colonel was not on leave from his country's

Curtis Cup team, and judged by the disdain evident on his face when he eyed the Swampmen he was not in favor of any Papa-Sans sharing the golf course with him.

"Damn this get-up," Hawkeye was saying to Trapper. "It doesn't do much for my backswing."

"Good," Trapper said, increasing the awkwardness of his own efforts.

"What do you mean, 'good'?" Hawkeye said.

"Keep your voice down," Trapper said, "because I think we're about to hook a live one."

"See here, you two!" the British colonel bleated, walking up to them at that moment. "I don't know who you think you are, but I think . . ."

"Think again," Trapper said.

"I want you to know I'm Colonel Cornwall."

"Cornwallis?" Hawkeye said. "I thought we fixed your wagon at Yorktown."

"I said Cornwall."

"Lovely there in the spring," Trapper said. "Rhododendrons and all that."

"Now see here!" the colonel said, red in the face now. "I don't know what you're doing here, but rather than make an issue of it, if you'll just step aside and allow us to tee off . . ."

"Look, Corny," Hawkeye said. "You just calm down, or we'll tee off on *you*."

"I'll tell you what we'll do, Colonel," Trapper said. "You look like a sporting chap, so to settle this little difficulty in a sporting way, we'll both play you a ten pound Nassau."

"I beg your pardon?"

"You heard him," Hawkeye said.

"Excuse me a moment," the colonel said, and he turned and rejoined his companions to get their opinion of the proposition.

"What do you think?" Hawkeye said.

"We got him," Trapper said, manufacturing as awkward a swing as he could without making it too obvious.

"Here he comes now," Hawkeye said.

"All right," the colonel said. "You're on, and we'll be watching every shot you hit."

The Swampmen hit drives designed to get the ball in play, with no attempt at distance, and they were down the middle about 225 yards. Trapper reached the green in two and got his par four. Hawkeye hit a nice five-iron but misjudged the distance and was long, hit a wedge back but missed a five-footer and took a bogey.

The second hole was a short par three that gave them no trouble. Both bogied three and four, however, as it became clear that driving range experience at the Double Natural had sharpened their hitting ability but done little for their judgment of distance or their putting. Nevertheless, the girl caddies were quite impressed, particularly by Trapper John, whose every move they watched with rapt fascination.

Approaching the seventh, a par five, they were both three over par, and as the day was getting warmer, Trapper took off the long, flowing top of his Papa-San suit and his hat. This left him with long hair, a beard, a bare torso, and long, flowing trousers, and seemed to move him up another notch in the eyes of the girls.

On the seventh, he was down the middle a good 260, with Hawkeye not far behind him. Hawkeye's second shot wasn't much, however, and he had a full five-iron left. Then Trapper cranked out an awesome two-wood with a slight tail-end hook which bit the hard fairway, bounced over a trap, and came to rest within two feet of the pin.

"Jesus!" exclaimed Hawkeye. The caddies, hearing this, looked knowingly at each other, and it dawned on the Swampmen what their mounting excitement was all about. Happily, Hawkeye had several of the autographed pictures in his wallet and, with a grand gesture, he bestowed complimentary copies upon the girls who, their suspicions confirmed, were overcome. Hawkeye had to lead them aside to calm them down, explaining as best he could that the Master's game was a little rusty and that He wanted to get in at least eighteen holes before making His comeback generally known.

"These bimboes," he explained to Trapper, approaching the eighth tee, "are on a real Christian kick, so don't disappoint them."

Trapper grabbed his driver, winced and looked at his hands. "Goddam nail holes," he complained.

The rest of the way around, Trapper played even par on the not too difficult and not too long course to finish with a seventy-three. Hawkeye couldn't figure the greens and found himself needing a ten-footer on the eighteenth for a seventy-eight. Trapper blessed the ball and the cup before Hawkeye essayed the putt, which went in like it had eyes. The caddies, bowing their way out, departed to spread the word.

"Now," Trapper said, "let's prepare to lighten Corny's load a little. If that hacker breaks eighty I'll take it to the World Court."

The Swampmen, with Trapper back in full uniform, found the bar. They were on their second Scotch when they noticed the Japanese faces peeking through the window and then Colonel Cornwall and his three colleagues pushing their way through the crowd at the door.

"I say now," the colonel was saying, brushing himself off. "Does anyone know what this is all about?"

"Ah, yes," Hawkeye said, motioning toward Trapper, who was bowing toward the faces at the window and door. "Mighty High Religious Personage is greeting followers."

"Of course, of course," the colonel was saying now, starting to rock with laughter. "I say! That's rather droll, isn't it?"

"What's that, sir?" one of his colleagues asked.

"Chap here," he said, nodding toward Trapper. "Why, the chap here's portraying John the Baptist!"

"Colonel," Hawkeye said, handing him one of the autographed pictures, "You can't tell the players without a scorecard."

"Oh, I say!" the colonel was roaring now. "That *is* good, isn't it? I *do* get it now. Say, you chaps, do have a drink on me. Oh, I say!"

The Swampmen had several drinks on him and, when they got around to comparing cards, the colonel, who had shot an eighty-two, paid up willingly.

"Corny," Hawkeye heard himself saying, "How about you and

these other gentlemen joining us for dinner at Dr. Yamamoto's Finest Kind Pediatric Hospital and Whorehouse?"

"Oh, I say!" the colonel said. "That sounds like sport!"

Shortly after 7:00 P.M., Me Lay Marston, idly sipping a martini in the bar of the FKPH&W, heard a commotion outside. Going to the door, he found Hawkeye, the British contingent and then Trapper John bringing up the rear. Trapper was trying to disentangle himself from the converts and the just curious.

"Me Lay," Trapper said, when he got inside. "I've had enough of this. Get me a pair of scissors and a razor."

In time Trapper John was shaved, shorn and showered, and dinner was solicitously served by the young ladies. While the visitors sipped after-dinner cordials, Me Lay excused himself to make his rounds at the adjoining hospital. In a few minutes he returned with a worried look.

"What had you guys planned for tonight?" he asked.

"Well," answered Trapper, "we thought we'd get some . . ."

"How about looking at a kid for me?"

"Look, Me Lay," Hawkeye said, "you're supposed to be the intern in this . . ."

"Shut up, and come look at this kid."

"What's the story?" asked Trapper.

"Well, one of our girls got careless, and two days ago she gave birth to an eight-pound Japanese-American male."

"What's wrong with him?"

"Every time we feed him, it either comes right back up or he coughs and turns blue and has a helluva time."

"We don't have to see him," Trapper said. "Call that half-assed Army Hospital and tell them to be ready to put some lipiodal in this kid's esophagus and take X-rays."

"But it's ten-thirty at night. We can't get everybody out for a civilian. They won't do it."

"How much you wanna bet, Me Lay?" inquired Hawkeye Pierce. "Get on the horn and tell them the pros from Dover are on their way with a patient. Better tell the OR to crank itself up, because I got a feeling that you're going to pass some gas while I help Trapper close a tracheo-esophageal fistula."

"Oh, I say," Colonel Cornwall wanted to know, "what's that?"

"It's a hole between the esophagus and the trachea, where it doesn't belong," Hawkeye explained.

"And you chaps can repair that?"

"Well," said Me Lay. "We can try."

At the 25th Station Hospital, the Officer of the Day received a call from Captain Marston saying that an emergency was coming in for X-rays. Soon after, Hawkeye and Trapper, in Papa-San suits and followed by Me Lay carrying the baby, entered the X-ray department.

Captain Banks, the O.D., arrived and asked, "What's this all about?"

"It's all about this baby," Hawkeye informed him. "We want to X-ray him and we want to do it right now, and we do not wish to be engaged in useless conversation by officious military types, of which you look like one to me."

"But, we can't . . ."

Hawkeye sat Captain Banks on the edge of a desk and handed him the phone.

"Be nice, Captain. Call the X-ray technician. If you give us any kind of a bad time, me and Trapper John are going to clean your clock. We are frustrated lovers and quite dangerous."

Captain Banks called. While awaiting the technician, Trapper and Me Lay placed a small catheter in the baby's esophagus. A few minutes later, radio-opaque oil was injected through the catheter. It revealed the abnormal opening between the esophagus and the trachea but no significant narrowing of the esophagus. This meant that anything the baby ate could go into his lungs but that, happily, once the opening was closed, the esophagus would be able to accommodate the passage of food. It required careful preparation, proper anesthesia, early and competent surgery and good luck.

"Me Lay, let's you and me get a needle into a vein," Trapper said, and then, turning to Captain Banks, he said, "You there, in the shiny shoes, tell the lab to do a blood count and cross-match a pint.

We won't need that much, but it's a term they'll understand. Then tell the OR to get set up for a thoracotomy. We're going to operate in about two hours. Hawkeye, you stick close to Alice, or whatever his name is, and see that he performs efficiently."

The Officer of the Day had no choice but to perform efficiently. The nurses were routed out, not at all pleased at the prospect of operating a second time with the pros from Dover. There was, in fact, outright grumbling which Hawkeye Pierce brought to a rapid conclusion.

"Ladies," he said, "we are sorry to get you out at this time of night. However, we stumbled upon this deal, and we can't walk away from it, no matter whose rules are broken. This baby will die if we don't fix him, so let's all be nice and just think about the baby."

Fortunately, nurses succumb to this kind of pitch. They gave up any show of resistance, particularly after they saw the baby, but Hawkeye caught Captain Banks calling Colonel Merrill.

"Now, Captain," he chided him, "I may give you a few lumps, but first I must call the Finest Kind Pediatric Hospital and Whorehouse."

So doing, he talked to Colonel Cornwall, explained their situation and made a few suggestions. Fifteen minutes later, as Colonel R. P. Merrill stormed into the hospital, he was met by four British officers who loaded him unceremoniously into their Land Rover and returned to the FKPH&W.

After Captain Banks had been stripped naked and locked in a broom closet by the two Swampmen, the operation was finally started. Me Lay's anesthesia was excellent, the nurses cooperated completely, and Trapper and Hawkeye indulged in none of the byplay that had marked their first local appearance. After an hour and a half of careful work, Trapper had closed the fistula. They shed their gowns and discussed the postoperative care.

"I think we better leave him here," said Trapper. "You can't take care of anything like this in that whorehouse hospital of yours, can you, Me Lay?"

"Not too well, but I don't see how we can keep him here. Merrill will be all over us in the morning."

"Leave the kid here," Hawkeye said. "We'll be in and out and can look after both him and the boy we did this morning. I know how to keep Merrill off our backs."

At 3:00 A.M., back at the FKPH&W, they had a drink with the British officers who told them that Colonel Merrill was upstairs asleep, having been coaxed into having a drink and a sedative.

"But what about when he wakes up?" asked Me Lay.

"Send a naked broad into his room and take some pictures," suggested Hawkeye.

"Oh, I say!" Colonel Cornwall said.

A few minutes later, Colonel Merrill began to stir and awaken as the girl joined him in bed. Witnesses to the scene filled the doorway while Trapper John leisurely shot a roll of film.

"I told you so! I told you so!" chanted Hawkeye. "He's a dirty old man. A disgrace to the uniform."

"The blighter should bloody well be cashiered from the service," asserted Colonel Cornwall indignantly.

"I'd say that depends on his behavior from now on," said Trapper John, pocketing the film.

The Swampmen were to tee off in the Kokura Open at ten o'clock the next morning. One of Me Lay's assistants was instructed to obtain proper clothing, since they did not wish to wear Papa-San suits forever.

Awakening at 8:00 A.M., weary but determined to be ready for the tournament, they drank coffee, ate steak and eggs served in bed by the ladies of the house, and donned sky blue slacks and golf shirts.

On the way to the course, they visited their two patients. The baby was far from out of the woods, but the Congressman's son was doing well. Before leaving, they entered the colonel's office.

"Where's that dirty old man?" Hawkeye asked the secretary.

The colonel came out, but he didn't roar.

"Colonel," said Hawkeye, "we've qualified for the Kokura Open so we're going to the course. We expect your people to watch that baby we operated on last night like he was the Congressman's grandson, which for all we know he may be. We expect to be notified of any change for the worse, and if we find anything wrong when we come back this afternoon, we'll burn down the hospital."

The colonel believed them.

They arrived at the golf course at nine-thirty, practiced putting and chipping, took a few swings and, with their English confreres there to cheer them on, they pronounced themselves ready to go. They weren't. The activities of the previous days, and nights, had taken too much out of them, and by the end of the third day, what with having to check repeatedly on the Congressman's son and the baby, they were hopelessly mired back in the pack.

"I guess that does it," Trapper said, as they sat in the bar at the club. "We might have a chance if three guys dropped dead and a half dozen others came down with echinococcosus."

"What's that?" Colonel Cornwall wanted to know.

"The liver gets so big you can't get your club head back past it," Hawkeye said, "so we've got no chance."

"We're proud of you anyway," the colonel informed them. "You gave it a good go, you did. I must say, though, I shouldn't give up surgery for the professional tour if I were you."

"I guess we figured that out already," Trapper said, "but what I can't figure out is what we're going to do about this baby we're stuck with."

"But you chaps have done all you can," the colonel said.

"No, we haven't," Trapper said. "After the big deal we made saving his life, what do we do now? Leave him in a whorehouse?"

"Leave it to me," Hawkeye said. "I think it'll be safe now to take the kid back to Dr. Yamamoto's Finest Kind Pediatric Hospital and Whorehouse."

They went to the 25th Station Hospital, said good-bye to the Congressman's son who was well on his way to recovery, and picked up their small patient. Riding the Land Rover back to the FKPH&W, Trapper had a thought.

"We oughta name the little bastard," he said. Hawkeye had considered this problem twenty-four hours earlier. He had even laid a little groundwork.

"I have named him," he said.

"What is it?"

"I'm not sure how much I can con Me Lay Marston into," Hawkeye said, "but the name is Ezekiel Bradbury Marston, VI."

"Oh, I say," Colonel Cornwall said.

"Obviously you are either nuts or you know something," Trapper John said eventually. "Which is it?"

"I know something. I know that Me Lay and the Broad from Eagle Head have one daughter and that's all the kids they're ever going to have. I'll save you the next question. Remember I was away for a while last night? I went to one of those overseas telephone places and called the Broad from Eagle Head, whom I've known longer than Me Lay has. To make a long story short, she agrees that a name like Ezekiel Bradbury Marston must not die!"

"Hawkeye, you are amazing," admired the colonel.

"For once, I gotta agree," agreed Trapper.

At the FKPH&W, they placed Ezekiel Bradbury Marston, VI, in a laundry basket, left instructions for his care and returned to the bar where they found the unsuspecting parent, Me Lay Marston.

"What are we going to do with this kid, Me Lay?" asked Trapper.

"I don't know."

"Well, Jesus, Me Lay, you're not much of a whorehouse administrator if you don't have some ideas on the subject."

"Good-looking kid," said Hawkeye. "What's his mother like?"

"A nice intelligent girl. She asked me this morning what we'd do with the baby. I've been looking into a few possibilities, but I'll tell you right now there aren't any good ones."

"Too bad. The little chap's half American," said Colonel Cornwall. "Any way to get him to the States?"

"Only one way," said Me Lay.

"What's that?"

"Get somebody to adopt him."

Hawkeye said, "Me Lay, why don't you adopt him?"

Me Lay looked miserable. He lit a cigarette and sipped his drink.

"That idea's been popping into my head ever since we operated on him," he said finally, "but how can I do it? Am I supposed to call up my wife and say I'm sending home a half-breed bastard from a Japanese whorehouse?"

"You don't have to," Trapper told him. "Hawkeye called your wife last night. The deal's set. All you have to do is arrange the details."

Hesitating only a moment, Me Lay got up, went to the hospital area, picked up the baby and brought him to the bar.

"What's his name, Me Lay?" asked Trapper.

"Gentlemen, meet my son, Ezekiel Bradbury Marston, VI, of Spruce Harbor, Maine."

Late that night a flyboy who'd been in Seoul earlier in the day brought word of increasing action on Old Baldy. The next morning the pros from Dover, having withdrawn from the tournament, but still clad in sky blue slacks and golf shirts, boarded a plane for Seoul.

The Ways of Life at the Country Club

ROBERT H. BOYLE

Robert Boyle is a veteran sports writer for Sports Illustrated, *where this piece originally appeared in 1962. Mr. Boyle is also a legendary figure in the environmental community, having fought battles against corporate polluters and as a driving force of the Hudson River Fisherman's Association.*

One of the distinctive hallmarks of our mobile, suburban society is the country club. The country club is a uniquely American institution. In its 80 years of existence it has undergone an evolution that amounts to a revolution. Originally a patrician playground loosely modeled on the great English country house with its leisurely weekend, the country club is becoming a year-round family fun center that has more resemblance to the local bowling palace out on Route 1 than to any plutocratic pleasure dome.

There are 3,300 country clubs of all kinds in the U.S. The membership totals 1.7 million. Approximately 3,000 of these clubs are the classic type, privately owned by the members. Nationally, they take in about $250 million a year in dues and fees. They sell $500 million worth of food and beverages. The average club has between 400 and 600 members, gross annual dues of $100,000 to $150,000 and a food and beverage sale of $150,000 to $250,000.

*   *   *

Surprisingly, the sociologists have largely ignored the country club. Only the novelists—Sinclair Lewis, J. P. Marquand and John O'Hara—have examined it in detail. Perhaps O'Hara, with his deadly social awareness, etched the sharpest picture of "the country-club set" in *Appointment in Samarra,* published in 1934. Brilliant as the novel was, O'Hara might have to change some things if he were writing it today. Sex, for instance, seems to be on the way out at the club (the growing family influence, you know), and gin rummy has supplanted bridge as the club's most popular card game.

Americans join country clubs for a variety of reasons, most of them intertwined with one another. The main reasons appear to be:

Golf. The game is at an all-time popular high, but it is almost impossible to play on a public course at one's convenience. There is now only one course for every 29,000 Americans, compared to one for every 21,000 in the early '30s. In the last decade alone the number of women golfers has jumped 44%.

Social prestige. Club membership firmly places a member and his family in the local hierarchy. It is tangible recognition of having "arrived." (In Chicago, Irish Catholics advertised their arrival by brunching at the South Shore Country Club after Sunday Mass.) "It's all prestige, the whole damn thing," says one club manager.

Emotional security. "We have become a nation of near-strangers through the impersonal urbanization process," writes Charles F. Hathaway, a Los Angeles club manager who studied more than 200 country clubs while doing graduate work at Michigan State. "When we are with our own kind, such as in our club, the threat of association with people greatly different from ourselves is greatly lessened." (In Chicago leading gangsters sought one another's companionship at the Mount Prospect Country Club. However, when the club ran into financial difficulties a few years ago, local residents, who at the start had joked about the Mafia Open, voted to buy it out.)

Business contacts. "Unless you belong to a country club, you're nobody in the eyes of some of your business acquaintances," says a Louisville railroad man. A Chicago executive says, "The club is really a kind of grease, like a fraternity. It makes it easier for you to pick up business." From coast to coast, business infiltrates the country club. A Boston advertising agency has a low-70s golfer whose only job is to soften up prospective clients on the course. A Seattle firm has hired "an Ivy League type" for the same purpose. "We have to have a man who can play a good game of golf and has all the social graces to bring in the business that's to be picked up around clubs," says a partner. "Our man does a fine job at it. He's no great shakes as a lawyer, but he doesn't have to be."

As early as the late 18th century there were signs of the country club to come. In 1795 Charleston had a golf clubhouse, and a decade later Augusta and Savannah each had one, in which members staged balls and parties. But these clubs were the creations of lonely Scotsmen longing for the ancient game, and none lasted long. It was not until the post–Civil War boom, when the U.S. was turning from a rural, agricultural nation into an urban and industrial colossus, that the country club came into existence to stay.

It seems odd now, but the early country clubs had no connection at all with golf. The first club formed was The Country Club in Brookline, Mass., in 1882. (It is a gaucherie of the worst sort to refer to the club as the Brookline Country Club. It is always The Country Club. As Dixon Wecter remarks in *The Saga of American Society,* The Country Club has never assumed a place name because "it is *sui generis,* like the roc's egg.")

The Country Club was the idea of James Murray Forbes, a Proper Bostonian and a well-known sportsman and horseman. One of the coaching set, Forbes looked upon the Brookline countryside as the logical terminus for the then fashionable tallyho drives. ". . . The general idea," went the original prospectus, "is to have a comfortable clubhouse for the use of members and their families, a simple restaurant, bedrooms, bowling alley, lawn tennis grounds and so on; also to have race meetings and, occasionally, music in the afternoon." Horse racing was one of the main attractions at the club; there is still a track surrounding the first and 18th fairways.

Two years later the Country Club of Westchester County began. A contemporary observer noted that it had "developed from a suggestion to organize a tennis club into a determination to found a club where all country sports could be enjoyed." The club had tennis courts, a polo field, a racetrack, baseball diamond, traps for live pigeon shooting, boats, bathhouses and a pack of hounds.

In 1886 Pierre Lorillard III, heir to the snuff and tobacco fortune, created the most sumptuous club of all at Tuxedo Park, 40 miles northwest of New York City. On 7,000 of the 600,000 acres he owned in the area, Lorillard, in collaboration with the architect Bruce Price, the father of Emily Post, built a water system, 22 donnered cottages weathered to medieval charm, a huge wooden clubhouse, stables, a swimming tank, a trout hatchery and a gatehouse that Price described as looking "like a frontispiece to an English novel." Tuxedo bespoke leisure and wealth; its initial cost was $1.5 million. Several years later Lorillard spent the balance of $2 million building a golf course, a racetrack and a mile-long toboggan slide lit by electricity. Only the best people—William Waldorf Astor, C. Oliver Iselin, Ogden Mills, Sir Roderick Cameron, the British consul in New York, and the like—were admitted, and from the beginning the club made social history. At the first of its annual Autumn Balls, which still signal the start of the New York social season, young Griswold Lorillard appeared in a tailless dress coat that the herd knows as a "tuxedo."

Given such a magnificent send-off, the country club became the rage. A great moment came in 1888 when John Reid, a Scot, banded together with five other congenial souls in Yonkers, N.Y. to build a golf course. They called their little group St. Andrews. The game caught on at established country clubs, whose members became enthusiastic about this latest sporting import from Britain. In Brookline, The Country Club, under prodding from such distinguished members as Arthur Hunnewell and G. E. Cabot, appropriated $50 for the construction of an experimental six-hole course. There is a legend that the spectators became quite bored watching the first match after one participant scored a hole in one on the first hole and the other players failed to duplicate the feat. In 1894 St. Andrews, The Country Club and three other clubs formed the U.S. Golf Association. The country club, energized by golf, was on its way. In Springfield, N.J., Louis Keller of the *Social Register* started Baltusrol, and up the Hudson River, Chauncey Depew and William Rockefeller helped to found the Ardsley Casino, forerunner of the present-day Ardsley Country Club.

The yellow press scoffed at these "howling swells" who golfed in scarlet jackets and leg wrappings, worn as protection against the nonexistent gorse, but to Henry James, returning to the U.S. in 1904 after a 30-year absence abroad, the country club was an object of admiration. It was the perfect place for the elite to relax. At the 19th hole of St. Andrews, Charles Schwab put together U.S. Steel by persuading Andrew Carnegie to sell out to J. P. Morgan. (Carnegie never lingered long at the club. Fearful of abduction, he always left the grounds before nightfall.) In Washington, William Howard Taft shrugged off Theodore Roosevelt's warning that golf was a dude's game and betook his bulk to Chevy Chase, where he built a cottage. At the same club Woodrow Wilson courted Edith Bolling Galt, and he was on the course when he heard of the sinking of the *Lusitania.*

All country clubs received a great deal of impetus from golf, and in 1913 golf received an impetus from Francis Ouimet, an ex-caddie at The Country Club. One of a host of Catholic youngsters who toted bags for the Brahmins, Ouimet popularized golf the country over when, at the age of only 20, he defeated Harry Vardon and Ted Ray, Britain's greatest, in the playoff round of the U.S. Open. By almost a literal stroke he made golf a game for the masses.

In the '20s the country club was carried to the farthest reaches. By 1929 there were 4,500 clubs in the U.S., the highest number ever attained. The city of Zenith in Lewis' *Babbitt* had two: the Tonawanda Country Club for the upper crust and the Outing Golf and Country Club for the aspiring business class. That go-getter real estate man, George F. Babbitt, a member of Outing, was wont to say with frequency, "You couldn't hire me to join the Tonawanda, even if I did have a hundred and eighty bucks to throw away on the initiation fee." Sociologist Mark Benny has speculated that golf became popular with the American businessman because it answers the needs of the independent capitalist. In hitting the ball from hole to hole, the golfer is symbolically directing his own destiny. Golf, in short, is a game of laissez-faire. It is not coincidental, Benny says, that both golf and Adam Smith came out of Scotland at the same time.

During the '30s the Depression forced a quarter of the private clubs to close. World War II put a further crimp in country clubs. Indeed, it was not until 1956 that the number of clubs held steady at 2,800 and then began to increase. Today clubs are being built at about the rate of 100 a year, and there would be more but for the expense involved. The National Golf Foundation in Chicago, which operates a planning service for persons wishing to start a country club, estimates that it costs on the average of $500,000 to $750,000 to build a clubhouse for 300 members and an 18-hole course.

Maintenance costs are at all-time highs. The latest annual survey of country club finances by Horwath & Horwath, an accounting firm that specializes in the club and hotel field, reveals that for the 12th straight year private country clubs are operating at a loss. (The current average deficit is 6%.) Golf is a steady loser financially, incapable of paying its own way. Harris, Kerr, Forster, another accounting firm in the field, reports the upkeep of the average golf hole costs $3,059, 56% more than it did in 1951. The dining room, which must be open for two or 200 guests, is another loser.

In general, country clubs have attempted to make up the deficit by increasing dues (the average club dues have almost doubled in the past 10 years, from $200 to $360), raising the initiation fee (the average fee has almost tripled to $1,000 in the same period of time) or simply assessing the members for the difference. Of course, none of these methods is popular with club members, who no sooner recover from one socking when they are slugged with another. To quell the protests, clubs have experimented with a variety of methods to increase income. Some catered to outside parties, but a year ago the Internal Revenue Service ruled that any private club that derived

25% of its income from nonmembers would lose its nonprofit tax status. Other clubs imposed a monthly minimum for food and drink, but again Internal Revenue ruled that all such charges were subject to the 20% federal excise tax.

To offset rising costs some clubs have sold their property outright and moved farther out. (Only in California have country clubs gotten a break on real estate taxes: a year ago voters approved an amendment to assess club land at the rate specified for recreational purposes rather than at building value.) What most clubs have done to bring in money is to encourage day-in, day-out participation by members. To do this they have increased the number of social memberships while keeping the golf memberships down. After all, only so many golfers can use the course, and the social members concentrate on only the last hole of the 19. As a result of the influx of social members, the bar till, in theory anyway, clinks merrily from morn to night.

Increased participation also means family participation. "At my club," says one manager, "golf has gotten to the point where the men are allowed to play on Wednesday and Saturday." In fact, a number of clubs now report more women than men use the course. "The women are fine," says another manager, "as long as you keep them off the house committee. They can't get together on colors."

To lure the family, clubs have built tennis courts and swimming pools. (One harassed male refers to the latter as "the cheapest baby-sitting service in the world.") Other clubs have added bowling alleys, which take up the slack in winter when the course is closed. The club is even changing architecturally. In place of the spacious timbered structures of the past have come glass and concrete pill boxes designed for maximum efficiency—and the maximum buck. In *Planning the Golf Clubhouse,* Harold J. Cliffer warns the lounge "should not be designed to provide seating for large groups gathered for affairs. As a matter of club economics, the space should be relatively small, not too amply furnished and accessible to the cocktail lounge. This acts as an inducement for people not able to find seating in the lounge to gather in the cocktail lounge and have a before-dinner or before-luncheon cocktail. Activity in the cocktail lounge is much more profitable from the standpoint of the management than having the lounge furniture warmed by non-patronizing members or guests." On no account, he adds, should the bar be placed in the dining room: ". . . the drinkers feel too inhibited about imbibing freely while exposed to the scrutiny of the diners, and as a result of too little patronage, the management has complained bitterly that the bar cannot make money in such a location."

In recent years an increasing number of clubs have turned to a professional manager to solve their problems. Club managing is the latest of American occupations to be upgraded to professional status. There is a Club Managers Association of America, with 2,200 members, a headquarters in Washington and a monthly journal. Several colleges offer majors in the field, the most notable of which is the School of Hotel Administration at Cornell. There budding country club managers are put through a four-year course, crowned by a Bachelor of Science degree, in which they study such subjects as Chemistry and Its Application to Food Preparation, Human Relations, Classical Cuisine and Sanitation in the Food Service Operation. Once a year Cornell and the CMAA get together in Ithaca for a week-long seminar on club problems. In a class session last September the managers were advised to use "chef recommends" on the menu for items that were either overstocked or unusually profitable and to avoid foreign names for dishes because they made guests hesitant to order.

To keep the club humming, managers have gone on a party spree. "Show me a successful country club and I'll show you one that gives parties and lots of them," Leonard Taylor, president of a party-favor firm, told club managers convened in Ithaca a few years ago. "A well-planned party is the push that gets families out of their homes and into the club. A party gives them the sip and taste of country club life and makes them want to come back."

The secret of a successful party is the knack of combining profitable food (drink is always profitable) with a theme that will bring the members out in droves. The most popular party is a Hawaiian luau. (The Elmcrest Golf and Country Club in Cedar Rapids, Iowa put one on for $1,537 and grossed $4,111.) Next in popularity is a Roaring Twenties party. (The Morris County Golf Club near Morristown, N.J. plastered the walls with old advertisements of sheet music and records and dressed the staff in Charlie Chaplin and Mae West costumes two weeks before the big event. "It was pretty hard to come to the club and not realize that something to do with the Roaring Twenties was going to happen soon," Taylor exulted.) Other favored parties are a Night in Paris, in which the invitations are mailed by postcard from France a couple of weeks before; a Night on the Steppes, in which a waiter dresses as a bear and cavorts to Russian folk tunes; a Balinese Purification Feast, featuring three large altars in the ballroom heaped with fruits, leaves and flowers; and a Night in Monte Carlo, in which the members gamble with "play money," which they actually bought beforehand and will cash later—sometimes for prizes. A most unusual party is the one given on Labor Day by the Meshingomesia Country Club in Marion, Ind. It is a Labor Union party. The theme is "something for nothing," with every fifth guest getting a free meal.

Country clubs today generally fall into six categories: top-status, middle-class, minority, rural, proprietary and industrial. The classic situation is for a city to have three clubs: top-status for the elite, middle-class for the strivers and just plain folks, and the minority club for the Jews.

Some top-status clubs are known nationally. Among these would be Chevy Chase, The Country Club, the Los Angeles Country Club, the Country Club of Detroit, the St. Louis Country Club and the Burlingame near San Francisco. These clubs are preeminent in their communities, though there may be a second club that is hard on their heels for prestige. In Detroit, for example, Bloomfield Hills runs a close second to the Country Club of Detroit, but since CCD has 10 of the Ford family as members to BH's one, CCD has a clear edge. "It's not how many Cadillacs you have in the garage," says an observer of the Detroit social scene, "but how many Fords at the party." The Country Club of Detroit was the scene of Charlotte Ford's $250,000 debut in 1959. Guests entered through an elegant corridor specially lined with pink-blooming topiary roses and alcoved French paneling that gave no hint that the men's locker room was behind the false front. In smaller cities a rough rule of thumb for spotting the top club is to find out where the Junior League meets.

Although, as E. Digby Baltzell, a University of Pennsylvania sociologist, points out in *Philadelphia Gentlemen,* membership in the top-status club is often an accurate social index, it is not necessarily an indicator of prestige in some cities. In Philadelphia, Baltzell writes, "the higher one goes in the social class hierarchy, the less important the role of the country club is in leisure-time activities. There are numerous first families along the Main Line and in Chestnut Hill who are never seen at country clubs even if they belong, and many do not. A Proper Chicagoan, who visits in Chestnut Hill, would meet his host's friends in their own houses; in Lake Forest, the Philadelphian would be more likely to meet his Proper Chicagoan's friends at various elaborate country clubs."

More often than not, top-status clubs exhibit certain traits. For example:

The top club is not necessarily physically impressive, much less elaborate. The grounds are neat, but the clubhouse is genteelly run down. The interior is subdued. "The highest prestige club," Hathaway writes, "holds to the older decoration themes. A front door, though worn and beaten, will be kept in place long after it has served its useful life, because it seems to have a unique character of its own. The middle-class clubs, on the other hand, are continually redecorating and attempting to keep furnishings as well as facilities up with a brand-new air about them."

The top club serves simple food. "The higher the prestige of a club, and thereby the social status of its members," Hathaway writes, "the less likelihood you will have of encountering showiness [in food]. At the top members resist any show for fear other members will think they are trying to impress them." It is in the middle-class clubs that one is likely to find flaming-sword dishes and glittering ice carvings. Thus in Houston, when Golfcrest, a middle-class club that attracts the successful used-car salesman, held an interclub match, *chili con queso* dip, crabmeat dip and guacamole salad were served between the ninth and 10th holes. When the top-status Houston Country Club was return host, its members simply served cheese and crackers. Hathaway says class tastes may also be discerned on a "hardsoft" scale. "The upper classes," he writes, "seem to prefer hard, firm bread, and the lower classes . . . softer rolls."

The top club has a strict sense of privacy. The Country Club of Detroit issues no membership roster at all. Bloomfield Hills lists only names. Other clubs, like Oakland Hills and Forest Lake, put out a complete list, with business and home phone numbers; Forest Lake also lists addresses.

The top club keeps its privacy despite the fiercest assaults of the press. A member of Burlingame would never reveal his golf score to a newspaperman, not even if he scored a hole in one. Officers of The Country Club have steadfastly refused to say what happened to the remains of an elderly lady, a Cushing, who requested that her ashes be scattered on the 18th green. White House reporters say they never saw President Eisenhower so angry as he was the day photographers invaded the sacrosanct trophy room at the Augusta National. "They are not going to take any pictures in that room!" he thundered. The photographers retreated en masse, though one discreetly snapped away "in case he toppled over." Later the President posed outside the clubhouse.

The top club has next to nothing to do with golf tournaments. Oh, Augusta has the Masters, but the Masters is the Masters, and the winner gets to wear the club's green coat. When The Country Club held the U.S. Amateur a couple of years back, some members threatened to resign. Only once in its long history has the National Golf Links of America in Southampton, "America's snootiest golf course," tolerated a professional tournament. That was in 1928, when the members may have been carried away by the bull market. At any rate, the professionals had a difficult time. They were kept out of the clubrooms and the restaurant, and only after an argument were they allowed to use the showers.

The top-status club prohibits business discussions. To talk business at The Country Club, *Fortune* once noted, "would be calamitous. As the background for a Boston business date, the Brae Burn Club, out Newton way, would be the choice. It's social, too, but most of the members have known what it was to make a buck the hard way." One exception to the rule is the Country Club of Detroit. Members would object to an outright sales pitch, but it is all right to talk shop about cars. "We eat and sleep autos in this town," says a steel executive. "It gets so that when you go to church you expect to see a car up on the altar." Of course, shop talk sometimes pays off well. Another executive once overheard a conversation that prompted his company to change the remodeling plans at one of its mills.

In its 80 years of existence the American country club has undergone many changes. Originally a preserve of the elite, it has now spread to the point where there are 3,300 country clubs of all kinds. In the main, the clubs fall into six categories: top-status, middle-class, minority, rural, proprietary and industrial. The top-status club, as we saw last week, has managed to retain much of its remoteness; hence, it is the middle-class club that most Americans know best. The Bellingham Golf and Country Club in Bellingham, Wash. is as typical as any in its development.

The Club, as it is always referred to locally, began in 1912 with a nine-hole course on leased land. The backers were the Very Best Families in town and the surrounding countryside—the Larrabees, the Demings, Woods, Bloedels, Welches, Campbells, Donovans and Goulds, in short, the fish-cannery rich, the lumber-mill rich, the big landowners whose roots reached back to before the turn of the century.

In the '20s the club bought the land and added a second nine holes. Members kept their Canadian whisky, always available through the town's top bootlegger, in their lockers for the entertainment of friends. During the Depression the club operated only occasionally as it struggled under a $20,000 debt incurred in buying the property. Club life was even more bleak during World War II. Food and equipment shortages kept the clubhouse closed, and greenkeepers were either in the armed services or in defense work. On weekends members mowed the course to keep it playable.

The early postwar years brought a change in the membership, finances, and club status. The Very Best Families lost interest: they had discovered a new way to entertain when Charlie, last of the Larrabees, subdivided the family estate into choice building lots. The Very Best Families promptly moved there, exchanging the club for the elegant new home, hi-fi, the powerboat (or, better still, the private plane) and a summer place in the San Juan Islands. Although they retained their memberships in the club, they were seldom present. In their place stepped a whole new middle class, and even lower middle class, who joined to drink at the bar—the state legislature had legalized liquor—or pump quarters into a newly installed battery of slot machines.

By the early '50s the club ran into difficulty. The slot machines, which had compensated for the loss of the big spenders, were outlawed. The members reorganized, selling social memberships for as little as $25 a year and raising the dues. They set out to attract the family crowd, and they did. In the last few years women have had increasing influence on club activities. For example, the men's stags have dwindled. (The club monthly, *Divots and Ice,* blamed "warmer weather, the longer days and the opening of the swimming pool" for the downfall of the stags, but the fact is the wives didn't like them.) The women have taken over with crazy-hat luncheons, fashion shows, card parties and golf contests in which the players are required to dress in the professional costumes of their husbands. (One winner was Sue Abrahamsen, wife of a deep-sea diver, who played 18 holes in the full gear, including helmet.) There are teen-age dances, tiny tot golf tournaments and a big come-one-come-all outdoor salmon barbecue.

The switch to the family doesn't appeal to everyone—some middle-aged golfers still gripe about the change in the 15th hole caused by the swimming pool—but since the club now breaks even it isn't likely to be changed. Although the club does not discriminate—Bellingham's small Jewish colony belongs—it still has its cliques: the members of the Very Best Families, rarely seen, treated like royalty, ignoring everyone but their own kind; the grumpy golfers; the pulp mill crowd, who come as close as anyone to dominating the club; the professional men and the strivers. A great point is made of trying to represent all groups on the governing boards.

Membership in the club is not as exclusive as it once was, though a great swath of the membership would like to think it is. The club is the center of the lives of many people, who are, all considered, comfortable in its atmosphere, pleased with the ice-cream bar for the kids and content that the menu has not one word of French. They move around as easily as they would in their own backyards.

The third type of American club is the minority club. Usually this means a Jewish country club, but in an older section of the country like New England it may also mean an Irish club or possibly a French-Canadian and Italian club. Springfield, Mass. offers a good cross-section of such ethnic stratification. At the top is the Longmeadow Country Club, whose approximately 400 members are upper-class Protestants, except for a very few Catholics. The Springfield Country Club has about 300 members, more than half of whom are Catholic, mostly Irish. (There are also a few French-Canadians and Poles.) It has an Elks Club atmosphere where any member who wants action can find card-playing as well as golfing companions. The Crestview Country Club, the newest and most lavish, has 300 members, all of them Jewish. The Ludlow Country Club is predominantly French-Canadian, Italian and Polish, and it is, says an observer, "about as exclusive as a neighborhood bar, drawing heavily from the non-prestige classes who want to get away from crowded municipal links."

In larger cities one sometimes finds two or more Jewish clubs, the top one composed principally of German Jews who tend to find eastern European Jews unacceptable. To many Jews, German or Russian, the restricted country club represents perhaps the sorest symbol of social discrimination. A Jewish community leader in Elmira, N.Y. told Sociologist John P. Dean of Cornell: "They'll call on me to lead their Community Chest campaign or help on the Red Cross. But when it comes to the country club, I'm not good enough for them."

In January, the Anti-Defamation League of B'nai B'rith issued the first report ever made on nationwide religious discrimination by social clubs. Of 803 country clubs surveyed, 224 were nondiscriminatory. Of the remaining 579, 505 were "Christian country clubs," 416 of which barred Jews completely. The other 89 had a quota. Seventy-four of the 579 discriminating clubs were Jewish. Seventy-one of these barred Christians completely, and the remaining three accepted them "in small numbers."

The ADL report contended that while discriminatory country clubs "have traditionally taken, and won acceptance for, the position that the . . . club is an extension of one's own parlor . . . (and) a man has a right to choose whom he will invite into his home," the practice of discrimination was unfair because if "the seat of power in any community discriminates against Jews, it may sound a note that will be taken up by others in the community. . . . Lower echelon civic groups, ears closely attuned to the note from on high, will find sanction for similar exclusions. The university, upon whose board of trustees sit members of the discriminatory club, will not protest a quota system, the fraternities will mimic their elders in exclusionary practices. Thus may a new generation, while still in its formative years, be schooled in the ways and benefits of social discriminations."

"Clearly," the report continued, "the problems raised by such exclusionary practices are not only social, but more frequently economic, political and sociological. The ultimate victim is not the man reaching toward the seat of power or toward the prestige of upper level social acceptance. Rather it is the youth who finds he is barred from job or school (and when he is older, from a home) simply and solely because he is Jewish."

The ADL report concluded that although "the extent of discrimination against Jews by clubs is far greater than the levels of discrimination against Jews in other areas such as education, employment, housing and public accommodations," the fact that a significant number of clubs "were 'Jewish clubs' that discriminate against Christians is eloquent testimony to the further institutionalization of religious prejudice. When, as and if Jewish community relations agencies conclude that the problem of the 'Christian club' merits their attention, they will inevitably have to cope with the other side of the coin—the 'Jewish club.'"

Discrimination aside, Jewish country clubs generally differ from their Christian counterparts in a couple of ways. For one, the Jewish clubs put great stress on charity; a prospective member is expected to be philanthropic (one club in the New York area requires that an applicant must have given at least $10,000 to United Jewish Appeal). For another, members of Jewish clubs habitually eat more and drink less than do Christian club members. It is possible to pick out the Jewish clubs from the clubs surveyed statistically in Horwath & Horwath's annual anonymous study simply by checking the food and beverage expenditures of the average member. In one Jewish club, for instance, the average member spent $455 on food and only $134 on drink. At a comparable Christian club the average member spent $275 for food and $240 for drink.

Significantly, of all the clubs surveyed by *Sports Illustrated,* the one most esteemed for its food was the Hillcrest Country Club in Los Angeles, a predominantly Jewish club drawing heavily on show business. (The Los Angeles Country Club does not accept Jews and avoids anyone remotely connected with the entertainment world. The sole actor member is Robert Stack, the Eliot Ness of *The Un-*

touchables, but Stack, who comes from a proper Los Angeles family, was admitted before he entered the movies.) "Hillcrest," Milton Berle, a member, once remarked, "is a dining club with golf." "Our food," says Sherrill Corwin, a theater executive who is the club's president, "is talked about the world over." A typical Saturday luncheon menu at the club includes chicken broth with matzo balls ($.75), grenadine of prime beef tenderloin on rye toast *garni* ($3) and smoked northern whitefish with thin-sliced onions and tomato ($2.60). "You should be here Sunday night," say members. The place to be seen is "the table" in the bar where Jack Benny, George Burns and Groucho Marx gather to banter.

Two Negro clubs, the only ones of their kind in the country, are located in North Carolina—the Meadowbrook Country Club outside Raleigh and Forest Lake Country Club in Greensboro. Forest Lake, which is slightly ahead in development, got going three years ago when a group of businessmen led by J. Kenneth Lee, an attorney, bought the 124-acre Burlington Industries Country Club for $90,000. Eighteen of the acres are developed. There are a clubhouse, tennis courts, stables and bridle paths. Three lakes are available for swimming, fishing and boating. There are now 60 family memberships costing $200 each a year, and the club runs a full schedule of events, down to parties for children. Most of the members are professional people; many are faculty members at colleges in the area. Fortunately, the club has been able to get by financially by renting out the clubhouse to local business and civic groups. There had been considerable talk of building a golf course, but now the city of Greensboro is planning to start a municipal course nearby, and the members are hopeful of playing there. To attract potential members, the club is circulating an illustrated brochure which bears the slogan, "Social Position Is Important."

In a class by themselves are the small rural country clubs that have sprung up in the Farm Belt in recent years. Farmers who used to scoff at the city-slicker game of "cow pasture pool" now play a fast nine waiting for the milk to cool. The clubs came about as the result of mechanization, which has freed the farmer from many of his chores, and a liking for Ike. Ike liked golf, and that was good enough for the farmer, no matter what Benson did.

The Logan–Missouri Valley Country Club, near Logan, Iowa (population 2,500), has been in operation since 1948. Yearly dues are $48. The entry fee is $100, and a payment plan permits members to spread this over a 10-year period. "I'm doing it that way," says Don Shrum, a telegrapher for the Chicago Northwestern Railroad, "and I pay the membership fee quarterly. That way it doesn't hit you all at once." The Missouri Valley Chamber of Commerce has asked storekeepers to close at 5 instead of 6 on weeknights "So folks can get in a round before dark." On occasion, challenge matches are held with teams from nearby Blair, Neb. The winners eat steak and the losers wienies. Afterwards, everyone pitches in to clean up.

At Alma, Neb. (population only 1,765), residents took over an abandoned depot just outside town so they could get that "outside-the-city country club atmosphere." To make sure that everyone meets everyone else at the Saturday night "mixers," dancers are required to change partners. "Country club life is part of living in rural Nebraska," says Cal Stewart, who was editor of a small-town weekly newspaper. "It's really down to earth. The guy who pumps gas in the banker's car plays golf with him on Sunday. If you want to have fun in a small town, you have to belong to the country club, and your station in life is no barrier."

The latest development in country clubs is the proprietary club owned by a businessman or syndicate out to make a dollar. There are now over 200 of these clubs across the country, and most of them are able to make money by catering to the masses at mass prices, in some instances anyway, and by such practices as central purchasing and soliciting outside parties. However, anyone interested in joining a proprietary club should be wary: in recent months a number of them have collapsed because of bad financing, leaving members holding the bag. As a general rule, anyone interested in a proprietary club should join only after the club has been built, never on the glowing promises of the prospectus. Prospective members should check carefully into any club offering life memberships at a flat bargain price. Flat fees attract suckers, not the income needed to keep the club going.

Although there are some semi-exclusive proprietary clubs, particularly in the retirement country of the South, generally anyone who has the money to hand over gets in. As far as is known, no Negroes have applied for proprietary club memberships, but one manager says, "I expect this will happen shortly." He adds, "The major golf associations have slowed down the admission of new clubs because they're afraid the clubs might admit Negroes. The golf associations are notoriously conservative, but you must have them because they issue all the official handicaps."

The promise of profit in a proprietary club is so strong that a number of golfers have become involved in them. Mike Souchak is building several in partnership with some businessmen in North Carolina, where he lives: and Dow Finsterwald's partnership in the Tequesta, Fla. club is one of the early successes along this line.

The leader in the field, if leader is the word, is George S. May, the flamboyant owner of Tam O'Shanter Country Club in Chicago. May got his start in life as a sharp Bible salesman—he used to follow Billy Sunday around the sawdust circuit—and both he and his club are living rebukes to the old-fashioned notion that a country club is a genteel place to relax. From its uniformed guards at its two gates to the eight bars—one of which is between the 9th hole and the 10th tee—Tam is designed to make money. The gaudy red-and-white clubhouse is a habitable jukebox. Tam has 300 regular golfers who pay a yearly membership fee of $750, 125 limited golfers who pay $450 and 441 social members who lay out $175 a year. For every $364 the golfer spends annually on food and drink, he receives a rebate of $50. For every $364 the social member spends, he receives a rebate of $25. (May arrived at $364 by figuring a member should spend at least a dollar a day. Christmas is on the house.)

Housing developers have been quick to see the money to be made in proprietary clubs. One such is Leon A. Katz, president of Golf Associates in New York. Originally a developer pure and simple, Katz is now also a country club man. Golf Associates has three clubs in operation, is building three more and has three others in negotiation. What Katz does is scout around for clubs that went broke during the Depression, buy them and restore the courses. Restoration is much cheaper than building anew. Once while he was commuting by helicopter from his home in Flushing to a club he was building in Westchester, he spotted what looked like the outline of an abandoned course in Armonk. Katz verified his aerial observation and bought the property from its startled owners.

Katz's clubs, which cost approximately $1 million each, average 300 families. The entry fee ranges from $400 to $500, and annual dues are $500. "We appeal to the public course golfer who can no longer get on a course and has a little money," Katz says. "They're hungry for golf." He keeps down maintenance costs by renting groundkeeping machinery and doing away with what he calls "frills." "The dining room is designed for average usage, not the crowd on the *Queen Mary,*" he says. "And we do not run a credit operation. We get a substantial return on our investment." One of the clubs will be surrounded by 300 houses. "It goes fast that way," he says. "In 10 years, everyone will look upon a club as a necessity."

Finally, there are the industrial country clubs, about 100 all told, and most designed for the working stiff. The Endicott Johnson Company has the En-Joie Country Club at Endicott, N.Y., the West Virginia Pulp & Paper Co. has the Westvaco Country Club in Covington, Va., and the Texas Company has the Texaco Country Club in Houston. One of the splashiest is the Du Pont Country Club in Wilmington, Del., with 9,300 members, three 18-hole courses, one nine-hole course, 16 tennis courts and one lawn bowling court.

Curiously, the oldest company golf club was started by Oneida Limited, manufacturers of silverplate, in Oneida, N.Y. The company is a descendant of a communistic (in the old utopian sense) society based on Christian principles. Founded in the 1840s by J. H. Noyes, the community disbanded in 1880 when outsiders objected to its radical views on marriage. A joint stock company was created to run the business enterprises established by the community. The company put into business practice Noyes's idealistic doctrines. As a result, the company began the golf club for employees 64 years ago and pioneered such other innovations as the coffee break and paid vacations.

Everything considered, the country club, be it industrial, rural or top-status, is probably the most accurate mirror of social trends in American life today. It offers the family a place to play and the businessman a place to be seen. If the country club has its flaws—and surely discrimination is one of them—it is not necessarily because the club system is unfair but because the society in which it flourishes has flaws of its own.

Chapter Four

1965–1973

A H, THE SIXTIES. I loved the Sixties, when everyone was on one side or the other, when life was so complicated, yet so clear.

Out on the Tour, it wasn't all Arnie and Jack and Gary making more money than any golfer had ever dreamed of. Before the Nike Tour and all the other bonanzas of today, there was "The Ghost Patrol of Golf," made up of the guys who didn't have exemptions and who were trying to qualify for any week's tournament openings.

Today, everyone over forty says they were a child of the Sixties, but the fact is, while the times they were a-changin', they weren't a-changin' that fast. For the great silent majority of kids, the Sixties didn't begin with Bob Dylan or the Beatles or even Woodstock. No, they began nearly a year later, when Billy Casper was teeing it up to win his Master's and Richard Nixon announced that he was escalating the war in Vietnam. Nixon escalated the war all right. Before that weekend in May, there were hippies and yippies and radicals and potheads and acidheads and greasers and preppies and all the rest, including golf pros and Bob Hope, with all the rest outnumbering the others by far. On May 6, though, the preppies and all the rest (except the golf pros and Bob Hope) joined the others, learned to smoke pot, grew their hair, and said "heavy, man."

I'd quit drugs the September before, courtesy of a game of golf my mother played. But in three years, starting in 1967, I went from espouser of my parents' Barry Goldwater beliefs to card-carrying member of SDS (possibly the only member to vote for Nixon in 1968) back to druggie, only to find Bill Clinton sitting in the backseat of my '65 Mustang as I drove Joe Duffey, running in Connecticut as a revisionist Marxist for the U.S. Senate, to campaign stops and meetings with corporate heads. With our help—more Clinton's than mine, I must admit—Duffey won the Democratic nomination and was barely beaten in the general election by longtime liberal Lowell Weicker.

Back to my mother's golf game, though. It was a Tuesday evening, and a friend had got some great acid he said would take an hour to do its work. We dropped, and he went down the street to get another friend, while I stayed at the house I was sharing to have some dinner. Within minutes, I was tripping wildly, and a few minutes after that, one of the kids in the house told me my mother was on the phone. Because my mother had only called twice in the two years I'd been in college, once to tell me her father had had a stroke, the other to tell me he'd died, I was sure my roommate was goofing on me. I took the phone and said hello. My mother said, "Hi, Love," and then proceeded to tell me about the golf tournament she'd won that afternoon. After listening to her detailed description of her play on three or four holes and wanting her to get to the point, I asked, "What are you talking about?"

"My golf game," she replied. "Is something the matter with you?"

"No," I said, "nothing's the matter with me. What's the matter with you?"

"Nothing's the matter with me. Are you on pot?"

"No, I'm not on pot," I said. "I'm tripping." And, in my altered state, the word sounded so good that I repeated it over and over, in a high voice and in a low voice, with every possible inflection: "Tripping, triiiiping, trippinnngggggg." It was a parent's nightmare. And the beginning of a very bad trip for a young man who wasn't exactly in the mood to question every aspect of his uncertain life. Luckily, my parents knew not to call the Catholic priest. Instead, they phoned the Presbyterian minister, who, despite his leftist leanings, was a good friend of theirs. He told them the worst thing they could do would be to drive up to see me, and he assured them I would be okay and would probably call when I came down from my trip, which I did.

Michael Murphy's *Golf in the Kingdom* probably comes as close as anything can to what it would be like to play golf on acid. Murphy, who started the Esalen Institute on his parents' estate at Big Sur, wrote the book in 1972, and the story of his one game with Shivas Irons and his subsequent journey to enlightenment is a classic. It stands alone in my book as testament to the Sixties, when everything changed and nothing changed, as the old French saying goes.

The Ghost Patrol of Golf

WALTER BINGHAM

Walter Bingham is a writer and editor for Sports Illustrated *and has been an avid golfer for over fifty years. He commutes between Truro, Massachusetts, and New York City. "The Ghost Patrol of Golf" appeared first in* SI *in 1970.*

They gather every Monday at dawn while fog still blankets the fairways and the greens are soaked with dew. They are dressed colorfully, in the fashion of professional golfers, which indeed they are. They are about to begin a tournament, one you won't see on television or read about in the papers. There is no purse at stake, no trophies or smiling victory photographs. The only gallery they'll see all day is made up of a few wives and friends.

Yesterday, Sunday, another tournament ended somewhere else—at Pebble Beach, maybe, or Pensacola—but these players weren't in it. Many of them don't even know who won there, nor do they care. What matters is today's tournament, because if they don't make it today there is no tomorrow. There's just a long drive to the next foggy Monday.

These men waiting nervously to tee off are members of golfing's Ghost Patrol, a collection of once-weres, never will-bes and young hopefuls called rabbits, a term sometimes applied loosely to the whole group. There are perhaps 200 of them here, trying to qualify for a shot at this week's paycheck, to gain a spot in the tournament that begins on Thursday, the one with the $150,000 purse, the one the Palmers and the Nicklauses play in. The odds are that only one in 10 will make it, maybe fewer than that. Of the 144 starting positions in most pro tournaments, as many as 130 may be filled by players who are exempt from qualifying. The remaining spots belong to the rabbits.

Exempt: that is the golden word on the tour. For a golfer, a year's exemption from pretournament qualifying is worth thousands of dollars, as well as freedom from a season of mental anguish and heartache. An exemption means a pro golfer can play in any tournament he chooses, no matter how many 75s he shoots the week before. It means he can sit down at the beginning of the year and plan. He can pick the tournaments he'll play, when his wife can join him, when he'll take a vacation. In short, it means he can live like a human being and not like a rabbit.

There are 15 types of exemption, but four of them cover the bulk of the field. In the charmed circle are those who have won a PGA Championship or a U.S. Open, which makes them exempt for life. This category takes in most of the game's superstars. Next in line are those who have won any official tournament which exempts them for the next 12 months. This exemption, as much as the $25,000 or so in prize money, is why you see such wide grins on the faces of the Tom Shaws and Larry Hinsons when they win their first tournament. When Hale Irwin, a rabbit, lost in the playoff to Billy Casper in this year's L.A. Open, he was less distraught over the difference in prize money ($20,000 vs. $11,400) than over the fact that he had missed a chance to free himself from Monday qualifying for the rest of 1970.

"I'd have gladly given up the money for that exemption," he said later. "Qualifying on Monday is the toughest thing there is in golf—except winning a tournament. After a while the body just can't take it, the mind can't take it—you go nuts."

The third major exemption goes to the top 60 money earners from the previous year, although this is to be replaced in 1971 by a more equitable point system based on this year's play, so that a

$300,000 Dow Jones Open is no more important toward gaining an exemption than the $100,000 Robinson Open. It is this category that keeps many pros out on the tour in November and early December, when they would rather be at home.

Johnny Pott, a tour veteran at 34 and 24th on the all-time money list, though exempt through much of last year as a member of the Ryder Cup team, discovered to his surprise that this exemption ended with the PGA tournament in August. Still, in 52nd place on the money list, he seemed assured of finishing in the top 60 for 1969 and so passed up the Hawaiian Open. He was aghast to find later that several players just below him on the money list had done well in Hawaii and he was now 62nd.

Frantic, Pott accepted an invitation to the Heritage Classic but failed to make the cut. He went to the Danny Thomas Classic, tried to qualify on Monday but shot a 73, which was not good enough. Any rabbit could have told him that. "I thought I'd blown it," Pott says. "I was about to go home when Steve Reid mentioned the West End Classic on Grand Bahama Island. It was a satellite tournament, but the money was official and you didn't have to qualify." Pott hustled over, shot a 64 in the first round and finished second, collecting $2,437, enough to put him back in the top 60. Pott wears the look of a reprieved man these days.

The fourth major exemption is for players who make the 36-hole cut in one tournament, automatically qualifying them for the next. This is the best hope of the rabbit. Winning a tournament or finishing in the year's top 60 may be the impossible dream, but making the cut is always a possibility. Most rabbits insist that it is easier to make the cut than to qualify on Monday.

"Sometimes it seems as if the whole world is out there playing on Monday," says Joe Schwendeman, an aide to Commissioner Joseph C. Dey of the PGA's Tournament Players Division. Even when the qualifying takes place on two or three courses—"dirt tracks," as one rabbit calls them—the players are turned out early, 7 o'clock, or as soon as the greens are playable.

The atmosphere is tense. "This is the first of what I hope will be three tournaments this week," says Bob Shaw, a young Australian. "The one today is the toughest. Then there's Thursday and Friday, when you try to make the cut. If you survive that, you play in your third tournament on Saturday and Sunday for the money. But Monday's the big one."

By the time they tee off every golfer knows how many spots are open for this week's tournament. It has been a subject of active speculation all the previous week, and the rumored number has fluctuated as often as the odds on a tote board. But nothing is set until Sunday at 6 p.m., the deadline for filing entries. Dave Hill, having shot three straight 74s, may have decided on Sunday morning that he was overgolfed and needed a rest. But a closing round of 66 has left him surprisingly refreshed, and he decides to sign up for next week. One spot gone. But Frank Beard, who intended to play, learns that one of his children has mumps, and so he goes home. One spot back. When the list closes Sunday night, perhaps 124 exempt pros have signed up. That means 20 spots for the rabbits.

There are often not enough caddies to accommodate so many entrants and so the club turns out its fleet of electric carts, with club members recruited to drive them. "I hate to use a cart," says George Johnson, a promising black player. "When I hit a bad shot, I need a few minutes to settle down. With a cart, I'm on to the next shot too soon."

The players go off in foursomes, one group every 10 minutes. No ropes are needed to hold the galleries in check, for there are seldom any galleries at all. No scoreboards record the progress of the event, no neat ladies in straw hats and red-and-white-striped skirts walk down the fairways keeping score. From the time the players leave the first tee until they return to the 18th green some four hours later, they battle in near privacy. The wives, in raincoats, scarves and golf shoes, trail behind and suffer.

"What makes it so brutal is that it's like sudden death," says Bob Shaw. "One bad shot can wipe you out."

"I always tried to play conservative golf on Monday," says Bert Greene, a graduate rabbit who escaped by finishing 22nd on last year's money list. "Figure one or two birdies on the par 5s and the rest pars. There's no prize for shooting 66. Of course, if you make a double bogey you have to change your game plan in a hurry."

As the players come off the 18th green, they hand in their scores to the TPD official in charge, either Wade Cagle, Ed Griffiths, George Walsh or Steve Shabala, four advance men who leapfrog from tournament to tournament. When each score has been recorded, it is also listed publicly on a board near the clubhouse. Those who shoot 67 can return to their motels knowing they will tee it up on Thursday. Those who shoot 73 may hang around, but it's a faint hope that they're in, and most leave.

The players who shoot somewhere in between—71 or 72—are the ones who must stand and wait. On the tour they call it the sweat box, the predicament of an early finisher with a 72. As each four-some rolls in, he watches closely as the scores are posted. When he finished, he was third from the top. Now comes a 71, then a 70. The open spots dwindle to seven, now six. And there are still three four-somes out on the course. It is a long wait.

The PGA has no record of when Monday qualifying was born, but tour veterans can recall qualifications for the L.A. Open and other West Coast tournaments—favorite havens for pros from the cold weather regions—during the '40s. With the explosion in golf during the 1960s, Monday qualifying rounds became standard practice.

Dave Marr, who has been around since the late '50s, recalls that it was easy to qualify then if you were able to play all. "They'd have maybe 130 guys out there on Monday, but there was room for 80. Shoot 75 and you still had a chance." This year it took a one-under-par 71 at Spyglass to be sure of a starting spot in the Crosby. "I'd hate to have to shoot a 71 at Spyglass," Marr says.

The line separating the rabbit from the regular tournament money-winner is a thin one. Every week the Ghost Patrol includes several golfers capable of winning. Last year Bunky Henry qualified on Monday for the Monsanto open, finished tied for 41st and won $322. The next week he tied for 78th at Jacksonville, earning $114. The third week, at the National Airlines in Miami, Henry shot 69-

73-66-70-278 to win the tournament, $40,000 and, most important, a year's exemption. With only minor differences, the same story could be told about Tom Shaw, Larry Hinson, Larry Ziegler and Steve Spray. Spray, for instance, had to qualify for the Sahara, made the cut, then won at San Francisco the following week.

"Those fellows," says Bob Shaw of the exempt pros, "are no different than a lot of us out here. A whole bunch of players in our group are capable of winning if they can just get to play."

Tom Shaw (no relation) tends to agree. "I was the world's worst qualifier," he says. "In 1968 I tried to qualify 15 times and failed all but three. Even so, I made $14,000. When I played, I made money."

Monday's nonheroes can be divided into two groups. About half the field, roughly 100 players at any qualifying round, are club pros who enter five or 10 tournaments a year, usually the ones within hailing distance of their home courses. The rest are touring pros, men who try to make their living from the $6.7 million bag of prize money offered on the tour this year.

The second category, the touring pros, is made up of three subgroups: the real rabbits, players in their first year or two of the tour; the older hands with small reputations built on wins or high finishes in things like the Azalea Open or the Magnolia Classic—guys like Monty Kaser, Babe Hiskey or Larry Mowry; and finally there is the fallen star, the player—like Jacky Cupit or Marty Fleckman or Al Balding—who made headlines once and may again. But not now.

The rabbits are the most anonymous, except to each other. "If Jack Nicklaus walked in here, he'd know me," says Dick Carmody, "but that's only because we played golf against each other in college. I doubt if he'd know many others out here." Carmody has known such modest successes as winning the Quebec Open, which earned him $2,500 but no exemption, since it was not a PGA event. Last year Carmody suffered the embarrassment of having his player's card revoked, a penalty of the TPD for bad play. Now he is back on the trail again as a Class A player, the category under which most club pros compete. He finished 39th in the L.A. Open but missed the cut at Phoenix, which put him back in the pit. At the Crosby qualifying round at Spyglass he shot a 73 in the rain, which would have been good enough except that it rained so hard the round was canceled. The next day he shot 72, which put him in a 16-way tie for nine spots, and a sudden-death playoff was scheduled Wednesday.

Carmody was awake most of the night worrying about the first playoff hole at Pebble ("It's a narrow fairway, and I told myself I had to keep the ball in bounds"), then delighted himself next morning by hitting his drive down the middle. Perhaps overcome, he knocked his approach wide of the green and out of bounds. End of tournament.

Most rabbits such as Carmody are sponsored, else they would not be able to afford the tour. Besides, the TPD insists a player show proof of support. Sponsors are generally wealthy club members who pass the hat until they have raised enough—usually $20,000 or so— to send their young assistant pro out on the tour for a year. A few celebrities—Lawrence Welk, for one, and Dean Martin and Glen Campbell—are currently backing golfers on tour. One promising rabbit, John Jacobs, talked his wealthy girlfriend into backing him.

One level above the true rabbit are the modest successes like Kaser, Hiskey and Mowry, with their horticultural wins at the Magnolia or Azalea, satellite events that rarely carry an exemption but whose money is official. Pete Brown, before his dramatic victory in the recent Andy Williams–San Diego Open, fell into this category. Although Brown had been on the tour for 16 years, he had won only one minor tournament. Last year he was 84th on the money list with $20,893, about $12,000 shy of getting him into the top 60. Brown has competed in qualifying rounds for years and got into the Andy Williams—despite missing the cut at the Crosby—by surviving the cut in the Crosby pro-am, a side-door exemption for which his amateur partner deserves as much credit as Brown. Brown later said all he could think about as he lined up his final putt in the last round at San Diego was "one putt for no more Mondays." He missed that putt but won the tournament in a playoff. No more Mondays.

The top level of qualifier is the veteran player who has made headlines, has won tournaments (but not recently) and who, in some cases, has come within a shot of earning a lifetime exemption. Jacky Cupit in 1963 had the U.S. Open all wrapped up until he double bogeyed the 71st hole and finished in a three-way tie with Arnold Palmer and Julius Boros. Boros won.

Now here is Cupit, seven years later, sitting in a golf cart waiting to tee off. He is not bitter, he says bitterly, adding that if he qualifies today he will phone his wife in Texas and have her come out for the tournament. Then he goes out and shoots 80.

Others who currently share Cupit's fate are Marty Fleckman, who as an amateur led the 1967 Open at Baltusrol going into the last round; Kermit Zarley, a former tour winner whom Bob Hope made famous by calling "the pro from the moon"; Labron Harris, the 1962 U.S. Amateur champion; and Al Balding. Less than two years ago in Rome, Balding, a lanky, gray-haired Canadian golfer of 45, teamed with George Knudson to win the World Cup. Balding was low individual. Balding has been on and off the tour for years, was eighth leading money earner back in 1957. Several weeks ago he had to qualify for the Andy Williams. He was having a coffee shop breakfast early Monday morning when a friend spotted him.

"Alsie," said the pal. "What the devil are you doing here?"

"Have to work today," said Balding.

"Work?" asked the friend. It took a moment for the meaning to sink in. "You mean. . . ?"

Balding's friend never finished the question.

"It's not in the code to mention qualifying," says Dave Marr, who has been permanently exempt since he won the PGA in 1965. "You see certain players on Thursday and you know they must have had to qualify to be there, but you never mention it. You just say, 'Hi, Pete, hi, George.'"

The brightest fallen star at the moment is Doug Sanders, golf's flamboyant dresser, who has won 17 tournaments in his career and is seventh on the all-time money list. But his last tour win was in 1967, and last year he was 64th in earnings with $30,311. So, technically, Sanders is not exempt. Yet he's never out there on Monday. Why? Because the rules allow sponsors of every tournament to exempt eight players not otherwise eligible—a ploy to insure the presence of local favorites, or players like Sanders, whose reputations outlast their putting strokes. At one time players were allowed to accept only three such exemptions a year, but now the TPD permits players to take as many as they want. The rabbits are restless over the rule.

"Everything is for the established pro," says one young player. "It kills you to see some of the guys who can't even swing anymore taking up spots that could be ours. Jerry Barber, Paul Runyan—some of these players with lifetime exemptions. And now this sponsor thing. Life's tough enough without that."

Tougher still is when a sponsor gives an exemption to an amateur—an *amateur,* mind you—usually one who has a big reputation (and no worse than a two handicap). Everyone wants to see how old Bill will make out against the pros, never mind that old Bill is taking up a spot that might otherwise go to someone struggling to earn a living. That's why Oscar Fraley of the Danny Thomas tournament became an instant hero among the rabbits last fall when he didn't use any of his sponsor's exemptions, but threw all eight spots to the qualifiers.

Now it is Monday afternoon, and the scores are all in. The successful qualifiers return to their motels and inform the desk clerk that they will be staying a few days longer, perhaps even for the whole week. Then they begin to scout around for a place to practice on Tuesday and Wednesday because, unlike the exempt players, Monday qualifiers are not allowed to play in Pro-Ams. But at least they get to tee it up Thursday.

What about the others, the 150 or so who didn't make it? "It's tough on them," admits Jack Tuthill, the TPD tournament director. "Nobody wants them. They aren't supposed to hang around for the tournament, and they sure aren't wanted at the next tournament course—tearing up the fairways and making spike marks on the green."

The experienced rabbit can usually find someplace to play because he has been around long enough to meet a lot of club pros. But the younger players, the ones on their first or second swings, often find themselves paying $.50 to hit a pail of balls on a driving range beside the highway between here and there. Bert Yancey remembers stopping his car by an empty lot, hitting his bag of practice balls and then shagging them himself. Not long ago Bob Shaw tried to play at a public course in Los Angeles where a qualifying round for the L.A. Open was scheduled. He was told pros were not welcome. Shaw offered to pay the greens fee. The answer was no. Desperately, Shaw offered $10 merely to be allowed to walk the course so he could get to know it. The answer was still no.

Another problem that comes with failing to qualify is keeping faith in your game. "After a while, you start to think bad thoughts," says George Johnson. "You get the idea you can't play."

"It's the most terrifying thing in golf," recalls Yancey. "It's worse than missing a cut or blowing a U.S. Open. When you miss on Monday, you haven't got anything."

The problems of the Monday qualifier have, of course, come to the attention of Joe Dey, whose policy board recently approved a change he recommended, making club pros who are not TPD members enter an 18-hole *pre*qualifying round on Friday. Only the top 20% from Friday are now allowed into Monday's round, reducing that field.

Perhaps more pertinent is the whole question of whether the rule is fair to club pros. Joe Dey thinks it is. "The regular touring pros have already earned the right to compete in qualifying rounds," he says. Besides, he points out, for an initiation fee of $50, plus $250 a year dues, any club pro can join the TPD and thus avoid the pre-Monday qualifying. The new system went into effect last month.

Commissioner Dey is toying with another solution, a periodic 36-hole qualifying round to replace the weekly one. This would establish a semipermanent ranking, from which available starting positions would be filled. If National Airlines had 24 open spots, the top 24 in the ranking would get to play. This system would give the top 10 or 12 a respite from qualifying every week, and it would permit those who are below 30 or so to return home to sharpen their games for the next 36-hole round. For those in between, unfortunately, it would mean another form of the sweat box, having to travel from tournament to tournament in hopes that enough exempt players decide not to enter.

A more agreeable solution to the Monday crush would be the long-dreamed-of solid "second" tour. Dey is thinking in terms of a kind of minor league golf, success in which leads to the major league tour. And staying up there might well depend solely on merit, *i.e.*, stroke averages or victories. Dey can understand the rabbits' resentment of lifetime exemptions, and may soon propose they be limited to 10 years. You can almost hear the growls already.

Until that happy day, that first Monday when all the rabbits can sleep in and still have their nibbles at pro golfing's lettuce patch on Thursday, the struggle goes on. They will continue to gather at dawn and by dusk most of them will have nothing to look forward to but a long wait till next Monday.

All Empires Decline and Fall . . .

CHRISTOPHER BRAM

Christopher Bram is the author of six novels. His fifth, Father of Franken-stein, *is soon to be released as a motion picture.*

All empires decline and fall. Empire. The word itself suggests the ephemeral and doomed. It was a word I disliked during my twenty-plus years in the Foreign Service, thinking it can't be applied to American interests, a cynical way of dismissing our good work. But nothing is forever, nothing is pure.

I own a golf ball autographed by Richard Nixon.

(Yes, that's closer to the note I want to strike. I sound like a pompous ass when I attempt to do George Kennan or Dean Acheson. In describing a career that was small potatoes, I should stick to the potato's eye view.)

This golf ball is not something I cherish. I never admired or even respected Mr. Nixon during my years with the government. His golf ball holds no place of esteem in my little house in the Maryland suburbs. In fact, it wanders about the house of its own accord, appearing now in the drawer of the desk where I write this, now in the bowl of coconuts on my TV set and VCR, now in the dish on my refrigerator where I keep my car keys, unpaid bills and free condoms. I suppose I should either have the thing sealed in Lucite for posterity or toss it in my bag of practice balls where time, my persistent hook and a patch of weeds will rid me of it for good.

I once played nine holes with President Nixon, in 1969 at the Wack Wack Golf and Country Club in Manila. More accurately, I played with Chip Adkins, then chargé d'affaires to the Philippines, while Nixon played with Ferdinand Marcos. The two heads of state strutted down the fairway twenty yards ahead of us, each with a club in his hand, chatting and pretending to enjoy themselves. Marcos gave the more convincing performance. All around us strolled an army of press people, Secret Service men dressed like Mormons despite the heat and Marcos bodyguards. Nixon played a very anxious, distracted game, but then nobody could really concentrate on sport in those circumstances. It was all one could do not to bean a reporter or Marcos goon on the head.

Nixon was in Manila after flying out to the Pacific for the splashdown of the first men on the moon. He toured the Far East to prolong his vacation from the pressure in Washington over the Vietnam War. Even then I was struck that there was so much history—an American triumph in outer space, a bloody quagmire a few hundred miles away—looming over something as commonplace as this quartet of middle-aged men in bilious knits and plaids knocking little white balls through the grass.

The Wack Wack was (and still is, I suspect) one of the most beautiful courses in Asia, a cunning series of vistas and hazards, Australian pines mixed with stands of bamboo along the fairways, palm trees towering over the greens like rubbery Roman columns. It was the same golf course where, one night three years later, Marcos staged an assassination attempt on a cabinet minister to give himself his final excuse to declare martial law. Machine-gun fire allegedly ripped through Juan Enrile's car as it drove past the thirteenth hole on the way back from the Malacanang Palace. It was later reported that Enrile and his men simply stopped the car on the back nine, got out and shot it up themselves.

Determined to win at everything he did, Marcos cheated at golf too. I once saw a goon surreptitiously scoot the boss's ball out of the rough for a better lie, and have heard tales from others involving duplicate balls and doctored scorecards. He did not cheat the day he played Nixon. He won honestly, but only by two strokes. Marcos was a bold man, not a stupid one.

We had time for just nine holes that morning before the rest of the day's scheduled events. We talked and laughed in the clubhouse locker room while we changed clothes, all regular guys. Marcos took his pants off himself, doing without his usual pair of valets. Nixon worked hard at appearing regular, going so far as to tell an off-color story, the punch line of which eluded everyone. I knew Nixon primarily as a face and voice on television. It was unnerving to undress so close to the jowls and square-tipped nose familiar to me from political cartoons, like undressing beside Mickey Mouse. Without meaning to suggest anything sexual, I admit I had a guilty desire to see the man naked. A peek would do. But no, Nixon slipped from his golf pants into his dress slacks as quickly as the shyest fat boy in gym class. I presume he waited until he got back to the Malacanang Palace to take a shower. He avoided looking at me and Adkins while we toweled off, although I do think I caught him checking out Marcos. (I can't believe I'm including all this.)

In suit and tie again, he called in one of his Secret Service men and sent him out for something. The man returned, utterly stonefaced in his sunglasses, a dozen golf balls cupped in the bowl of his hands. "Mementos for the boys," Nixon explained. Sitting on a bench, he wrote his name on each ball and passed them to me, until I had my hands full of a slippery pile of white dimpled spheres. "Distribute them to the caddies," the Chief Executive told me. "Something they can pass on to their grandchildren." He laughed as he capped his pen, not nastily, but as if he suddenly appreciated the comedy of the gesture, the absurdity of fame. Or maybe he realized from the looks on Adkins's face and mine what a stupid act this really was. Marcos assured him that it was for such thoughtfulness and generosity that the Philippine people loved President Nixon.

Even with my big hands, I had difficulty carrying so many balls without spilling them. I hurried through the heat and glare to the caddy pen, a clay courtyard out behind the clubhouse with an open latrine and a porch roof of green corrugated fiberglass. The "boys," the youngest of whom was over twenty, sat in the green shadow of the porch, drinking San Miguel and listening to Nancy Sinatra on a transistor radio. "From the American president," I announced as I approached. They jumped to their feet and came forward, expecting a handsome tip. They saw only golf balls, and stopped. Then, baffled yet polite, they each took one, turning the balls around and around in their fingers, as if there might be a trick involved. One of them laughed and said in Tagalog, "What I want are Marcos's balls." Nobody else laughed; a Marcos man stood among them, given away by his silk shirt and alligator shoes. I wanted to laugh, but could not let America lose more face with these people than we already had. Keeping all doubts and irony to myself, I still earnestly played the game that summer.

When I was through, I had three or four balls left. Nobody asked for the extras. I didn't know what else to do with them, so I loaded them into my pants pockets, thanked the caddies again and rejoined the others. I did not know how to return Nixon's unwanted balls to him. (The masculine analogy in all this certainly gets tiresome, doesn't it?) I spent the rest of the day tumorous with golf balls, unable to take them out until I put on my tux that night for the lavish dinner given in the Nixons' honor. They flew on to Japan the next day and we were able to get back to the quiet business of quarreling among ourselves.

Over the following week, I gave away balls, I can't remember to whom. I know I gave one to the Sullivan kids, who lived in Manila with their mother while their father was attached to the embassy in Saigon. No dependents were allowed in Vietnam and here was another family with whom I could play Uncle Jim. I may have given one to Rosalita, my cook, although I can't imagine what she'd want with it. In the end, I kept one for myself, assuming a nephew or niece might get a kick out of having the president's scrawl to show friends. It was three years before I got back to the States and saw my sister's family again. In the meantime, the ball disappeared and I forgot all about it. During that long sabbatical which I thought was permanent, I kept most of my things in storage. Not until I retired for good and bought this house did I unpack the many boxes of accumulated junk. I found the golf ball in a box full of Balinese woodcarvings, amateur tennis trophies, an ornate brass lamp base hammered out of the casing of an artillery shell and other debris one was reluctant to throw away.

Here it is, a Titleist 500, probably never used, with an illegible name circling it in blue ink, written as well as one can write anything on a small, lightly cratered globe. As with the world, so with a golf ball. It can't be worth any money; I don't know how an autograph dealer would go about authenticating the darn thing. But it still bounces. (There. I bounce it off my kitchen floor, which sits on cold concrete slab.) It hasn't gone dead yet, not as a golf ball anyway.

If there's a moral to all this, it eludes me. Except that I have no business writing a memoir. I may send these pages to you, the best of a bad lot, just to show you I *did* try. Your uncle is no writer. Reading what I've written, I fear my humor doesn't always come through and I alternate between the pompous and the smart-aleck. There are patches as cheerfully callous as the worst Watergate confessional. And I was never callous. Stupid or romantic, but never callous. Having been so blind about my life while I lived it, I can't bear the thought of being blind again on a second go-round.

The truth of the matter is I have no juicy anecdotes to tell, no state secrets to reveal, no story of my own. All I have is the tale of a career played out in the no-man's land between public events and private pathology. The latter might interest students of organizational behavior, but the habit of discretion forged by years in the State Department dies hard. There's much I'm reluctant to discuss, even with you. (Not the sexual. I certainly couldn't write about it, but you and I have no secrets in that department.) Let me leave history to the famous and you historians. I was there only on a brief visit, a tourist in the empire, a houseguest of history. That last phrase might look nice on my tombstone.

Good grief, Meg. Here I am at fifty-plus, already planning my own funeral. You see how attempting this has spoiled my equilibrium. I will forget the past, go out into the world and finish installing the new weatherproof gutters. Wisdom should express itself in silence.

Jim set the pencil down and sat back in his chair. Chair and desk were in the kitchen and it was cold there, despite his plaid flannel shirt and the sunny day outside. Framed in the window above the sink, the red leaves of a maple tree streamed in the wind like paper flames. The sky was a bright, pure blue. All around him, his empty house softly whistled and droned, as if with the sound of the Earth swerving through space.

Jim ran both hands over his scalp, wanting the thinning hair to assure him he really was old and therefore wise. He was not quite silent, though. He flipped through the pages in the yellow legal pad covered with tiny seismic zigzags, wondering what he had hoped to accomplish here, why the effort left him feeling so depressed. He hadn't actually wanted to write a memoir or meditation on history or whatever this was supposed to be. He couldn't remember where he had let this turn into a letter.

"Love, Jim," he wrote on the last sheet and gently tore the pages out. He folded them and wedged the bundle into a business envelope. Sending it on to his niece who taught history gave the exercise some kind of purpose, and got the evidence of failure out of the house. He addressed the envelope. He peeled off his reading glasses and set them on the desk, a pair of oval windows that watched him with their arms coolly crossed. He bounced the golf ball one last time against the floor before he dropped it in the drawer, then went out to the mailbox with the letter to his confidante, friend and accomplice.

Singing the Praises of Golf

MICHAEL MURPHY

A Stanford University graduate, Michael Murphy is the founder of the Esalen Institute, and the author of what The San Francisco Times *called "A masterpiece on the mysticism of golf." His* Golf in the Kingdom *has been one of the most popular books on golf for over twenty-five years and will undoubtedly remain so for years to come.*

Liston the barman was lighting a fire in the clubhouse bar as we entered. A few moments later I was sitting in front of the blazing logs, whisky glass in hand, listening to Shivas and his friends sing Scottish golfing songs. The fire in front of me and the subtle fire of Shivas's presence were warming me inside and out. I listened to them singing in their rich Fife accents,

> *. . . among the heather and the gorse,*
> *ye must remember of course,*
> *not tae lose yer balls at ol' Sin Tondress. . . .*

listened to their laughter and raillery, to the sounds of golfers stomping grass from their cleats, then a cheer from the eighteenth green—sounds that reminded me of a special Christmas when I was a child. I was filled with gratitude, my eyes filled with tears as I looked around that glowing room. The mood that had come over me out on the course, that sense of an enormous presence suffusing the world, was with me still. I could feel the wild and mysterious terrain of the Burningbush Links, those immense worlds waiting, but this warm place was at the center of my feelings now, the convivial faces and friendly words, the songs, the walls covered with dancing firelight. I felt as if I had found my way home at last.

For more than an hour I watched the club members come and go, and gazed into the fire as I savored that incredible round. Shivas was greeting friends at the bar. I could hear his voice above the rest from time to time, giving encouragement or answering a friendly gibe; his presence seemed as important to them as it was to me.

During that hour no problems existed. But then questions began to form, began intruding themselves as they inevitably do. The aura of utter well-being was fading, and I began the return to my ordinary state of mind.

What was this strangely impressive man really up to? What was he doing on the thirteenth tee? There had been something uncanny about that hole, something I could not quite bring into consciousness. What had the bartender meant when he taunted him about "defiling the old men of Burningbush"? Later that evening some of these questions would be answered and others would be compounded.

He had invited me to dinner, interrupting my ruminations with a sudden shout from the bar. "Michael, ma good lad," he said, coming over and putting his hand on my shoulder, "'tis time ye're exposed to the true complexities o' the gemme." I would soon find that the thoughts which had begun to disturb me were being developed at length by others.

The meal was to be at the home of the McNaughtons, he said as we left the clubhouse. I was surprised and flattered at the sudden invitation, and sensed his excitement about the gathering that was soon to take place. He had changed into a white crew-necked sweater, and either because of the clothes or a change of mood had a different look about him. He seemed less massive and concentrated, even a little smaller in size. His wind-burned face contrasted sharply with the sweater's whiteness, making him more handsome than ever.

He hummed a tune as we walked along, some old Scotch ballad, I think, with a vaguely Oriental air, that mysterious longing and joy you catch sometimes in the wailing of the pipes.

The strange melody trailed off as we approached our destination; he seemed to be distracted. When we arrived at the McNaughtons' house, he touched my shoulder vaguely and murmured something about needing to be alone for a moment. "Ye go ahaid, Michael, they'll understand," he almost whispered the words, then wandered off down the street. Startled and embarrassed, I explained to the handsome woman who answered the door that Shivas Irons had invited me to dinner and that now he had gone off down the street. She asked me to come in. As I stepped through the doorway, I looked back and saw him sitting on a window ledge looking up into the evening sky. He seemed to be lost in thought.

"Did ye play gowf with him today?" the handsome lady asked as she ushered me in. "He sometimes brings his playin' partners here afterwards." She introduced herself as Agatha McNaughton. Following her up the narrow staircase, I couldn't help noticing what a great figure she had—she moved ahead of me up the steep passageway with slow pleasurable steps.

The other guests had arrived and were sitting with their drinks around a stone hearth that framed an inviting fire. Above the mantel an ancient-looking pair of crossed swords gleamed in the firelight. The men stood to greet me. Peter McNaughton, Agatha's husband, was a vigorous-looking red-faced man in his fifties, perhaps twenty years Agatha's senior. He shook my hand, pulling me toward him with two muscular jerks. "Welcome to our guid cafe," he said with gusto. "What did ye do with our unpredictable friend?"

"He went for a walk. . . ."

"Waitin' for the moon to rise perhaps," he said and smiled, cutting me off in mid-sentence as if to save me embarrassment. "He may stay out thair for an hour or more. But here . . ." He introduced me around to the others—an imposing craggy-faced old Scotsman named Julian Laing, an English couple named Greene, and Peter's sixteen-year-old son, Kelly. Laing, it was explained to me, was the town's "main doctor"; he had delivered five thousand of the town's ten thousand inhabitants. He was also, I was to discover, a psychiatrist of sorts with remarkable, highly eccentric theories. As he shook my hand he winked enigmatically and asked if Shivas had brought me "through the eye of the needle." I wasn't exactly sure what he meant.

The Greenes were visiting from Cornwall, up to study the ecology of the Firth of Forth and tell Shivas their new theories about golfing links. Spirited, bouncy little people not much taller than five feet, they reminded me of a pair of elves from Tolkien's trilogy. His name was Adam and hers was Eve, they were meant for each other, they said. Everyone laughed at the familiar joke, which must have been trotted out for the hundredth time. Adam Greene taught "cosmic ecology" at a London "Free University." God knows how he supported himself. I think he had been an engineer or inventor before his turn to philosophy.

Peter McNaughton acted as master of ceremonies with enormous zest and a sense that this was a special gathering indeed. It was obvious that he was very proud of his friends. His son, Kelly, was over six feet tall, had a kind of sardonic whisky brogue, and blushed whenever he smiled. He smiled and blushed when he shook my hand.

"Did ye git the traitment today?" he asked. The remark carried all sorts of insinuations. I mumbled something like "Yes, I did have quite a round, how did you know?" evoking a laugh from everyone.

"How do we know!" exclaimed Agatha, with a warm, richly textured brogue. "Why, that bad man wouldna' just let ye play an ordinary round of golf!" I felt like I'd been taken into the clan.

We sat around the fire drinking whisky and trading pleasantries. I couldn't stop thinking about Shivas down there on that window ledge, but no one else seemed concerned. There was excitement underlying the hospitable remarks, a sense of anticipation about this gathering. "And what do ye do to keep the body alive, Mr. Murphy?" Agatha asked. She wore a light brown woolen blouse that showed the contour of her breasts. I said something about being a student and aspiring writer. They wanted to know what school I went to and I told them. Old Laing then got the conversation going in earnest.

"Well, Murphy," he intoned with his gnarled burr, "as an aspiring man of words, will ye tell me whether words have a future? They've had a dismal past." He raised his brambly eyebrows and peered over his glass at me. He then looked around at everyone else and came on with another conversation opener. "Wuidna'all of ye agree tha' all logic, all human history, all our experience compel us to recognize tha' the only thing in life worth doin' is the will of God?" I hadn't expected that kind of statement. I thought of some people in my home town, Salinas, from the First Church of God of Prophecy.

No one seemed disposed to reply. Any further remarks would have to carry some metaphysical force. There was a long silence as we drank our Scotch and looked into the fire.

"Well, Shivas would agree with ye," Kelly said at last with his sardonic inflection.

"Aye, we've discussed the matter for years," the old doctor replied, "but ye ken how he is. Tomorra' he'll be tellin' Murphy heer that believin' in God is dangerous. He's the dangerous one, o' course." He repeated the words with affectionate irony, "He's the dangerous one." There was affection in the old man's voice as he invoked his friend's presence, but with it there was an unmistakable sense that Shivas Irons was indeed dangerous.

"As long as we're talking about him, shouldn't we tell him it's time to eat?" Eve Greene broke in. The McNaughtons replied, almost in unison, that there was no use disturbing him now, that he would come in good time. "Ye know how he is," they said protectively, and ushered us into their dining room. It was a long, low candlelit room with latticed windows and wood beams across the ceiling. The dining table was some 20 feet long, and 4 feet wide, a table for a banquet. Seated around it we seemed yards apart.

The McNaughtons' hospitality, the happy anticipation I felt among this group of friends, the whisky, and the winds of Burningbush had all had their effect upon me. I was warmed and lifted high.

Peering down the table at those faces in the candlelight I began to smile. It must have been an idiot smile. "Ye look so happy, Michael," Agatha said, "a round of golf with Shivas will do tha' to ye."

"Oh, where is he, where is he?" Eve Greene persisted, looking hopefully about the room over her attractive upturned nose. Her head barely made it over the edge of the table. Both she and Adam needed cushions to reach their dinner. "We've been looking forward to seeing him for weeks. Our theories about golf and evolution are growing larger every day."

"Aye, ma guid Greenes, yer theories were enormous awready," said Peter, lifting his glass high. "Let us drink a toast to all theories round, let us sing the praises of gowf." His always ruddy face was red with pleasure. "To gowf!" he exclaimed, and we all raised our glasses—of water, milk, or whisky, a makeshift but inspired toast to golf and the good life.

Agatha then brought in a large tureen of broth, full of dumplings. For a moment we ate in silence, savoring the aroma of that ancient Scottish potion. It smelled to me like heather and the breeze above the thirteenth hole, warmed with bullion and flour dumplings.

Suddenly, there was a loud knocking at the front door and Shivas's stentorian voice shouting, "Open up in the name o' the law." Peter hurried down the stairs and we could hear them talking below. Then Shivas appeared at the dining-room door. He was flushed and radiant.

"Ah, ma guid cronies, Ah see ye've waited for me. Is thair anything at a' left to eat?" He embraced Agatha with a bone-crunching hug and held her for a moment while she tried to squirm away. "Adam and Eve, love birds still," he grasped their hands, "what new theories have ye now? Julian Laing, protector o' Burningbush and ma very own soul!" He went round the table as he greeted everyone. "And *you*." He squeezed the back of Kelly's neck and the tall boy punched him playfully in the stomach. "What d'ye think o' this group, Michael? A motley lot, wouldn't ye say?"

He was strikingly handsome, tanned and ruddy in his white

sweater and golden pants. Something had given his spirits a tremendous lift.

"I see that I've gotten here at the right moment. Lay on, Mrs. McNaughton," he said in his booming voice. And we all began eating the impressive meal that Agatha laid in front of us. What a wife she was, I thought, lucky Peter. Shivas obviously appreciated her too. "Agatha, Agatha, ye remind me o' what I'm missin'," he said as he demolished a plate of stew.

It was somewhere between the stew and the dessert that the conversation we had all been secretly waiting for finally began. Peter proposed that we all take our turn describing the game of golf. Since the Greenes were here with their new theories and as this was a gathering that was not likely to recur for a while, if ever, he said, we should each in turn tell what the endlessly mysterious sport was really about. The Greenes were by now virtually standing on their chairs, which seemed so much lower than the rest, to talk about their discoveries. They had been waiting for weeks for the occasion. Shivas was enthusiastic too. "'Tis time tha' we did justice to the subject," he said, "and this is just the group tae do it. But I want tae hear yer ideas first. I shall speak last, plagiarist that I am, and, Michael, I want ye tae remember it all for posterity. Now, Peter, begin. Ye're the host."

"No, Agatha is," protested the good husband, "this is her party."

"Then Agatha, *begin*," boomed Shivas.

"No, Peter is the one with ideas," said our handsome hostess, and everyone began talking at once.

Eventually Peter began. "All right, my friends," he said, leaning forward and looking round at us all, his graying temples reflecting the candlelight. "I'm not an intellectual sort like the rest o' ye, so ye're not goin' tae get any fancy theories from me. And I'm goin' to keep this speech very short, for I'm sayin' my farewell to the game. I've suffered enough with it."

Peter's seemingly decisive statement was met with a round of hoots and gibes. Apparently he had made such renunciations before.

"Let us drink a toast to Peter's imminent departure," said Shivas, lifting up his glass, "and to his predictable retoorn." There was a round of laughter as we all lifted glasses toward our host.

Kelly got up from the table and went into the sitting room. He returned with an old wooden-shafted club that was taped together with wads of black binding tape. "Break it noo," he said, offering the golfing stick to his father, "it'll bring everyone luck."

Peter smiled and took the club with both his hands. His face was bright red now from drink and what seemed to be a sudden embarrassment, "Ye see, ma friends," he said, holding up the stick, "we call this our wishbone. Ye can each make a wish." Then he stood up and broke it with an enormous crack across his knee. He stood at the end of the table, sheepishly holding up a broken piece in each hand. "We do this, ye see, whenever I give up the gemme. Did ye make yer wishes?" There was another round of laughter and our host sat down.

The surprising performance had happened so swiftly that I had not had a chance to make a wish. But the first thought that had flashed in my mind, I can still remember it, was an image of a golf pro at the Salinas club who had come from Oklahoma, a colorful man with gigantic temper, throwing a sand wedge at me by mistake. It whirled like a vicious helicopter blade as it came right for my face—I ducked and it grazed my scalp. It was the closest I had come to being killed or maimed and now the image had surfaced as Peter broke his club.

"What did ye wish, Mr. Murphy?" Kelly asked in his whisky brogue from the other end of the table.

"That no one kills me with a golf club," my reply popped out. Everyone thought it was a great wish.

"Ye see, that is why I *break* my club," Peter grinned. "To save ye all from disaster."

"Oh, McNaughton, ye'll be back," Shivas's voice resounded above the rest, "but finish yer speech." The rest of the group urged Peter to continue.

"Awright, I'll tell ye what I think, for through my sufferin's a certain understandin' has developed." He looked with sad eyes around the table and winked at Julian. "If I've learned one thing about the game it is that 'tis many things to many people, includin' the many ones in my very own head." He tapped his temple. "We've certainly seen them come and go through Burnin'bush. Tall ones, short ones, scratch players, and duffers from the end o' the wardle. Intellectual sorts and workin' men, pleasant tempraments and mean ones, the MacGillicudys and the Balfours, the Leviases, the St. Clairs, the Van Blocks, the gentlemen from Pakistan—in terms of origin and character and ideas, a most diverse and complex lot. For each has his peculiar understandin', his peculiar theory, his peculiar view o' the world, his peculiar swing, God knows. Get them here on the links, and all their parts fall oot." He smiled sadly again and shook his head. "Gowf is a way o' makin' a man naked. I would say tha' nowhere does a man go so naked as he does before a discernin' eye dressed for gowf. Ye talk about yer body language, Julian, yer style o' projectin', yer rationalizashin', yer excuses, lies, cheatin' roonds, incredible stories, failures of character—why, there's no other place to match it. Ye take auld Judge Hobbes, my God, the lies he told last week about that round o' his in the tournament, 'tis enough to make ye wonder about our courts o' law. So I ask ye first, why does gowf bring out so much in a man, so many sides o' his personality? Why is the game such an X-ray o' the soul?

"Now let's take this thing ye call projection," he looked again at Dr. Laing. "One man sees the Burnin'bush Links as a beautiful thing, the next sees it a menacin' monster. Or one man'll see it friendly one day and unfriendly the next. Or the same hole will change before his very eyes, within minutes. What d'ye call that ink-blot test, Julian?"

"A Rorrshock, Peter, that's what ye're talkin' aboot."

"Yes, a Rorrshock, that's what a golf links is. On some days I love these links of ours, on others I hate them. And it *looks* different, by God, it *looks* different dependin' on my mood. Agatha heer says I go through the same kind o' trouble with her, guid woman." He reached toward his wife. "Like marriage it is, like marriage!" The idea seemed to have struck him for the first time. He and Agatha looked at each other in silence for a moment. The sounds of silverware striking plates and the slurping of broth quieted as the two of them exchanged secret knowings. All heads turned up from the dinner and looked to the end of the table. Peter and Agatha were sharing untold numbers of insights and feelings regarding the relationship of golf and marriage, and the group seemed to be awed by the sight. Six faces waited expectantly in the candlelight.

"Just like marriage," Peter said at last, in a quiet solemn voice. Then he turned toward us with a small boy's smile of discovery. "Why, Agatha's like a Rorrshock too." There seemed to be a dozen "r's" in the word Rorschach. "Just like a Rorrshock," he said again, turning back to look at her with his child-like smile. "Marriage is a test of my devotion and my memory that things will be all right."

Words of approval and congratulations sprang from all sides of the table. We all wanted to cheer them on. I could see that Agatha was his mother and young lover and God knew what other incarnations in the Rorschach he saw. The same complexity seemed to be true for her.

"A good marriage is as rare and complex and fragile as the world itself," said Shivas, "and very like the game o' gowf. Ye're right, Peter, ye're right." I remembered that he was a bachelor and wondered if he had ever been married.

Then our host and devoted husband broke into an impassioned speech comparing marriage to golf. The connection had sprung some trapdoor of insight and lyricism in his heart, and all his sufferings and enthusiasms poured forth. Like golf, marriage required many skills, he said, "steadiness of purpose and imagination, a persistent will and willingness to change, long shots and delicate strokes, strength and a deft touch," the metaphors were tumbling in all directions now, "good sense and the occasional gamble, steady nerves and a certain wild streak. And ye've got to have it *all* goin' or the whole thing goes kaflooey." He clenched his fist and turned his thumb down. "Any part o' the game can ruin the whole. Ye've got to have all yer parts and all yer skills, yer lovin' heart, yer manhood, and all yer subtleties. Not only are ye naked to yerself and to yer partner, but ye've got to contend with yer entire self, all yoor *many* selves. Nowhere have I seen the Hindoo law of Karma work so clearly as in marriage and in golf. Character is destiny, my friends, on the links and with yer beloved wife." He took Agatha's hand and they exchanged unspoken thoughts again. "Get me another glass o' whisky, darlin'," he said, "this clarity is frightenin'."

Perhaps the insight regarding marriage or perhaps the whisky Agatha brought him cast another light on the game for Peter. Like a barometer of his mood, his complexion had become bright red again with pleasure.

"There is somethin' benign about the game after all," he said expansively, "we can read it in our history. It's recorded that after the Treaty of Glasgow in 1502, which ended our worst wars wi' the English, James the Fourth bought himself a set o' clubs and balls. The prohibitin' laws against the game, which he had renewed because the fields were needed for war practice, were dropped tha' year since there would be nae mair fightin'. Then he married Margaret Tudor the followin' year—bought himsel' some clubs and married the daughter of the English king—wha' d'ye think o' that! Marriage and golf again, both recorded for posterity! Tis curious, ye'll have to admit, that all o' this has been remembered in our history books."

Some of us asked how he knew all that. "He reads all he can about the game," said Kelly, "thinks he'll finally read the secret."

"Now I've often thought about James the Fourth," Peter went on undeterred, "how he signed that treaty and bought himself those clubs. Reminds me o' President Eisenhower." He looked at me. "It's not a warlike man that loves the game so much." I felt constrained to say that Ike was getting a lot of criticism for all the time he was spending on the course. "Well, I'll admit that a man like that could get more done, but at least he probably willna' get ye into wars or silly ventures, seein' how much time he needs for his leisure. I think the very *thought* o' liftin' that prohibitin' law led James the Fourth to sign the Glasgow treaty. He couldna' have played unless the war was over, since they needed all that links-land for practicin' their bows and arrows." Julian Laing and Shivas both laughed at this proposal.

"Yer history's a Rorrshock," the old doctor rumbled with a smile that revealed several golden teeth. "O' course history aye has been."

But the challenge only seemed to fuel our host's passion for his subject. He claimed that men who loved games "did not have to use other human beings for their sport"—or lord it over private lives and morals. After the union of the Scottish and English crowns James Six and One proclaimed that Sunday sports were to be permitted in Scotland. Peter recited a declaration by the king, which he had memorized, something to the effect that on Sunday "our good people be not disturbed or discouraged from any lawful recreation such as dancing, leaping, or vaulting." Those good Presbyterians could now leap about the streets after divine service. "And, moreover, that was the year the featherie ball was invented!" he exclaimed. "A ball that could fly further than any before it." The coincidence of those two events—the discovery of the "featherie ball" and the relaxation of the sabbath prohibition against sport—was significant, for every improvement in leisure got into laws and treaties and politics generally. The first international golf match, between the Duke of York (later James the Second of England and Scotland) and John Patersone, the shoemaker, against two English noblemen, "a match much remembered and in the spirit of the Restoration," was held at the Leith Links sometime later in the century; its importance as a public event showed how games encouraged the meeting of men in a peaceful manner. He said that the house John Patersone built with his winnings from the match still stood in Edinburgh, that we could all see it for ourselves. Then he talked about the first golfing societies, the competition for the silver club at Edinburgh, and "the banding together of the brothers." With the English wars lessening, Scotsmen could now join to fight the elements and the "demons of their souls" at the Royal Aberdeen Club, the Royal and Ancient Club, the Honorable Company of Edinburgh Golfers, or the Musselburgh Club. All these fraternities made their rules, started their competitions, adopted their emblems and uniforms. Black jackets, red jackets, tartan jackets, and even more colorful outfits became obligatory for club festivities and play on the various golfing links. "Ye were fined if ye didna' wear the uniform—and why was that?" he asked. "To form a band o' brithers, that's why. *It was a way for men to join in peace and mak' it vivid to themselves.*" He pounded fiercely on the table for emphasis, rattling the dishes. "About the time o' the first clubs even the English and Scottish parliaments joined together, completin' what the Treaty o' Glasgow started two hundred years before. So ye see, at every important joinin' o' the English and the Scots golf played a part. At the very least, the memory of these great events of golf and politics were joined in our memories and imaginations and history books. Now extend this to all the history o' games and leisure. In golf our spears—and my friends, the Scots have had some fierce ones—get beaten into gowfin' sticks. Now we would beat the good earth instead of our fellow man."

At about this point in the conversation, I told the group about my friend Joe K. Adams' proposing a Gymnasium for the Production of Dionysian Rites and other Health-Giving Rituals. Adams claimed that body chemistry was altered during wild dancing and other emotional sports. He claimed that dancing helped the bodily functions in general and opened up the mind. Julian thought it was a good idea. He had developed a theory that certain kinds of psychosis came from a lack of proper exercise.

"Better games would empty entire wings o' oor mental 'ospitals," he said in his broad Scots burr. His wispy silver hair glowed like a halo in the candlelight, giving his face an iridescent quality. "I've cured several myself with nothin' mair than games and dancin'. And listenin' to the pipes can blow the mind free, too." He then described the "perfect golf links." It would include music on certain holes. All sports, he said, are improved when you can hear the right music, with the inner ear if possible, or with bagpipes and bands if you couldn't. Ecstasy produced beneficial vitamins, it seemed.

"Oor brain is a distillery, pumpin' strange whiskys into the bloodstream to produce a permanent intoxication. Ye've got to feed the right things to the distillery, or ye get some bad green whisky." He made a retching sound and spit into his plate to emphasize the point. Eve Greene flinched and Adam pretended not to notice.

"But not gowf, Julian," Peter broke into the old doctor's speech, "not gowf. Gowf is for quietin' the mind, not stirrin' it. Look what happened when ye sent poor Campbell aroond the links with that dancin' step ye showed him. The members wanted to lock him up." Apparently Julian had prescribed an eighteen-hole Highland Fling for one of his patients.

"Oh, oh, oh." Julian leaned away from the table and his voice rose, "but look wha' happened to the man. 'Twas a cure, wouldna'ye say?"

Peter and the others agreed it had been a cure. Campbell had eventually gone off to the South Seas to write a book. But the argument continued. Peter and the Greenes took sides against Julian, maintaining that the beauty of the game lay in its poise and decorum, in its Apollonian virtues. The fierce old doctor took the Dionysian line; the game was meant for dancing, he said. "Noo look at ye, Peter, ye play against yer emotions, with yer emotions, through yer emotions. Wha' about the names ye have for yer different selves?" It was true. Peter McNaughton, like many others, had different lines for his different golfing selves. I cannot remember them exactly, but they went something like "Old Red," for a mean and choleric one that broke clubs and swore viciously at his wife; "Divot," for a spastic one dangerous to onlookers; "Palsy," for another with floating anxiety, tremors of the hands and huge nervousness on the first tee. He seemed to have a certain detachment about them, referring to them as if they were familiar presences. He talked to them apparently. Agatha and Kelly knew who they were. Dialogues were held with them at dinner. Peter was a foursome all by himself.

"Tae me," said Julian, "yer a livin' example o' what the game is all about. What is it but the comin' together of our separate parts? Ye said it yerself, Peter, just a little while ago when ye compared the game to marriage. Our inner parts want to marry too."

I looked at Agatha. She was nodding in agreement, like many wives I have seen who pray for their husband's integration. Her hands involuntarily formed a prayerful attitude.

"Well, 'Naught' has taken ower now," said Peter with sudden vehemence. I think he sensed the group was ganging up on him. "There is nae mair gowf while 'Naught' is in command." He had rejected these uncontrollable sub-personalities, along with golf and the whole business. Julian asked him what was left. "Oh, my friends, this lovely family, my sanity, my peace o' mind," he said with unconvincing gusto.

"Now, Peter 'Naught,' I think yer many sel's will return ere long over another game, over another dinner, in the midst o' this very family. There is nae banishin' them," said Julian with a sinister smile.

Peter was getting angry. He rose from the table. "Here, poor gowfin' addicts," he said, "drink up and arm yersel's against yer madness. I've said my piece. Ye can see I love the game, have my theories just like you, even my historical understandin's. But I'm leavin' it all behind. We will heer nae mair o' 'Palsy' and 'Divot.'" There was a finality in his voice that none of us wanted to question. It was someone else's turn to speak.

Agatha proposed that we go into the sitting room; perhaps she sensed that we needed a respite from so much talk. We found seats for ourselves while Peter stoked the burning logs. For a moment there was silence. There was a hint of embarrassment as we looked around at each other. Shivas spoke up first. "Now, Adam," he said, "ye've been tellin' us about yer theories the night, heer's yer chance. I ken they're goin' tae be guid ones." We all looked at the little man, who was almost invisible now in the shadows of the couch. I remember hoping that he would make a long speech that would give me some ideas for my own. But his enthusiasm and bouncy spirit seemed to have left him; he looked at us shyly as if he were afraid to say anything. We all sensed his discomfort. When he finally spoke his voice was so low none of us could hear what he said. Julian leaned forward with a hand cupped to his ear. "Wha' was that, Adam," he asked, "wha' was that ye said, did ye say the supermind?"

Adam nodded. It was painful to watch his embarrassment but we still wondered what he had mumbled. The entire group turned toward Julian. "What did he say?" someone asked.

"I think he said that golf is the *supermind*," the old man answered, scratching the back of his head. We all turned back to Adam. The bashful little figure whispered another inaudible sentence. We all turned to Julian again, as if he were our interpreter. The old man shook his head and leaned toward Adam. "Adam, ye'll have tae speak up," he said. "Did ye say the *supermind?*"

The little man raised himself an inch or two on the couch and spoke again. We could barely hear him. "Golf is the new yoga of the supermind," the bashful voice said.

"Good man!" Shivas exclaimed. "I can see that I'll enjoy this." Apparently he was the only one who understood. Everyone else looked puzzled. Then Adam sank back into the shadows of the couch. It was going to take more encouragement to get him going in earnest. Eve reached over and put a reassuring hand on his arm.

"Well, now, that's certainly an interestin' beginnin'," said Julian. The rest of us nodded in agreement. There was still no response from the declivity in the couch.

"The yoga of the supermind," someone said as if he were just comprehending the meaning of the phrase, "yes, I see what he means."

I felt myself nodding in agreement. Yes, the yoga of the supermind, ye . . . es, I see.

Then Adam spoke again. The only words I could hear distinctly were "the next manifesting plane." I closed my eyes to ponder the gnomic phrases. There must be something to them, Shivas certainly seemed to think so. Supermind, a term from Aurobindo, but golf being "the yoga of the supermind," that was a little hard to follow. And "the next manifesting plane," what was that? As I pondered thus I heard a small commotion across the room. I opened my eyes and lo!—there was Adam standing on the couch. He stood in the flickering shadows bouncing gently on the cushions of his seat.

Then he began to speak. "Golf recapitulates evolution," he said in a melodious voice, "it is a microcosm of the world, a projection of all our hopes and fears." I cannot remember all the phrases, but his words were an ecstatic hymn to golf, not golf the game I knew, but golf as it might appear in the Platonic World of Ideas, the archetypal game of games. As he talked I wondered what his course in "cosmic ecology" must be like. No professor of mine at Stanford had ever talked like this.

He told about the technological changes in the game and how they brought new powers and awarenesses into play for those who pursued it with a passion. With its improved clubs and balls and courses, golf reflected man's ever-increasing complexity. It was becoming a better vehicle for training the higher capacities. And so it was becoming the yoga of the supermind, the discipline for transcendence. As he gave this incredible speech I wondered if he played the game himself. Being no taller than five feet four, he must have had a difficult time if he did. I wondered how far he could hit the ball, if he could reach a green in regulation figures.

"Golf is played at many levels," he was almost chanting now as he swayed in the firelight. "Take our love of the ball's flight, the thrill of seeing it hang in the sky." He made a sweeping gesture with his arm, tracing an imaginary trajectory against the fire's glow. "How many games depend upon that thrill—archery, football, golf—the thrill of a ball flying to a target, have you felt it? The ball flying *into* the target; it's a symbol, of course. And here, friends, my theory leads. . . ," he stepped down from the couch and crossed the room to the fireplace, ". . . my theory leads to the simultaneity of past and future. For everything has a past *and* future reason for being. Projectiles for example, our urge to see them fly is derived from our paleolithic past, from the hunt, we love to see the spear or stone in flight. But," he stood on tiptoes and his voice rose, "it is also an anticipation. The flight of the ball, the sight of it hanging there in space, anticipates our desire for transcendence. We love to see it curve in flight as if it is free—why else do we hit a fade or draw? We love to see it hang there, that is why we love to hit our drives so far. The ball in flight brings dim memories of our ancestral past *and* premonitions of the next manifesting plane."

He rocked slowly back and forth, occasionally making a wide, sweeping gesture with an arm. We were all staring at him now with amazement. "The thrill of seeing a ball fly over the countryside, over obstacles—especially over a stretch of water—and then onto the green and into the hole has a mystic quality. Something in us *loves* that flight. What is it but the flight of the alone to the alone?"

He was tilting back his head and his black eyes were dancing. One sensed that his shyness had given way to a passion tinged with madness. A few moments before I had wanted to draw him out and give him support, now I was beginning to think we should try to slow him down. He was not the first person I had seen grow strangely intense while attempting to account for the game's mystery.

"The theory of golf," he continued, "which Eve and I have evolved, is the most elaborate and complete one ever invented to account for the game. I think it explains *everything*."

I was suddenly aware of Julian. He was frowning and glancing from time to time at Shivas. I wondered what he saw in Adam's behavior. He had said that he was generally in favor of madness, but now he looked concerned. Though I was fascinated by the speech emanating from the fireplace I was glad we had a doctor around.

"Have you ever pondered the mystery of the hole?" the swaying figure asked. "What are its past and future connotations? Think about that one. And a *hole-in-one*, have you ever thought about that!" He looked around at us with a wide-eyed look full of portent. "*A hole-in-one*," he intoned the term as if it were the holy of holies, "the flight of the alone to the alone."

Julian turned in his armchair to look at Shivas. "Ye incourage 'im in this kind o' thinkin' now and ye see where it leads 'im." Shivas did not answer; he only looked at Julian with a grave inscrutable look. The old man turned back to Adam. "The flight o' the alone to the alone, do ye equate the average gowfer wi' Plotinus noo? It's a dim connection, Adam."

"But it's *so real*," the little man answered solemnly, with a glint in his eye. He stood on the hearth as if to get more height into his words. "All of our experience is full of anticipations, we love what we might be. That is why we love a low-sailing two-iron or a three-hundred-yard drive."

I wondered if he had ever hit a two-iron shot like the one he described—or a 300-yard drive. He was indeed describing the Platonic Game of Golf. "We know in our bones what we are meant to be, so we are attracted by any glimpse of greater possibilities. There are moments in every golfer's game when he gets off a Promethean shot or when he feels a marvelous state of mind. Do you know what I mean?" he asked, suddenly looking down at me.

I thought of my shots on the back nine that day and nodded, in spite of my fears for him. Yes, I knew what he meant, how could I forget? There was logic in his madness.

"Some players embody that feeling," he said in his melodious voice. "Bobby Jones did. If someone else does, we will love him too. So . . ." he paused in mid-sentence as if pondering the next turn of his thought ". . . so because evolution is always at work, golf is becoming a better and better vehicle for it all."

This last generalization was all Julian could take. "Humbug, it's all humbug," he growled. "There is nothin' awtaematic about evolution or gowf or any other thing. Adam, it's you that's awtaematic when ye talk like that."

I was surprised at the old doctor's anger and direct confrontation to Adam's logic: my impulse had been to listen and hope for the best. But Adam now had too much passion to be deterred. He launched into another line of reasoning about the inevitability of life's unfoldment, arguing that any human activity that received the investment golf did was bound to reflect more and more of the human situation with all its hopes, fears, loves, ways of coping, struggles for survival, aspirations for God—the works. Therefore, it had to reflect the always upward tendency of life. "Golf is a microcosm of the world," he said. "When you invent new clubs, you get new attitudes. Replacing divots only began when courses were built from scratch instead of being marked off across links-land. Replacing the divot means a change in consciousness. . . ."

"Now, Adam," Julian broke in, "ye dinna' mean tae tell me tha' the replacin' o' the divot shows an improvement o' the spirit. It only shows me that the herds o' public gowfers realize they're about to overrun wha's left o' the green." Peter nodded in agreement. The two of them were a dour contrast to Adam's incredible optimism.

But Adam Greene sailed on. "I look for signals of transcendence in golf as in everything else." He smiled triumphantly and stepped down off the hearth. "I ask you to think about your own experience. If you are honest—even you, Julian, you—will have to admit that I'm right."

"If I'm goin' to be honest, Adam Greene," Julian replied, "then I've got to talk about the signals o' the damned along wi' the signals o' transcendence. Ye can see any signals ye want in the game."

"Well, Julian, if you had eyes to see . . ." Adam threw his hands up.

"But there is more to it," Eve Greene interrupted, coming to her husband's rescue. They had talked so much about these things, these speculations were so important to them. Their eyes shone in the firelight. "The environment is so crucial," she said. "Our playing partners, the course, our state of mind, our whole life affect our game so much. Whenever we play Burningbush we feel something special, the kind of thing Shivas and Seamus talk about. We think the thirteenth hole is haunted."

Haunted? I thought of my own experience there. "Who is Seamus?" I asked.

"We'll not be bringin' Seamus MacDuff into this," said Peter vehemently. "I can't stand the man."

"Now, Peter," said Shivas, "now, Peter—Seamus is our great good friend." He smiled at our host and reached over to squeeze his arm.

"Who is Seamus MacDuff?" I asked the question louder this time.

"Seamus MacDuff," said Eve Greene, "is the local madman, or a very *wise* man, depending upon your point of view. He and Shivas are very special friends."

"Who is he?" I persisted. There seemed to be no end of strange characters in this innocent-seeming town.

"Well, Ah'll tell ye, Michael, if ye promise to keep it a secret noo," Shivas fixed me with a solemn look. "Seamus MacDuff is the man who invented the game so long ago. He's workin' on it still, perfectin' it ye might say. And blessin' our town here by choosin' our links to do his special work." He leaned toward me. "And Seamus it is who teaches me most o' what Ah ken about the game."

There was a long silence. The ghost of Seamus was with us. I began to wonder if I had seen him on the course. I seemed to remember a seedy-looking character walking back and forth along the far edge of that treacherous ravine on the thirteenth hole. Then—weird sensation—I realized I *had* seen him! The glimpse I had gotten had not been important then, absorbed as I was with our play. But now I remembered him vividly. I could have sworn he was wearing a tattered black tail coat! "Did we see him on the thirteenth?" I whispered to Shivas.

"Noo did ye see him there!" he answered loudly, pulling back from me with a wide-eyed look. "Did he speak?"

"Well, he did seem to be saying something," I answered. To my amazement I now remembered that he *had* spoken. "But I can't remember what he said," I went on vaguely.

Had he been talking to us? How could I repress such a vivid perception? I had been totally preoccupied with my game after Shivas's strange performance and my own extraordinary shot. But to have my recognition of Seamus MacDuff totally obscured. . . . At that point I asked Agatha to get me another glass of whisky. There was a long silence. Finally Shivas spoke.

"I like yer theories, Greenes," he said. "Speakin' o' environments, I've aye wanted to play at the Tuctu gowf course in Peroo. 'Tis the highest in the world, they say. 'Tis said tha' the game is played there from mountaintop to mountaintop. There wid be yer environmental effect, now widn't? The ball wid fly a mile."

"I thought ye wanted to play in Tibet," said Kelly.

"Well, Tibet [he pronounced it Ti'but] wid be a place a'right, but this is the worst yeer in their history and I dinna' think we'll have much o' a chance tae do it," he said gravely. That was 1956, the year the Chinese overran Tibet. I learned that this had affected him deeply. "But gowf has been played there, o' that we can be shair noo." He said this last with great conviction.

"I always said ye shoulda' played wi' the Sodom and Gomorra' Gowfin Society on the Dead Sea," rumbled Julian from the depths of his armchair. "Noo there yer ba' would nae 'ave gone very farr," he rolled his r's as if he were savoring them. "Nae verry farr at a'. Twelve hundred feet below the sea, their li'l coorse was. Played the thing maself before the war. Like playin' in the inferno. The inferno itself. Only the English woulda' thought of doin' a thing like tha'."

"The Sodom and Gomorrah Golfing Society!" Eve exclaimed. "There was such a place?"

"Indeed there was, in a town called Kallia, upon the Dead Sea," Julian said.

"Now, Julian, you must admit that playing such a course affected your game," said the pixilated lady, ever hopeful for her husband's theories.

"Well, I'll tell ye, Eve," he replied, "it left an indelible impression on me that the English could stick it out in hell and niver know the difference."

The whisky now was having its effect, and the conversation bobbed along as if we were shooting the rapids of the Colorado. Adam and Eve continued to elaborate their sweeping theory of evolution. They talked about successive levels of mind, the opening up of supramental powers and awarenesses, and somehow came around to gardens. "The history of golf and the history of gardens are interlocked," they said. "The golf links here in Burningbush are an exploded garden." Then they explained the relationships between gardens and certain states of mind, how the English made the formal European gardens more like nature, made them gentler and more random. I said that nothing in England or Scotland could rival Pebble Beach for sheer grandeur, that the famous California golf course should certainly produce some wonderful states of mind, though I had never heard of any actually occurring there. Then the conversation came round again to Seamus MacDuff.

"He's an embarrassment to the city and a royal pain in the ass," said Peter abruptly. "Why they let him live out in that ravine, I'll niver know."

"Does he actually live out there?" I asked.

"Let us say he spends a good deal o' his precious time there," said Shivas. "He's studyin' the game at all times, workin' on his theories o' the wardle."

It was uncanny how much I could remember now about that scroungy-looking character. I seemed to remember him gesticulating in our direction as he walked along the far edge of the gully.

"It's reputed that he's writing a book which will be published after his death," said Eve. "But no one knows for sure."

"Oh, he's mad as a loon and why d'ye all pretend to take him so serious?" said Peter. "Ye're makin' fun o' him just like everybody else. That's what ye're really doin', just makin' fun of him."

"I niver make fun o' the man," said Shivas gravely. "And he has a book indeed, a great book. *The Logarithms of the Just,* it's called, bein' first notes for a physics o' the spirit. I've seen it twice. So dinna' tell me that I'm makin' fun of 'im, Peter. He's my truest teacher."

"What kind of theories does he have?" I asked, my curiosity growing with each statement.

"Apparently he's studying gravity," someone said. "His theory explains the alignment of human consciousness with the physical forces of the universe."

"Is he a mathematician?" I asked.

"In the Pythagorean tradition," said Shivas. "Ye see, Michael, he's had to tip the balance of his mind to study gravity. He's floatin' free now to get a better fix upon this world of ours." In a few hours I would discover Shivas's own formulations relating gravity to the subtle forces of the human soul.

"Seamus MacDuff is the one sane man among us," Julian slapped the arm of his chair. "The only sane man among us. In a world gone completely off the target he's readjustin' his sights. What if it takes a lifetime, are any o' us here doin' any better?"

Chapter Five

1974–1982

THE MID-SEVENTIES were dark days. American industry was coming apart at the seams, inflation was rampant, the future unknown. In golf, as in the country, nascent technologies few saw or even dreamed of were about to change everything. I was working in the letters department at *Newsweek,* which, after the glory days of Watergate, needed a Jonestown or a Squeaky Fromme to give it life. My parents sold the house they'd owned since 1948 and almost everything in it, including my golf clubs. I gave up golf, partly because without my parents paying, it had become too expensive, but mostly because it represented what I considered a failed life. I didn't want any part of it. All around I saw dreams crashing to the ground, so I married a beautiful, older woman. In reporting on *The Americans* from across the sea, Alistair Cooke captured us in his inimitably optimistic way. As always, John Updike saw the conundrum of our society—certainly of my life—and reported it in a masterly fashion in "Thirteen Ways of Looking at the Masters."

My parents rebounded, from my wedding as well as from their lives. They moved in with my mother's aunt, and with what was left from the sale of the house, they bought a cheese shop and went to work waiting on the swells of Bedford, New York, many of whom my mother had once golfed with. For the first time in years, my parents seemed to be enjoying themselves and were actually loving and happy to be with one another. In one of those ironies life often deals us, my father, who'd run a low-grade fever for months, was found to have cancer. My father, an old newspaper junkie, had always said not to die on a Friday because no one reads the papers on Saturday, died on a Friday, the Friday of Columbus Day weekend no less. What struck me more than the obvious grief of our family was how disconsolate the members of the Bogey Club were. My father was the first of their group to die.

A year after my father's death, my mother sold the cheese shop. For the first time in her life, she struck out on her own, moving to Ponte Vedra, Florida, and going in on a dress shop with two friends. Soon thereafter, the Arvida Corp. decided to build a gated community and golf course. They called it Sawgrass, after the razor-sharp blades they had to get rid of to put it in. Somehow, my mother, living on ten thousand dollars a year, was able to become one of Sawgrass's first members and to join the Ponte Vedra club. There I took up golf again on our trips south. The Florida sun opened my eyes to a world I'd shut myself off from, just as the great James Ellroy's *Brown's Requiem* opened my eyes to a new kind of writing.

In 1981, I had a play produced off-off Broadway. Objectively speaking, I can say that six producers were calling every day to express their interest, the audience very much enjoyed the show, and attendance built every night—until *The New York Times* gave it a bad review. My mother, who had never thought much of my play-wrighting, thinking it came out of a drug-induced state, traveled from Florida to see the play, which surprised me. She enjoyed the show, which amazed me, and she said I should keep writing no matter what Mel Gussow said, which astonished me.

Workers, Arise! Shout Fore

ALISTAIR COOKE

A gifted speaker, known to millions as the host of Masterpiece Theatre, *Alistair Cooke has also conquered the written word. He spent many years as a correspondent for* The Manchester Guardian *and the BBC, and has authored several books. He is also a golf fanatic, and this amusing story from* The Americans, *which shows the potential pitfalls facing the first golf course to be built in the (then) Soviet Union, only serves to further his reputation as a master of the written word.*

There is something I ought to talk about and something I must talk about. What I ought to talk about is the end of the annual General Assembly of the United Nations, a leaden piece of Christmas cake I have obediently chewed on for the past thirty-odd years. What I must tell you about is an encounter I recently had with the Russians that is altogether cockeyed and hilarious, but it is not without deep significance of a ritual kind. Let us skip the cake and come to the icing.

A few weeks ago I was staying in San Francisco, and I had a call one morning asking me to lunch with the Russian Consul General and his deputy. The invitation came from an unlikely host, a friend, a lawyer, an affable and fastidious gent, a Republican, and a first-rate golfer to whom the great game is not only a major exercise in military strategy and tactics but also a minor rehearsal of the Ten Commandments. He is, indeed, the chairman of the championship committee—and will without doubt soon become the president—of the United States Golf Association. His pairing with the Russian Consul General seemed improbable in the extreme. Where, I asked, shall we meet? "At the golf club, of course," was his mad reply. But why, why? "It is very important," he said, "I should surmise that the Consul General is coming under orders, and the whole point of the lunch is to talk golf." This was like being invited by a rabbi to lunch with the Pope to discuss stud poker. I accepted instantly.

The co-host was a young American, a boyish type, who is associated with his famous father in the most successful golf-architecture firm on earth. Golf architecture is the art and science of designing and building golf courses, and it involves much knowledge of landscape, soils, grasses, water drainage, engineering, meteorology, and sometimes—I feel—black magic. Let us call the young man Mr. Jones, for that happily is his name.

It seems he had recently got back from Moscow, where he and his father had responded to what must have sounded like a joke more unlikely than the reason for our lunch: a call from the Mayor of Moscow to consider building the first Russian golf course. The impulse, apparently, had come from a Soviet diplomat who had been exposed to the decadent West and had become one maniacal golfer. This in itself should give us pause. I should have guessed that any Russian who had yielded to such a capitalist diversionary activity as golf would have been, on his first homecoming, bundled off to Siberia, where he'd have been condemned to play golf with a red ball and a snow sled. But he was a close friend of the Mayor of Moscow. When he returned from a foreign, western, post, he came into the airport carrying a golf bag. The customs men—as also, I imagine, the military and the narcotics squad—examined the weaponry, but reluctantly gave him the benefit of his diplomatic passport. Somehow the man sold the Mayor of Moscow on the idea of a city—public, of course—golf course. I don't suppose things rested there. The matter went up to the Kremlin. And, from all I could gather, Mr. Brezhnev gave the nod.

Well, we sat down to lunch, and the Consul General—a stocky

man in the regulation Sears Roebuck suit—turned out to have a puckish humor. When we asked him if the Russians would take to golf, he said. "I think, because, you see, the Russian people like quick games." Somebody said, "Like chess." He came back on the hop: "Yes, we like a quick win." He plainly and admittedly knew nothing. But he asked everything. And to help him with the rudiments—of building rather than playing—young Mr. Jones put on a lantern lecture, with color slides showing rice paddies in Bangkok being transformed—slide by slide—into a bulldozed mess, then into terraced ground, then into ground being planted with gravel and soil and seed, and eventually emerging as a pastoral golf hole. Through a series of other slides we went to Hawaii and Florida and Scandinavia and, in the end, to the five sites around Moscow from which they will choose the one on which to build the course.

After that, the Consul General was given a lesson in weaponry. ("Golf," said Winston Churchill, "is a game whose aim is to hit a very small ball into an even smaller hole, with weapons singularly ill-designed for the purpose.") We went off in electric carts, like a little motorized battalion, to the eleventh tee on the noble San Francisco Golf Club course, a swaying landscape of lush green meadows flanked with towering cypresses and pine and occasional stands of eucalyptus.

The eleventh hole is a par three: that is to say, you are required to hit the green with your first shot and then sink the ball with two putts.

Our lawyer host, Mr. Frank (Sandy) Tatum, straightened his waistcoat (all *ex officio* members of the United States Golf Association board are very sensitive to the ancient amenities and insist on playing in ties and waistcoats, like the respectable Scots in the old prints). Offhand, I would bet that this Tatum, on that hole, would hit the green ninety-nine times in every hundred. He hit about six inches behind the ball, which rose in an unsteady arc and landed about 150 yards away, well short of a cavernous bunker. "Dear me," he said with splendid restraint.

"So," said the deputy consul (a pretty fresh type, I thought), "the first pancake is never any good." Ignoring this gem of Russian folk wisdom, Mr. Tatum set up another ball, and this time was comfortably on the green. Now, with many open-handed gestures and facetious bows, the Consul General was motioned to "have a go." He took off his jacket, looked down at the ball, gripped the club with all ten fingers (the so-called baseball grip, which about one professional in a thousand uses). His two hands were far apart. He missed the ball at the first swipe, but at the second it fell just a little short of Tatum's first effort. There was general applause. "A natural talent," purred the gallant Mr. Tatum. "Please!" said the Consul General.

Then the deputy had a go, and he slithered the ball about thirty yards along the ground. "That deputy," one of our group whispered, "he sure knows what he's doing." Well, then we all departed for the clubhouse, had our pictures taken, and the Consul General was presented, by young Mr. Jones, with a copy of an article I had once written on the origins of golf. Mysterious, this. "Why?" I asked young Jones. He looked for a second over his shoulder. "Don't you see," he hissed, "it supports the main argument?" And what would that be? "What we kicked around at lunch."

I realized then why I had been seated at lunch next to the Consul General. He had dropped several uncomfortable hints that he knew golf was a rich man's hobby, and I sensed that Moscow has asked him to check on this repulsive legend. I hastened to disabuse him with—young Jones later assured me—deeply moving eloquence. "No, no," I said, "that used to be so long ago, even then only in England and America, never in Scotland." I painted a picture, all the more poignant for being true, of poor little boys going off with their sticks and paying a few pennies to play some of the most hallowed courses on earth. "In Scotland," I said, "the people learn to play golf as simply as they learn to drink tea. And St. Andrews, which is the Vatican—pardon me, the Kremlin—of golf is a public course. On Sundays they close it so that little old ladies and dogs and babies can frolic—can walk around—for it is a public park *absolutely for the people.*" "No?" said the Consul General. "Yes," I said.

"What," he asked, "will our people do, will they succeed at this sport?" No question, I said, "ten years from now"—we were well along with the vodka martinis—"I swear to you the British or American Open champion" ("Open? What means this open?")—"the golf champion of Britain or America will be a Russian. After all, not so many years ago you sent a Russian basketball team, and Americans shook with laughter. Until you wiped the floor with both the Americans and the Canadians."

"Wiped?"

"Beat, trounced, massacred, defeated!"

"It is so," said the Consul, looking gloomily into his vodka.

"Very well, then," I went on, "maybe the big switcheroo will come sooner than ten years. Maybe four, five years from now, there will be a match between the best player in the world, Jack Nicklaus, and Nicholas the Third."

"There was never any Nicholas the Third," said the knowing Deputy.

"But there will be," I cried, "and he will win!"

"Iss possible?"

"Is certain."

I went back to town feeling I had done creditably on my first assignment as ambassador without portfolio. There were, of course, certain little nuisances: of having to learn to play the game (from whom?), to find courses to learn it on, pros willing to spend a couple of years teaching the first Russian golfer how, for God's sake, to hit a golf ball straight. I thought of Nicklaus, at the age of eight, going on the practice tee every day for a year to have his head gripped for an hour on end by the hand of an assistant pro so he could learn to keep his head still. Perhaps I should have stretched the apprenticeship period to ten or twenty years.

Still, if they get around to building the Jones course, I like to imagine Mr. Brezhnev or his successor, or *his* successor, standing on the first tee and approaching a ribbon with a mighty pair of shears. He will carry in his hand a note or two from our San Francisco Summit, and he will proclaim to a vast assembly of the peoples of all the Russias: "So! I have the extremely great honor to say to the citizens of our Soviet Socialist Republics —let us begin to play Goalf! The pipple's sport!"

Caddie's Day

JEANNE SCHINTO

The bottle is sticky around the spout. Do not pick it up by its spout. Keep your hands far away from the spout. A caddy's mouth has germs.

Two brown ants run around the rim of it. The caddy who threw it left a sip. Maybe the golfer was calling him to come on along. So he flung it beyond the caddy path, and it would have broken if he hit a rock. Behind those rocks caddies hide their bicycles. Caddies steal from one another.

I don't often walk along this path during the day. I come out here after supper. The golf course is empty of everyone then, but not sounds: the sprinklers tick around. And I take the flag out of its hole and march and sing. Sometimes I drop the flag and run because the darkness falls so soon. I run and climb the chain-link fence behind our house without cutting open my hand. My sneaker toes fit into the fence holes exactly. In a year or two they'll be too big. I do not tear open my hand, because I'm careful.

My mother thinks I am walking home the other way. On the road. I usually do. But today I have dirty paw prints down the front of my new dress, and I'm sneaking. I'd like to sneak into the house the cellar way so my mother won't see me and scream. Maybe I can take my dress off outside and bury it under the leaf pile in the corner of the backyard. If my mother says why don't you wear that little party dress Aunt Rhoda gave you anymore, I'll say I will next time, next time. And then I'll think of it rotting. And if she looks for it in my bedroom closet and doesn't find it and asks me where it is, I will say I don't know, it's not in there? It's not? And I'll start to look for it too.

The path is dusty, the color of a dog. The dust rises up. Over the bunker, on the green, the grass is short. Short as hair. As short as the milkman's. He told my mother: I don't even have to comb it when I get out of bed in the morning. Lucky duck! Sometimes the milkman pinches my cheek. It hurts. I give him a look. Then my mother gives me a slap. What'sa matter? He's saying he likes you.

On the green, a golfer is down on his knees, with his cheek on the grass. He's looking to see which way it's growing, my father said. He doesn't play golf, but he knows the greenskeeper, Mike, and Mike knows plenty. He runs the machines and he's very tall and dark, with a smile like an open tractor shovel. He talks to policemen all the time, and in summer, he has a crew of boys working for him. Members' sons, my father says, and this makes him shake his head and look sorry.

Change falls from the golfer's pocket. Nobody sees it but me. Not the golfer and not the other three with him. If the golfers had caddies, the caddies would see, but they have carts instead. And after they are going up the fairway, I scramble over the bunker. I pick up the coins—there are three—quarters, so big and round and silver. They looked funny lying on the grass. After the coins are in my pocket, the men look back and see me and wag their fingers. These are the two of them who are walking. The other two have driven the carts far up the fairway. And they say no, you better not play here, little girl. A ball could come and knock you on the head. Dangerous. Someone will hurt you, little girl. And don't be walking on that green.

Back on the path, I think, that's what they always say, and a ball hasn't hit me yet. I'd like to see them try and hit me with such a tiny ball. I'd go up on the fairway and stand. And I'd bet them, and I'd win. If I saw the ball coming close, I would duck, and they wouldn't see me. They would be too far away. And God would forgive me. He wouldn't want me to be killed. He loves me and watches out for me and knows the number of hairs on my head. He sees everything. And if I pulled one out by the roots? He'd see, even if he was busy. Even if he was busy saving someone from drowning. I would not be killed. Heaven is scary.

I see the caddy shed. From here it looks like a shoebox. And I hear the caddies' voices. They are swearing, but do not be afraid.

I'm not afraid, but I stop to read each tree. They are carved deep with initials, names, and hearts with arrows through them. My mother says that will kill the poor trees, gouging out bark with knives, and where do those boys get knives anyway? My father says the letters will grow, stretch right along with the bark. I'd like to see that. And I'd like to carve my initials here, but I don't have a knife. Some night after supper, I'll take one from the drawer in the kitchen.

The caddies' voices get louder as I walk along. It sounds like they are having a fight. Maybe they won't see me, and I'll sneak past them like a ghost. They'll be too busy spitting, shouting, shoving each other. On Caddies' Day they play golf themselves, and I hide behind the bunker and watch. They have fights, spit their words, raise their clubs. In the fall the bunkers burn. I used to think the caddies did it, and I cried. Our house would be burned. Then I saw Mike, the greenskeeper, with his torch. Fires burn black right to the path.

Not all of the caddies are young. Some of them are men my father's age, but they do not look like him. They look like his friends, the ones my mother says are vulgar. I do not see them yet. They are on the other side of the caddy shed, but I can hear them and I can picture them. They sit on two long wooden benches, their backs up against the shed. Unless they are playing cards, and then the benches face each other. Their shirts have wet marks under the arms. Hair curls around their ears. They smoke, hold their cigarettes between their teeth when they have to throw a card down. Sometimes they take the cigarettes from their mouths and call out to me. Comeer, little girlie. Sit on my lap, little girl. Other times they don't see me at all, and I walk the rest of the way home with my heart beating right out through my shirt.

And today? I think I will be safe! I will crawl past them unseen! They are all standing, shaking their fists, shouting, pointing to the benches. Both of the benches have been dragged out from their places up against the shed. One of the benches has been kicked over, legs up. Yes, I think, I will be safe! And I stride along. But then something happens.

A boy holding a card between his fingers swaggers to the center of the crowd. He wears a black T-shirt and his pants are too short and a curl of hair hangs in his eyes. He holds the card up, shows it, each side, as if it's a moth he's caught. He flicks it, watches it flutter down, turns and walks away.

Half of the caddies follow him, walking backward and swearing at the others, who stay behind. Passing the fallen bench, they lift it high onto their shoulders. They walk with it to the carved trees and are about to set it down. But then the boy in the black T-shirt sees me.

He nudges the others, lifts his chin, looks behind him, smiles. I smile, too, a little. Then he takes the bench up himself, lifts it over his head, walks to the path with it, and sets it down across it.

The fence runs the length of the path. It runs all around the golf course. I could climb it right here and then walk home on the road. I would go in the kitchen doorway, and my mother would see my dirty dress, and I don't care. But the caddies all are watching me. They would watch me climb. They would see my underpants. They would see if I fell. And if I cut my hand on the twists of wire at the top of the fence? I wouldn't want to run to them and ask them to make it stop bleeding.

Besides, on the road there are dogs I'm afraid of. They are not like the dog at the party. One of them bit me, a tiny dog, no bigger than a cat. But its teeth were like a rat's. It was a Chihuahua. My mother told me a dog can smell fear, and I must have had the smell on me that day. My father said next time give it a good kick in the teeth. Should I? A dog that small. God wouldn't like it. One of his creatures. They all have their purpose. What should I do?

I could go around them on the other side, on the golf course grass. The golfers would scream, but I would explain. They would give me time. Then they would come back to the caddy shed and scream at the caddies. I've seen them scream at them before. Men with red faces, red pants, red shirts, potbellies like they're expecting. White belts around them, white shoes, little hats. My father calls them fairies. I ask him what do you mean? He laughs. My mother makes a smirk. Sometimes the golfers hit the caddies. Well, I saw that once. And when it rains, a storm, golfers don't share their umbrellas with the caddies. The golfer takes the bag and walks ahead and the caddy walks behind—or runs. Or stands under a tree. My father says that's one way to get his hair curled but good when the lightning strikes him. I watch them shivering under the trees. No wonder caddies are so mean.

One of them comes up to me. His shirt is striped, his pants cuffs drag, he is holding a bottle. His palm is flat to the bottom of it, one finger stops up the spout, and he tips the bottle sideways and watches the bright red soda slosh. I watch it too, and then I see there is something else inside. It is filled with tiny brown ants riding on the surface of the red. They make a ship inside the bottle, inch-high, climbing over one another. Below, some have sunken into the red and are drowning.

I look up into the caddy's sweaty face. He is as tall as a tree and smiling. One of his front teeth is chipped. All of his teeth are yellow and must have germs, but you can't see them. Germs are invisible. He says, "Hey, girlie, you gotta pay the toll," and he turns and points his chin back over his shoulder at the other caddies on the bench across the path. The one in the black T-shirt gets up and starts coming toward me. "Don't walk backwards," he says to me. "You might trip over something. A tree root. See those roots behind you?" He laughs and the one with the ants in the bottle laughs too.

And then I laugh. I cannot help it. I cannot stop the laugh. I try to make my eyes look mad, but they are laughing too. Sometimes when my father's friends tell a joke my mother tries to frown, but I can see her smiling, laughing behind her frown. Once, I was kissing my doll and I could not stop it either.

I feel a tickle. The caddy in the black T-shirt is tickling my neck. Then he tries to brush the dirt from the front of my dress. And he straightens my bow. If he were my father or my mother or my aunt, he would tell me to twirl and show him how far the skirt goes out. Well, that was when I was smaller. But he doesn't ask me to twirl. He is talking, like the other one did, about the pay toll ahead. He asks me if I have any money while the other caddies from the bench gather around. I tell him no with a shrug. I shrug and shrug to each question he asks, because that eases the tickle. His hand is still tickling my neck.

He asks me, "What are you doing walking down the caddy path anyway? This is for caddies only. Didn't you know that? And nobody should leave the house without at least a couple pieces of change. Didn't your mother even give you a dime for a phone call in case you got lost? And how'd you get your dress front all dirty?"

Sweat.

I sweat from my upper lip, from my forehead, my chest. I like to feel the first sweat of summer. It happened in the schoolyard this year. I was playing jump rope: high-water, low. A girl everyone hates was holding the rope, and she tripped me, and everyone sneered at that girl and came to see if I was all right. With all of them standing around me in a circle, I started to cry. I was not hurt very badly, no blood, but I knew they wanted me to cry. I knew. They wanted to see me hurt good enough to cry so they could make the other girl scared, feel bad, worry that we would tell the teacher. And we did. And I cried some more when she came over. I wonder if I should cry now. Wonder if that is what the caddies want me to do.

"Hey, girlie, how 'bout a little kiss?"

I do not look into their faces. I look at their knees spread wide. One of them has his hands out.

After supper my father puts his hand palm up on the table, and I'm supposed to put my hand inside it. And I do. This is an old game. I'm too old now. But he makes me play. And I do. And he says, "How much do you love me?" And I say, "Five hundred." "How much?" He squeezes my hand. "A thousand." "How much?" "Ten thousand!" "How much?" "A million!" "That's better," he says. Then he lets go. One of them puts a hand on my shoulder. It is heavy as an iron. I used to not be able to pick up my mother's iron. She used to tell me to stay away from the board when she was ironing. Once, I was playing underneath it. That was my house. I was hiding. She was on the phone. When she walked back into the room and found me, she screamed.

They are whispering among themselves. Maybe I can walk away. My feet in my shoes are sweaty—they will squeak. But if my feet were bare they would make little footprints in the dust. And then the caddies would follow them right to the cellar door and up to my room.

Their voices are like low rumbles of thunder. I look up and watch the Adam's apple of the one with the bottle of ants. It looks as if it will soon burst through. It looks as if it hurts him. The hand on my shoulder is squeezing hard. It's the hand of the black T-shirt boy. Then it's lazy—resting, not holding. I start to walk away. Then I run. And a shout goes up. And everything changes.

My ankles hurt me. My nose hits their knees. I am upside down. They hold me by the ankles and laugh, thumbs pressed into my bones. Then money drops. Coins on the ground. They are dropping their money? No. It's the money I found on the green. I forgot about it.

"No money for the toll, huh? What's this? What's this?"

Someone picks up the coins. Snaps my underpants. I try to cover them with my dress. Someone takes my hands.

Sometimes I walk around my room with a mirror under my eyes. Everything is upside down. And I walk in the world upside down. I like to do this best when my room is messy and my mother says clean it up, it's a pigsty, clean it up now! And I take the mirror and instantly it's clean! The ceiling-floor so white and neat makes my room instantly picked up! I want my mother to look into the mirror with me, but she won't. I know without asking. Besides, there's only room for one pair of eyes at a time.

I want to cry. Will my mother hear me? I don't want my father to see. He would come and kill them with steak knives from the kitchen drawer. I would stand behind him and plead: they don't mean any harm. Passing me from one to the other. It's a game. They are laughing. Hear them laugh! My ankles hurt, and my nose. But they don't know it. They think I like it. I am laughing, too. Sometimes when you squeeze my hand, it hurts, and I say nothing. I laugh. And you, mother, nod, and say that's a good girl, and you laugh. Look at their faces! What do you think? Maybe they're saying they like me.

Then they put me down.

My feet feel funny on the ground. I'm dizzy and do not walk away. They are waiting, watching me to see what I will do next. They look a little afraid. That is funny, too. I think they think I'm going to do something back to them. What could it be?

The boy in the black T-shirt whispers something to the one with the ants in the bottle and gives him a smack on the shoulder to send him on his way. The ant boy throws his bottle down—it doesn't break; it rolls—and he goes back to the caddy shed, hands in his pockets, head down. The rest of the caddies are all around me, watching and waiting still. There is an opening in the circle. I could walk out of it, but I don't—even though I know that they wouldn't stop me if I tried.

When the ant boy returns, he has a new bottle of soda. He hands it to the black T-shirt boy, who hands it to me. It's orange. My favorite. How did he know? The bottle is icy and clean. I want to put it to my cheek, but they are waiting for me to take a sip.

I take a small one. The black T-shirt boy says, "You're okay, right, girlie? Right?" And he's frowning, and I'm scared again but I know what to do. I nod. And all of the caddies smile. And I smile, too, and sip again.

Two of the caddies sit down on the bench and start to deal the cards. A couple more go get sodas of their own and bring them back to the path and drink them. I am getting full, but I keep drinking, even when a golfer comes over. "Who's this? Who's this?" he asks. "What is going on?" But all of us keep drinking our sodas. We are celebrating something.

Thirteen Ways of
Looking at the Masters

JOHN UPDIKE

John Updike attended Harvard College and the Ruskin School of Drawing and Fine Arts in Oxford, England, where he honed the skills which made him one of the finest writers of the post-1960s period. His eloquent tales of suburban life have won him numerous awards, including the American Book Award for Fiction, the National Book Critics Circle Award, and most notably, the Pulitzer Prize for Fiction in 1982 for Rabbit Is Rich.

1. As an Event in Augusta, Georgia

In the middle of downtown Broad Street a tall white monument—like an immensely heightened wedding cake save that in place of the bride and groom stands a dignified Confederate officer—proffers the thought that

> *No nation rose so white and fair;*
> *None fell so pure of crime.*

Within a few steps of the monument, a movie theater, during Masters Week in 1979, was showing *Hair,* full of cheerful miscegenation and anti-military song and dance.

This is the Deep/Old/New South, with its sure-enough levees, railroad tracks, unpainted dwellings out of illustrations to Joel Chandler Harris, and stately homes ornamented by grillework and verandas. As far up the Savannah River as boats could go, Augusta has been a trading post since 1717 and was named in 1735 by James Oglethorpe for the mother of George III. It changed hands several times during the Revolutionary War, thrived on tobacco and cotton, imported textile machinery from Philadelphia in 1828, and during the Civil War housed the South's largest powder works. Sherman passed through here, and didn't leave much in the way of historical sites.

The Augusta National Golf Club is away from the business end of town, in a region of big brick houses embowered in magnolia and dogwood. A lot of people retire to Augusta, and one of the reasons that Bobby Jones wanted to build a golf course here, instead of near his native Atlanta, was the distinctly milder climate. The course, built in 1931–32 on the site of the Fruitlands Nursery property, after designs by Dr. Alister Mackenzie (architect of Cypress Point) and Jones himself, has the venerable Augusta Country Club at its back, and at its front, across Route 28, an extensive shopping-center outlay. At this point the New South becomes indistinguishable from New Jersey.

2. As an Event Not in Augusta, Georgia

How many Augusta citizens are members of the Augusta National Golf Club? The question, clearly in bad taste, brought raised eyebrows and a muttered "Very few" or, more spaciously, "Thirty-eight or forty." The initial membership fee is rumored to be $50,000, there is a waiting list five years' long, and most of the members seem to be national Beautiful People, Golfing Subspecies, who jet in for an occasional round during the six months the course is open. When Ike, whose cottage was near the clubhouse, used to show up and play a twosome with Arnold Palmer, the course would be cleared by the Secret Service. Cliff Roberts, chairman of the tournament from its inception in 1934 until his death in 1977, was a Wall Street investment banker; his chosen successor, William H. Lane, is a business executive from faraway Houston.

A lot of Augusta's citizens get out of town during Masters

Week, renting their houses. The lady in the drugstore near the house my wife and I were staying in told me she had once gone walking on the course. *Once:* the experience seemed unrepeatable. The course had looked deserted to her, but then a voice shouted "Fore" and a ball struck near her. The ghost of Lloyd Mangrum, perhaps. The only Augustans conspicuous during the tournament are the black caddies, who know the greens so well they can call a putt's break to the inch while standing on the fringe.

3. As a Study in Green

Green grass, green grandstands, green concession stalls, green paper cups, green folding chairs and visors for sale, green-and white ropes, green-topped Georgia pines, a prevalence of green in the slacks and jerseys of the gallery, like the prevalence of red in the crowd in Moscow on May Day. The caddies' bright green caps and Sam Snead's bright green trousers. If justice were poetic, Hubert Green would win it every year.

4. As a Rite of Spring

"It's become a rite of spring," a man told me with a growl, "like the Derby." Like Fort Lauderdale. Like Opening Day at a dozen ballparks. Spring it was, especially for us northerners who had left our gray skies, brown lawns, salt-strewn highways, and plucky little croci for this efflorescence of azaleas and barefoot *jeunes filles en fleurs*. Most of the gallery, like most of the golfers, had southern accents. This Yankee felt a little as if he were coming in late on a round of equinoctial parties that had stretched from Virginia to Florida. A lot of young men were lying on the grass betranced by the memories of last night's libations, and a lot of matronly voices continued discussing Aunt Earlene's unfortunate second marriage, while the golf balls floated overhead. For many in attendance, the Masters is a ritual observance. Some of the old-timers wore sun hats festooned with over twenty years' worth of admission badges.

Will success as a festival spoil the Masters as a sporting event? It hasn't yet, but the strain on the tournament's famous and exemplary organization can be felt. Ticket sales are limited, but the throng at the main scoreboard is hard to squeeze by. The acreage devoted to parking would make a golf course in itself. An army of over two thousand policemen, marshals, walkway guards, salespersons, trash-gleaners, and other attendants is needed to maintain order and facilitate the pursuit of happiness. To secure a place by any green it is necessary to arrive at least an hour before there is anything to watch.

When, on the last two days, the television equipment arrives, the crowd itself is watched. Dutifully, it takes its part as a mammoth unpaid extra in a national television spectacular. As part of it, patting out courteous applause at a good shot or groaning in chorus at a missed putt, one felt, slightly, *canned.*

5. As a Fashion Show

Female fashions, my wife pointed out, came in three strata. First, young women decked out as if going to a garden party—makeup, flowing dresses, sandals. Next, the trim, leathery generation of the mothers, dressed as if they themselves were playing golf—short skirts, sun visors, cleated two-tone shoes. Last, the generation of the grandmothers, in immaculately blued hair and amply filled pants suits in shades we might call electric pastel or Day-Glo azalea.

6. As a Display Case for Sam Snead and Arnold Palmer

Though they no longer are likely to win, you wouldn't know it from their charismas. Snead, with his rakishly tilted panama and slightly pushed-in face—a face that has known both battle and merriment—swaggers around the practice tee like the Sheriff of Golf County, testing a locked door here, hanging a parking ticket there. On the course, he remains a golfer one has to call beautiful, from the cushioned roll of his shoulders as he strokes the ball to the padding, panther-like tread with which he follows it down the center of the fairway, his chin tucked down while he thinks apparently rueful thoughts. He is one of the great inward golfers, those who wrap the dazzling difficulty of the game in an impassive, effortless flow of movement. When, on the green, he stands beside his ball, faces the hole, and performs the curious obeisance of his "side-winder" putting stroke, no one laughs.

And Palmer, he of the unsound swing, a hurried slash that ends as though he is snatching back something hot from a fire, remains the monumental outward golfer, who invites us into the game to share with him its heady turmoil, its call for constant courage. Every inch an agonist, Palmer still hitches his pants as he mounts the green, still strides between the wings of his army like Hector on his way to yet more problematical heroism. Age has thickened him, made him look almost muscle-bound, and has grizzled his thin, untidy hair; but his deportment more than ever expresses vitality, a love of life and of the game that rebounds to him, from the multitudes, as fervent gratitude. Like us golfing commoners, he risks looking bad for the sake of some fun.

Of the younger players, only Lanny Wadkins communicates Palmer's reckless determination, and only Fuzzy Zoeller has the captivating blitheness of a Jimmy Demaret or a Lee Trevino. The Masters, with its clubby lifetime qualification for previous winners, serves as an annual exhibit of Old Masters, wherein one can see the difference between the reigning, college-bred pros, with their even teeth, on-camera poise, and abstemious air, and the older crowd, who came up from caddie sheds, drove themselves in cars along the dusty miles of the Tour, and hustled bets with the rich to make ends meet. Golf expresses the man, as every weekend foursome knows; amid the mannerly lads who dominate the money list, Palmer and Snead loom as men.

7. As an Exercise in Spectatorship

In no other sport must the spectator move. The builders and improvers of Augusta National built mounds and bleachers for the crowds to gain vantage from, and a gracefully written pamphlet by the founder, Robert Jones, is handed out as instruction in the art of "letting the Tournament come to us instead of chasing after it." Nevertheless, as the field narrows and the interest of the hordes focuses, the best way to see anything is to hang back in the woods and use binoculars. Seen from within the galleries, the players become tiny walking dolls, glimpsable, like stars on a night of scudding clouds, in the gaps between heads.

Examples of Southern courtesy in the galleries: (1) When my wife stood to watch an approach to the green, the man behind her mildly observed, "Ma'am, it was awful nice when you were sittin' down." (2) A gentleman standing next to me, not liking the smell of a cigar I was smoking, offered to buy it from me for a dollar.

Extraordinary event in the galleries: on the fourth hole a ball set in flight by Dow Finsterwald solidly struck the head of a young man sitting beside the green. The sound of a golf ball on a skull is remarkably like that of two blocks of wood knocked together. *Glock.* Flesh hurts; bone makes music.

Single instance of successful spectatorship by this reporter: I happened to be in the pines left of the seventh fairway on the first day of play, wondering whether to go for another of the refreshment committee's standardized but economical ham sandwiches, when Art Wall, Jr., hooked a ball near where I was standing. Only a dozen or so gathered to watch his recovery; for a moment, then, we could breathe with a player and experience with him—as he waggled, peered at obtruding branches, switched clubs, and peered at the branches again—that quintessential golfing sensation, the loneliness of the bad-ball hitter.

Sad truth, never before revealed: by sticking to a spot in the stands or next to the green, one can view the field coming through, hitting variants of the same shots and putts, and by listening to the massed cheers and grunts from the other greens, one can guess at dramas unseen; but the unified field, as Einstein discovered in a more general connection, is unapprehendable, and the best way to witness a golf tournament is at the receiving end of a television signal. Many a fine golf reporter, it was whispered to me, never leaves the set in the press tent.

The other sad truth about golf spectatorship is that for today's pros it all comes down to the putting, and that the difference be-

tween a putt that drops and one that rims the cup, though teleolog-
ically enormous, is intellectually negligible.

8. As a Study in Turf-Building

A suburban lawn-owner can hardly look up from admiring the
weedless immensity of the Augusta National turf. One's impression,
when first admitted to this natural Oz, is that a giant putting surface
has been dropped over acres of rolling terrain, with a few apertures
for ponds and trees to poke through. A philosophy of golf is expressed in Jones's pamphlet: "The Augusta National has much more
fairway and green area than the average course. There is little punishing rough and very few bunkers. The course is not intended so
much to punish severely the wayward shot as to reward adequately
the stroke played with skill—and judgment."

It is an intentional paradox, then, that this championship
course is rather kind to duffers. The ball sits up on Augusta's emer-
ald carpet looking big as a baseball. It was not always such; in 1972,
an invasion of *Poa annua,* a white-spiked vagabond grass, rendered
conditions notoriously bumpy; in remedy a fescue called Pennlawn
and a rye called Pennfine were implanted on the fairways and greens,
respectively, and have flourished. Experimentation continues; to
make the greens even harder and slicker, they are thinking of re-
building them on a sand base—and have already done so on the adjacent par-three course.

From May to October, when the course is closed to play,
everything goes to seed and becomes a hayfield, and entire fairways
are plowed up: a harrowing thought. The caddies, I was solemnly assured, never replace a divot; they just sprinkle grass seed from a pouch
they carry. Well, this is a myth, for I repeatedly saw caddies replace
divots in the course of the tournament, with the care of tile-setters.

9. As Demography

One doesn't have to want to give the country back to the Indians to
feel a nostalgic pang while looking at old photos of the pre–World
War II tournaments, with their hatted, necktied galleries strolling up

the fairways in the wake of the baggy-trousered players, and lining the tees and greens only one man deep.

The scores have grown crowded, too. The best then would be among the best now—Lloyd Mangrum's single-round 64 in 1940 has not been bettered, though for the last two years it has been equaled. But the population of the second-best has increased, producing virtually a new winner each week of the Tour, and stifling the emergence of stable constellations of superstars like Nelson-Hogan-Snead and Palmer-Player-Nicklaus. In the 1936 and 1938 Masters, only seven players made the thirty-six-hole score of 145 that cut the 1979 field to forty-five players. Not until 1939 did the winner break 280 and not again until 1948. The last total over 280 to win it came in 1973. In 1936, Craig Wood had a first-day round of 88 and finished in the top two dozen. In 1952, Sam Snead won the Masters in spite of a third-round 77. That margin for intermittent error has been squeezed from tournament golf. Johnny Miller chops down a few trees, develops the wrong muscles, and drops like a stone on the lists. Arnold Palmer, relatively young and still strong and keen, can no longer ram the putts in from twenty feet, and becomes a father figure. A cruel world, top-flight golf, that eats its young.

10. As Race Relations

A Martian skimming overhead in his saucer would have to conclude that white Earthlings hit the ball and black Earthlings fetch it, that white men swing the sticks and black men carry them. The black caddies of Augusta, in their white coveralls, are a tradition that needs a symbolic breaking, the converse of Lee Elder's playing in the tournament.

To be fair, these caddies are specialists of a high order, who take a cheerful pride in their expertise and who are, especially during Masters Week, well paid for it. Gary Player's caddie for his spectacular come-from-nowhere victory of 1978 was tipped $10,000—a sum that, this caddie assured an impudent interrogator, was still safe in the bank. In the New South, blacks work side by side with whites in the concession stands and at the fairway ropes, though I didn't see any in a green marshal's coat. I was unofficially informed that, at the very time when civil rightists were agitating for a black player to be invited to play even if one did not earn qualification—as Elder did in 1975—blacks were not being admitted to the tournament *as spectators*. I wonder about this. On pages 26–27 of the green souvenir album with a text by Cliff Roberts, one can see a photograph of Henry Picard hitting out of a bunker, behind him in the scattering of spectators are a number of ebony gentlemen not dressed as caddies. At any rate, though golf remains a white man's game, it presents in the Masters player and caddie an active white-black partnership in which the white man is taking the advice and doing the manual work. Caddies think of the partnership as "we," as in "We hit a drive down the center and a four-iron stiff to the pin, but then he missed the putt."

11. As Class Relations

Though the Augusta National aspires to be the American St. Andrews, there is a significant economic difference between a Scottish golf links thriftily pinked out on a wasteland—the sandy seaside hills that are "links"—and the American courses elaborately, expensively carved from farmland and woods. Though golf has plebeian Scottish roots, in this country its province is patricians. A course requires capital and flaunts that ancient aristocratic prerogative, land. In much of the world, this humbling game is an automatic symbol of capitalist-imperialist oppression; a progressive African novelist, to establish a character as a villain, has only to show him coming off a golf course. And in our own nation, for all the roadside driving ranges and four o'clock factory leagues, golf remains for millions something that happens at the end of a long driveway, beyond the MEMBERS ONLY sign.

Yet competitive golf in the United States came of age when, at The Country Club, in Brookline, Massachusetts, a twenty-year-old ex-caddie and workingman's son, Francis Ouimet, beat the British legends Vardon and Ray in a playoff for the U.S. Open. And ever since, the great competitors have tended to come from the blue-collar level of golf, the caddies and the offspring of club pros. Rare is the Bobby Jones who emerges from the gentry with the perfectionistic drive and killer instinct that make a champion in this game which permits no let-up or loss of concentration, yet which penalizes tightness also. Hagen acted like a swell and was called Sir Walter, but he came up from a caddie's roost in Rochester. The lords of golf have been by and large gentlemen made and not born, while the clubs and the management of the Tour remain in the hands of the country-club crowd. When genteel Ed Sneed and Tom Watson fell into a three-way playoff for the 1979 Masters title, you knew in your bones it was going to be the third player, a barbarian called Fuzzy with a loopy all-out swing, who would stroll through the gates and carry off the loot.

12. As a Parade of Lovely Golfers, No Two Alike

Charles Coody, big-beaked bird. Billy Casper, once the king of touch, now sporting the bushy white sideburns of a turn-of-the-century railroad conductor, still able to pop them up from a sand-trap and sink the putt. Trevino, so broad across he looks like a reflection in a funhouse mirror, a model of delicacy around the greens and a model of affable temperament everywhere. Player, varying his normal black outfit with white slacks, his bearing so full of fight and muscle he seems to be restraining himself from breaking into a run. Nicklaus, Athlete of the Decade, still golden but almost gaunt and faintly grim, as he feels a crown evaporating from his head. Gay Brewer, heavy in the face and above the belt, nevertheless uncorking a string-straight mid-iron to within nine inches of the long seventh hole in the par-three tournament. Miller Barber, Truman Capote's double, punching and putting his way to last year's best round, a storm-split 64 in two installments. Bobby Clampett, looking too young and thin to be out there. Andy Bean, looking too big to be out there, and with his perennially puzzled expression seeming to be searching for a game more his size. Hubert Green, with a hunched flicky swing that would make a high school golf coach scream. Tom Weiskopf, the handsome embodiment of pained near-perfection. Hale Irwin, the picture-book golfer with the face of a Ph.D. candidate. Johnny Miller, looking heavier than we remember him, patiently knocking them out on the practice tee, wondering where the lightning went. Ben Crenshaw, the smiling Huck Finn, and Tom Watson, the more pensive Tom Sawyer, who, while the other boys were whitewashing fences, has become, politely but firmly, the best golfer in the world.

And many other redoubtable young men. Seeing them up close, in the dining room or on the clubhouse veranda, one is struck by how young and in many cases how slight they seem, with their pert and telegenic little wives—boys, really, anxious to be polite and to please even the bores and boors that collect in the interstices of all well-publicized events. Only when one sees them at a distance, as they walk alone or chatting in twos down the great green emptiness of the fairway, does one sense that each youth is the pinnacle of a buried pyramid of effort and investment, of prior competition from pre-teen level up, of immense and it must be at times burdensome accumulated hopes of parents, teachers, backers. And with none of the group hypnosis and exhilaration of team play to relieve them. And with the difference between success and failure so feather-fine.

13. As a Religious Experience

The four days of 1979's Masters fell on Maundy Thursday, Good Friday, Holy Saturday, and Easter Sunday. On Good Friday, fittingly, the skies darkened, tornadoes were predicted, and thousands of sinners ran for cover. My good wife, who had gone to divine services, was prevented from returning to the course by the flood of departing cars, and the clear moral is one propounded from many a pulpit: golf and churchgoing do not mix. Easter Sunday also happened to be the anniversary of the assassination of Abraham Lincoln and the sinking of the *Titanic,* and it wasn't such a good day for Ed Sneed either.

About ninety-nine percent of the gallery, my poll of local vibes indicated, was rooting for Sneed to hold off disaster and finish what he had begun. He had played splendidly for three days, and it didn't seem likely he'd come this close soon again. When he birdied the fif-teenth and enlarged his once huge cushion back to three strokes, it seemed he would do it. But then, through no flagrant fault of his own, he began "leaking." We all knew how it felt, the slippery strug-gle to nurse a good round back to the clubhouse. On the seven-teenth green, where I was standing, his approach looked no worse than his playing partner's; it just hit a foot too long, skipped onto the sloping back part of the green, and slithered into the fringe. His putt back caught the cup but twirled away. And his putt to save par, which looked to me like a gimme, lipped out, the same way my two-footers do when I lift my head to watch them drop, my sigh of relief all prepared. Zoeller, ten minutes before, had gently rolled in a birdie from much farther away. Sneed's fate seemed sealed then: the eighteenth hole, a famous bogey-maker, waited for him as in-eluctably as Romeo's missed appointment with Juliet.

He hadn't hit bad shots, and he hadn't panicked; he just was screwed a half-turn too tight to get a par. The gallery of forty thou-sand felt for him, right to the pits of our golf-weary stomachs, when his last hope of winning it clean hung on the lip of the seventy-second hole. It so easily might have been otherwise. But then that's life, and that's golf.

Brown's Requiem

JAMES ELLROY

James Ellroy is the best-selling author of over ten novels including The Big Nowhere, White Jazz *and* L.A. Confidential, *which was recently made into an award-winning motion picture. But take note, gentle reader, this selection from* Brown's Requiem *is rife with the language of the street, and may not please those with fair sensibilities.*

I

He sat down beside me on the front seat, and gave me a warm handshake. His hand was greasy and he smelled of dry leaves and sweat, the price of outdoor living. "Shoot it to me, Jack," he said.

"It's like this," I said, "I've been tailing your sister and Kupferman. Not long enough to establish any routine, but long enough to tell you there's no hanky-panky going on." It was a lie, but a kind one. "More importantly, I've talked to a former associate of Kupferman's and checked him out with the fuzz. I can tell you this: a long time ago, Kupferman was a money man for organized crime. An accountant, actually. He was a material witness to the grand jury twice, when they were investigating bookmaking. That was back in the 50's. I get the distinct impression that he's been clean for a long time."

"So where do you go from here? What else are you gonna do?"

"That's up to you. I can subpoena the grand jury records. That takes time, plus money for an attorney. I can continue my surveillance, which will probably yield no dirt. I can talk to other people who know Kupferman and see what they have to say. That's about it."

"You go to it, man. This is important to me."

"There's the question of money, if you want me to continue. I'll give you a flat rate. One week of my time, an even grand. That includes expenses. It's a good deal. I'll submit you a written report on all the shit I've dug up. One thing, though, I need the money tonight. And another, I'm going on vacation at the end of the week. No business, okay? You got the bread?"

"Yeah, but I'm not holding it. I never do at night. Too many psychos around. You ain't safe, even sleeping outside. We got to take a ride for the moolah. Okay?"

"Okay. You've got it in cash, right?"

"Right."

"Where do we go?"

"Venice."

Venice, where the debris meets the sea. It figured my canine friend would do his banking there.

I took surface streets to give me time to converse with my client. He was far more interesting than either of the people I was investigating. Mob minions gone legit and amateur musicians were commonplace, but caddies who slept on golf courses and carried around six or seven thousand dollars were rare, and probably indigenous to only L.A. I decided to do some polite digging in the guise of small talk. "How's the looping business, Fat Dog? You making any money?"

"I'm doing all right. I've got my regulars," he said.

"When I was a kid, my dad used to drive us by Wilshire Country Club every Saturday on the way to the movies. I used to see these guys carrying golf bags on their shoulders. It looked like a lot of work. Don't those bags get heavy?"

"Not really. You get used to it. You work Hillcrest or Brentwood though and you break your balls. Them kikes got cement in their bags. And none of 'em can play golf. They just like to torture their caddy. They pay you a few bucks more, but it's just so they can feel superior while they torture you."

"That's an interesting concept, Fat Dog. Sadism on the golf course. Jewish golfers as sadists. Why do you dislike Jews so much?"

"Dislike ain't the word. I never met one who kept his word, or could play golf. They rule the country and then complain how they can't get into good clubs like L.A. or Bel-Air. When I'm rich though, I'm gonna have me a whole caddy shack full of Jewish goats. I'm gonna get me a big fat Spalding trunk and load it down with umbrellas, golf balls, and extra clubs. The bastard's gonna weigh about seventy-five pounds. I'm gonna have a nigger caddy pack it on the front nine, and a Hebe on the back. I've got a friend, a rich guy who feels like me. He's gonna have a bag just like mine. We're gonna make these fuckin' Jews and niggers pack us double. Ha-ha-ha!" Fat Dog's laughter rose, then dissolved into a coughing attack. Tears were streaming down his cheeks. He stuck his head out the window to catch some air.

I prodded him a little. "You ever caddy for Kupferman?"

Regaining his breath, Fat Dog gave me a quizzical look. "Are you kidding? He had a coon pack his bag. Jews and niggers are soul brothers."

We were on Lincoln now, heading south. On Venice Boulevard we turned west, toward the beach. Within a few minutes we were on the edge of the Venice ghetto, known to Venetians as "Ghost Town." Fat Dog told me to stop on a street named Horizon. It wasn't much of a horizon, just dirty wood-framed four and eight flats with no front yards. It was trash night and garbage cans lined the sidewalk. Spanish voices and television battled for audial supremacy. There was no place to park, so Fat Dog told me to let him out and come back in ten minutes. I had other ideas.

He hopped out. Through my rear-view mirror, I watched him trot around the corner to my left. As soon as he was out of sight, I jumped out and tore after him, leaving the car double-parked. I slowed to a walk as I reached the corner. Fat Dog was nowhere in sight. I walked to the end of the block, looking in windows and checking out driveways. Nothing. I got back into my car and circled the streets surrounding Horizon at random. When I returned to the spot where I had dropped Fat Dog, he was standing there. He handed me a roll of bills as he got in.

I counted the money. There were twenty fifty-dollar bills. Nice new crisp U.S. Grants. "One week, Fat Dog. No more, no less. After that, it's farewell."

"It's a deal. Fritz is a German name, right?"

"Right."

"Are you German? Brown ain't no German name."

"I'm of German descent. My grandparents were born there. Their name was Brownmuller. When they came to America they shortened it to Brown. It was good they did. There was a lot of discrimination against Germans here during the First World War."

"Fucking A!" Fat Dog said. I could feel him getting keyed up. "It was the Jews, you know that. The Germans wouldn't take none of their shit. They owned all the pawnshops in America and Germany, and bled the white Christians dry! They—"

I started the car and pulled away, trying not to listen. I turned right on Main Street and headed north. It was getting to be too much; I was getting a headache. I turned to Fat Dog. "Why don't you can that shit, and right now," I said, trying to keep my voice down. "You hired me to get information for you, not to listen to your racist rebop. I like Jews. They're great violinists and they make a mean pastrami sandwich. I like blacks, too. They sure can dance. I watch *Soul Train* every week. So please shut the fuck up." Fat Dog was staring out his window. When he spoke he was surprisingly calm. "I'm sorry, man. You're my buddy. My friend is always telling me not to sound off on politics so much, that not everybody feels like we do. He's right. You go around shooting off your mouth and everybody knows your plans. You got no surprises left for nobody. I'm the man with the plan, but I got to cool it for now."

I was curious about his "plan," maybe a Utopian vision of unionized caddy fleets, blacks and Jews excluded, but I decided not to ask. My headache was just abating; "Tell me about yourself, Fat Dog. I was a cop for six years and I never met anyone like you."

"There ain't much to tell. I'm the king of the caddies, the greatest fucking looper who ever packed a bag. I'm strictly a club caddy, and proud of it. Those tour baggies ain't nothin'. Carrying single bags for a good player ain't jack shit. Two on your back and two more on a cart, that's the real test of a goat. I know every golf course in this city like the back of my hand. I'm a legend in my own time."

"I believe you. That was a pretty hefty roll you whipped out on me yesterday. With that kind of dough, how come you sleep outside?"

"That's personal, man. But I'll tell you if you tell me something. Okay?"

"Okay."

"How come you quit the police force?"

"They were about to can me. I was drinking heavily, and my fitness reports were shot to hell. I was too sensitive to be a cop." It was approximately a third of the truth, but my remark about my "sensitivity" was an outright lie.

"I believe you, man," Fat Dog said. "You got that look, nervous like, of a juicehead on the wagon. I could tell you was by all the coffee you was drinking the other day. Juicers on the wagon are all big coffee fiends."

"Back to you, Fat Dog," I said. "Why the outdoor living?"

He was silent for a minute or so. He seemed to be formulating his thoughts. We had made our way up to Sunset, and I was maneuvering eastbound in heavy traffic, around wide curves and abrupt turns. When he spoke his voice was tighter, less boisterous, like someone trying to explain something intrinsic and holy. "Do you dig pussy?" he asked.

"Sure," I said.

"Have you ever wanted to have a broad that could give you everything you've ever wanted? That you never had to worry about? I mean, you never had to worry about her fucking no other guys, you just knew she was loyal? And this broad, she's *perfect*. Her body is exactly like the one you've always dreamed of. And she's even nice to be around after you've fucked her? That's how I feel about golf courses. They're beautiful and mysterious. I don't sleep good inside. Nightmares. Sometimes when it rains, I sleep underneath this overhang next to the caddy shack at Bel-Air. It's dry, but it's outside. It's peaceful on golf courses. Most of the ones in L.A. got nice homes next to them. Big old-fashioned ones. The people leave their lights on sometimes 'cause they think no one's looking at them. I seen all kinds of strange shit that way. Once when I was camped out on Wilshire South, I saw some dame beat up her dog, just a little puppy, then get it on with another dame, right there on the floor. These rich cocksuckers who belong to these clubs, they think they own their golf courses, but they just play golf on them, and I live on them, all of them! The courses around here are the primo land in L.A., worth billions of bucks, and I've got them all for my personal crash pad. So I pack bags and I'm the best, and I know things that none of them rich assholes will never know."

"What kind of nightmares do you have?"

Fat Dog hesitated before he answered. "Just scary shit," he said. "Monsters, dragons, and animals, out to get me. Never getting to see my sister again."

"I tailed your sister today. She withdrew some money from a bank, then visited some people in the Valley and around Vermont and Melrose. Do you have any idea who these people are?"

"No!" Fat Dog screamed. "You're the private eye, you find out! I'm paying you a grand to find out! You find out about that Jew bloodsucker Kupferman, too! I'm paying you! You find out!"

I turned on to the golf course access road, stopped the car, and looked at Fat Dog. He was red-faced and shaking, his eyes pinpoints of fear and hatred. My client was insane. I started to speak, something consoling, but he started screaming again. "You find out, you cocksucker! You're working for the Fat Dog, don't you forget that!" He got out of the car and walked up to the fence. He started to scale it, then turned around to give me a parting salvo. "You ain't no German, you fuck. Nigger lover! Jew lover! You couldn't even keep a job with the fuzz, you . . ."

My headache came back, full force, and I got out of the car. I ran to the fence and pulled Fat Dog off by his belt. As he landed, I spun him around and hit him in the stomach, hard. He doubled over, gasping, and I whispered to him, "Listen, you fucking low-life. Nobody talks to me that way, ever. I took a look at your rap sheet today, and I know you're a weenie-wagger. You've got two choices as of now. You can apologize to me for what you said, and I'll continue to work for you. If you don't apologize, I'll throw a citizen's arrest on you for indecent exposure. With your two priors it means registration as a sex offender, which is not pleasant. What's it going to be?"

Fat Dog recovered his breath and muttered, "I apologize."

"Good," I said. "You've got one week of my time. I'll leave a message at the bar if I need to get in touch with you. You'll get my best job. At the end of the week I'll submit a written report." I gave him a boost and he managed to make it over the fence. I watched him walk into the darkness of his sanctuary, then drove away, my revulsion cut through with the strangest, sickest sense of fascination.

II

The L.A. south course was flatter than Bel-Air, and more urban bound. The lights of the Century City business monoliths about a half mile away cast an eerie glow on the trees and hills. Stan was directing me to the spot where he thought Fat Dog was most likely to be: the eleventh tee. Our flashlights played over the terrain, picking out scurrying rodents. In the distance I could hear the hiss of a sprinkler.

Fat Dog was not residing on the eleventh tee. Somehow I didn't care. I was astounded that I had lived in Los Angeles for over thirty years, had prided myself on my knowledge of my city, and had missed out on all this. This was more than the play domain of the very rich, it was quite simply another world, and such diverse types as caddies, wetbacks, and bummed-out ex-cops had access to it, on whatever level of reality they chose to seek. Golf courses: a whole solar system of alternate realities in the middle of a smog bound city.

I decided to explore all the city's courses, with my cassette recorder, on future sleepless nights. After Fat Dog Baker was safely locked up in the pen or the loony bin, of course.

I trained my light on a pair of wooden benches next to the tee. "Let's sit down," I said. I opened the thermos of coffee and poured Stan a cup, drinking mine directly from the container.

"You like it here, don't you?" Stan asked.

"Yeah," I said, "I'm surprised it took me this long to discover it."

We sipped coffee and stared into the darkness. We were facing north. Wilshire was a narrow strip of light in the distance. Cars glided silently along it.

"There's something I have to tell you," I said. "I'm not a cop. I'm a private investigator. I shanghaied you out here illegally. You can take off, or I'll drive you wherever you want to go."

I could feel Stan the Man staring at me in the dark. After a few moments, he laughed. "I knew there was something funny about you, I knew it, but I just couldn't put my finger on it. How come you're looking for Fat Dog?"

"I'm working for him. He hired me to do a little work for him."

"What kind of work?"

"It's confidential. Do you want to split? I'll drive you home."

"Naw, I like it here too. What kind of cases do you handle?"

"Mostly I repossess cars."

Stan laughed, wildly. "Now that's really funny," he said. "I used to steal cars and you repo them. That's a fucking scream!"

"Tell me about looping," I said.

"What about it?"

"Everything."

Stan the Man thought for a minute. What he had to say surprised me: "It's kind of sad. You show up and sign the list in the morning. If there's play, you work. Basically you carry two bags, one on each shoulder. You usually get twenty bucks for eighteen holes. The ladies stiff you about half the time. Some of the men do, too. Some members pay real good, but the caddy master's buddies get those loops. The way you make money in the looping racket is by getting regulars who take good care of you, and by pressing thirty-six holes, which is a lot of fucking work. Or you get foursomes, two on your back and two on a cart, and you make up to forty scoots. Or you get high-class putter jobs with gamblers and high rollers who know how to pay. But it's the guys who suck ass with the caddy master who get that action. Me, I just push thirty-six four days a week and spend the rest of my time fucking off. That's the great thing about looping. You can take off all the time you want, as long as you show up on weekends and for tournaments. It's also why you get so many bums as caddies, there's always cash on hand for booze or dope or the horses.

"We get some young college kids out at Bel-Air now. They got that young golfer image. The members eat it up and whip out heavy for those snot nose cocksuckers. None of 'em know shit about golf, they just know how to hand out a good snow job. They snort cocaine and blow weed out on the course. There's also the horseplayer clique. The caddy master is a bookie, and the guys who bet with him get primo loops. But caddies never save their dough. They either blow it on booze or pussy or gambling or dope. They're always broke. Always coming out to the club to make a measly twenty bucks to get drunk on. Loopers is always hobnobbing with big money, and they never have jackshit themselves.

"For instance, there's this Brentwood goat named Whitey Haines. He's an epileptic and a big boozehound. He used to loop Bel-Air, but he got fired 'cause he kept having seizures out on the course. It shook up the members. Anyway, the Bel-Air pro, he felt real guilty about eighty-sixing Whitey. Whitey ain't doing too good over at Brentwood; them hebes like their goats healthy.

"You see, Whitey is always going on two-week drunks. Them seizures scare the shit out of him, and the booze fixes him up, temporarily. Right before he goes on a drunk, he comes back to Bel-Air and cries the blues to the pro. Tells him he's got to see his dying aunt, or go to the hospital for some tests, or have hemorrhoid surgery, some line of horseshit like that. He puts the bite on the pro for two and a half C's and then splits. After he gets back from his drunk, he starts paying him back: ten here, fifteen there, twenty there. As soon as he gets his debt all paid off, Whitey comes back and puffs the same routine all over again: 'I got cancer of the armpits, pro, lend me two-fifty so I can get it cured.' The pro whips it out on him, and they're off and running again.

"Now the pro knows that Whitey is lying, and Whitey knows that he knows, but they play that charade over and over, 'cause the pro is a caddy who made good, who was good at playing golf and sucking up to money, and guys like Whitey Haines eat him up. He thinks, 'Jesus, if I didn't have such a sweet smile and a sweet swing, I might have ended up like this asshole, packing duck loops and on the dole.' So what's two hundred and fifty scoots on permanent vacation from your pocket if it makes you feel like a humanitarian?

"Looping continues to fucking amaze me. If you think Whitey Haines is a sad case, you ain't heard nothing yet. Take Bicycle Pete. He's dead now. He got fired from Wilshire for never taking a bath. He stunk like a skunk. Rode a girl's bicycle all over town and wore a Dodger cap with a propeller on top. Lived on Skid Row. Everybody thought he was retarded. He kicked off of a heart attack in his room. When the ambulance guys came to take his stiff away, they found over two hundred grand in diamonds in his closet.

"Then there's Dirt Road Dave. The ugliest guy I ever seen. Got this lantern jaw that sticks out about two feet. Used to hit all the invitationals. No caddy master would let him loop regular. He couldn't even work Wilshire, and that's the bottom of the line. So he'd loop invitationals to supplement his welfare check. He had a regular routine: at the end of the day, when all the loopers were hanging around the caddy shack, he'd chug-a-lug a half pint of bourbon, get up on a card table and suck his own dick. We used to throw quarters at him while he did it. He was one of the most famous caddies on the West Coast. Then he made his big mistake. He started doing it in public. The public didn't understand. Only caddies and perverts could dig his act. Old Dave's in Camarillo now.

"It's the loneliness, that's what gets me about looping. All these sad motherfuckers with no families, no responsibility, don't pay no income tax, nothing to look forward to but the World Series pool at the Tap and Cap, the Christmas party in the caddy shack, the next drunk, or the big horse that never hits. We got this college kid, a real smart kid, who loops weekends, and he says that caddies is 'the last vestige of the Colonial South. Golf course cotton pickers lapping at the fringes of a strained noblesse oblige.' He said that we were a holdover from another era, that we were a status symbol, and it was worth it for clubs to keep us around, to uphold their image.

"Caddies on the pro tour is absolutely necessary, of course, but that's another story. The club caddy is on his way out. Carts is coming in. Riviera went cart three years ago. Caddies is gonna blow it. They're too unreliable. Never showing up, or showing up drunk. I'm lucky. If worst comes to worst, I can always do reupholstering. That's my trade, but I hate it. I like looping for the freedom. I'm my own boss, except for the time I'm picking cotton. Besides, it ain't too late for me to change my life. I'm only thirty-nine, like Jack Benny."

Chapter Six

1982–1990

THE EIGHTIES WERE look-back years—the Roaring Twenties for the baby boomers—when we all got serious about our careers and our fun. People were dying—of AIDS, as well as of those things that were only supposed to strike old people: cancer, heart attacks, strokes, and other bizarre things like deadly blood clots from simple cuts. It was time to enjoy life, to do what you'd always wanted before it got away from you. For those who'd missed out on the cocaine blitz of the late Seventies, drugs came back into fashion.

It was also the golden age of the old fogey. World War II vets took to the roads in their gas-guzzling RVs, took to Medicare and social security,—but don't, don't ever call it welfare—and took to the White House, too. I have to admit, as much as I sometimes hate what he says or does, I'm a sucker for Bob Hope, and when I read about Bob with Ike and Bob with Gerald Ford in his *Confessions of a Hooker,* I'm like putty in his hands.

In the mid-Eighties, an older guy took to my mother (she was getting up there herself) and took her around the world as part of an organization called People to People, which as far as I could see was just an excuse to take rich people on trips to India, Scotland, and New Zealand to play golf. My mother married the guy.

I began my career at *Sports Illustrated,* and with a group there, I took to playing different courses around New York on Tuesdays and Wednesdays, our weekends. Courtesy of my stepfather, Howard, I got to play Sawgrass, the TPC Course, and Marsh Landing; the last I found the most enjoyable of the three. However, at Sawgrass and TPC, I did enjoy watching the drives of the Young Turks, those macho guys who teed off from the blues. Invariably, one of their foursome quietly hit a beautiful drive 250 yards out, whereas the others, followed by diatribes of curses and discourses about their swings, their clubs, or their balls, hooked or sliced out of bounds or sculled the ball so it barely dribbled to the white tees. On every hole of their six-hour round. Cart girls appeared out of nowhere to refuel the thirsty men. For, yes, golf was still a man's game.

And I was still a man, though I left my wife and then took up with a man. Soon after I told my mother, which was not an easy task, several of my brothers, another of whom is also gay, and I had dinner with my mother and stepfather. Howard, an old-school kind of guy, made some remark about faggots, at which point my mother said, "You'd better be careful, dear, there might be some of them right here at this table."

The "masters of the universe" all played golf. One of my favorite stories is about the guy from Salomon Brothers who took the hit for the company's misdeeds and landed in a Club Fed with forty million dollars in his cash account. A member of the Apawamis Club in Rye,

New York, he was, while incarcerated, voted to the greenskeeping committee. Seems the club members who were getting away with it figured that, because he was mowing the fairways at Club Fed, he knew more about greenskeeping than any of the rest of them. Such is the kind of fun when you're a master of the universe.

Confessions of a Hooker

BOB HOPE

Star of American radio, television, and film for over sixty years, Bob Hope continues to be a comic icon well into his nineties. He is also a noted golf enthusiast, having played rounds with U.S. Presidents and hosting his own PGA tournament, the Bob Hope Chrysler Classic in Palm Springs, California. This selection from Confessions of a Hooker, *was originally published in 1987.*

On May 8, 1953, I spoke at the White House Correspondents Dinner. Ike, of course, was there. I kidded him about his golf, about all those divots on the White House lawn. Not to mention the divots he'd been tearing up down in Augusta. I guess that's what the Republicans meant when they said they'd break up the Solid South.

Then I gave them the caddie joke that goes like this:

Ike was playing down at Augusta National the other day and he hit a bad shot. His caddie remarked, "You certainly goofed that one, mister." The other caddie in the group scolded him. He said, "You don't talk that way, LeRoy. That's the President of the United States!"

On the next hole Ike hit one out of bounds. The chastised caddie said, "You certainly freed that one, Mr. Lincoln."

Ike was a golfer to warm every weekender's heart, playing with gusto and determination. He fumed over his bad shots and exulted over his good ones, scrapping for every dollar on the line.

When Ike was President I played with him at Burning Tree, against General Omar Bradley and Senator Stuart Symington. On the 1st tee we discussed wagers. "Well," Ike said with that infectious smile, "I just loaned Bolivia $2 million. I'll play for a dollar Nassau."

I played terribly and we lost. The next day I teamed with Senator Prescott Bush against Ike and General Bradley. I was back on my game and shot 75. I beat Ike for $4.00 and I'll never forget the sour look on his face when he pulled out his money clip and paid off. He looked me in the eye and grumbled, "Why didn't you play this well yesterday?" He wasn't laughing, either.

Another course Ike liked to play was Eldorado, in Palm Springs. During his two terms as President he often came out to the desert during the winter, and never failed to get in a round or two. Eldorado has grapefruit trees in the rough, where Ike spent a lot of his time, and he was always picking up grapefruits while looking for his ball. One day he got really exasperated and said, "When I get back to the White House, if anyone serves me grapefruit they're fired!"

One of Ike's strongest rivals for the 1952 Republican presidential nomination was Robert Taft, who was also a dedicated golfer. Ike won the nomination, and shortly after he and Taft had a reconciliation round of golf at Burning Tree. The next day a friend of mine was in the Senate gallery, with his two sons. Down on the floor, engaged in earnest conversation with a couple of other senators, was Robert Taft.

My friend told his sons, "Look, boys, there's Robert Taft, one of the great Americans of all time. He's probably discussing some of the most important issues of the world with those men, issues that will affect all of our lives."

At that moment Taft pushed the men aside and went into his golf swing.

Ike liked to tell the story about two golfers in front of the green. One lay eight, the other nine. The one who had taken nine strokes said, "It's your hole. My short game is lousy."

When I got involved with the Desert Classic in 1965 Ike became an important part of the tournament. He really enjoyed watching the competition, and he always participated in the presentation ceremonies. In 1965 Billy Casper made a four-foot birdie putt on the final hole at Bermuda Dunes to beat Arnold Palmer by a stroke. At the awards program Ike turned to Billy and said, "That was a real knee-knocker." Will Grimsley of the Associated Press picked it up and it made every paper in the country the next morning.

In 1968, Ike's last year at the Classic, we arranged a little surprise for him. He was sitting in the bleachers with Mamie behind the 18th green at Bermuda Dunes. Over on the 1st fairway, unknown to Ike, General Bill Yancey, who was then the tournament's executive secretary, was assembling a combination of army, navy and air force bands.

The moment that play was completed, the bands moved into position on the 18th fairway and marched in unison toward Ike, playing all of his favorite songs. Ike was deeply moved. Mamie told me, "That's the first time in years I've seen tears come into his eyes."

Ironically, Palmer and Deane Beman, later to become commissioner of the PGA Tour, had tied after 90 holes and had to go into a sudden-death play-off while the bands were playing. The play-off started on 14. Yancey was worried that the play-off might get to 18 before the bands were through playing. Arnold took care of that by closing it out on 16.

Ike played quite a bit of golf with Arnold at Augusta National, where Palmer had won the Masters four times. They became close friends. Ike, Mamie and Winnie Palmer cooked up a little surprise for Arnold on his thirty-seventh birthday, September 16, 1966. Arnold was reading in the den of the Palmer home in Latrobe, Pennsylvania, when the doorbell rang. "Arn, why don't you see who that can be?" asked Winnie. When Arnold opened the door, there was Ike, that big smile spreading across his face. "Happy birthday, pro," he said. "Could you put up with another guest?" Mamie joined them a couple of hours later.

The birthday gift Ike presented to Palmer that day was one of his paintings, a rural scene in Pennsylvania. Ike loved to paint. I al-

ways kidded him that he preferred painting to golf because it required fewer strokes.

I don't suppose anyone has ever done more to popularize golf
than Ike. He was truly hooked on the game. It was no coincidence
that golf enjoyed a widespread burst of growth during Ike's years as
President. He brought a sort of White House sanction to the game,
a conviction of belief that it could be vastly enjoyed by middle-aged
men with middle-age handicaps.

Golf Digest magazine got a tremendous promotion when it dis-
persed thousands of circular badges with Ike's picture and the words
DON'T ASK WHAT I SHOT. The truth was that Ike played a perfectly respectable game. And no one every enjoyed it more. During his
White House years there was a rumor going around that the new
dollar bill would have Ben Hogan's picture on it.

It was always an honor to play with Ike. Playing golf with
America's Presidents is a great denominator. How a President acts in
a sand trap is a pretty good barometer of how he would respond if
the hot line suddenly lit up—and some of his language proved it.

Of all the golf Ike played around the world, I believe many of
his happiest rounds were with Freeman Gosden, the "Amos" of
"Amos 'n' Andy," after he left the White House and retired to Palm
Springs. Ike lived on the 11th fairway at Eldorado in those years. He
and Freeman were great pals. Freeman would call Ike in the morning and say, "Can you play today, Mr. President?" and Ike would reply, "Freeman, I'll meet you on the 1st tee at Eldorado in half an
hour." They had some wonderful times together.

The last time I saw him was at Walter Reed Hospital in Washington. I visited with him for about half an hour and then talked
with Mamie for a while out in the hallway. As I was about to go,
Mamie said, "You'd better say good-bye to Ike before you leave." As
I walked back into his room I was trying to think of a joke to tell
him, because I always told him every golf joke.

Ike looked tired, but he smiled when he saw me again. "Did
you hear about the guy," I said, "despondent over his round, who

walked into the locker room and loudly declared, 'I've got to be the worst golfer in the world.' There was another guy sitting there and he said, 'No, I am.' The first guy said, 'What did you have on the first hole?' 'An X.'"

"'You're one-up.'"

Ike laughed so hard I thought he was going to fall out of bed.

If I were ever backed into a corner and forced to name the people whom I've most enjoyed playing golf with it would, of course, be a difficult task. I've had so much fun on the golf course with so many persons. But very high on any list would be Gerald R. Ford, thirty-eighth President of the United States, genuine good guy and the most dangerous 14-handicapper in the land—in more ways than one.

Jerry Ford's fame as an erratic hitter, capable of beaning anyone within a range of 260 yards, is richly deserved. He's rattled a number of shots off heads and backsides of the fearless followers in his gallery. The President doesn't really have to keep score. He can just look back and count the walking wounded.

I play maybe fifteen or twenty rounds a year with the President, mostly at Pro-Ams on the PGA Tour including, naturally, the Bob Hope Desert Classic. We also get together at his invitational tournament, which has pros and amateurs, each year at Vail, Colorado. And sometimes we'll just go out and play a social round in Palm Springs, with no gallery except his Secret Service personnel. It's a little different playing with those guys around. I once saw him hit a shot off line and a cactus threw it back onto the fairway.

In the last half dozen years or so President Ford and I have become very close friends. I love the guy. He's so human, so natural. He gets so happy when he hits a good shot or sinks a long putt, and I can tell you that he's pretty good at both. But he's also got a temper, and I've seen him fume after missing a shot.

Ford plays golf with the same fierce determination he showed on the football field for the University of Michigan back in 1932, '33, and '34. He battles you all the way for a $1.00 Nassau. He reminds me a lot of Ike in that way. Ford has never shaken one habit of his football days when he played center—he still putts occasionally between his legs.

I've gotten a lot of mileage out of my Jerry Ford jokes. The public enjoys them, because they know that the President does hit a bunch of wild shots, that he loves to play golf as few men do and that he contributes so much to the game. The PGA Tour, in fact, made him an honorary member.

So it's fun to introduce him at dinners with lines like "You all know Jerry Ford—the most dangerous driver since Ben Hur." Ford is easy to spot on the course. He drives the cart with the red cross painted on top.

Whenever I play with him, I usually try to make it a foursome—the President, myself, a paramedic and a faith healer. One of my most prized possessions is the Purple Heart I received for all the golf I've played with him.

But he can play. The President is a considerably longer hitter than I am. I've seen him consistently drive the ball 250 to 260 yards. On the first hole of the Dinah Shore Pro-Am in 1983, when we were paired with JoAnne Carner, the longest hitter on the women's tour, Carner busted one. She beamed at the gallery's applause and went hoofing down the fairway after her ball. I thought Ford had struck his drive pretty well, too, and when we got out there, Ford's ball was 20 yards out ahead of Carner's. JoAnne couldn't believe it. She said, "Mr. President, that's the longest shot I've ever seen an amateur hit in any pro-am." It was also the straightest he hit that day.

In the Jackie Gleason tournament a few years ago, before one of the largest galleries I've ever seen, Ford was on the green in regulation and putting for birdies on the first 3 holes. He was really happy. Walking over to the 4th tee, I told him, "You know, wouldn't it be funny if you won the U.S. Open?" Ford smiled a little and said, "If I had made one of those birdies I might consider it."

You must remember, however, to be on the alert when you're playing with him. The only safe place is right behind him. He was playing in a charity tournament at Minneapolis in 1974, when he was Vice President, and on the 1st hole he struck a spectator on the head with his drive. Naturally the spectator was standing in the rough. The papers made a big thing out of that.

After all the years of my public needling, Ford is starting to strike back. At banquets he's using lines like "When Bob Hope sings 'Thanks for the Memory,' it reminds him of the last time he broke 90—on a miniature course." Now he's after me for new material he can use on the dais, my jokes about him that he can use on himself.

Every pro-am in the country would love to have him. After all, there are very few unemployed Presidents playing golf. He's a big draw, and the people want to see him. They know what an exciting kind of golf he plays. There's a family living just to the right of the 17th fairway at the Muirfield Village Golf Club in Dublin that has three of Jerry Ford's golf balls. He knocked each of them out of bounds, into that family's backyard, during the Pro-Ams of the last three Memorial tournaments.

Since he left the White House in 1977 the President has maintained a busy schedule. He's on at least half a dozen corporate boards, and travels all over the country giving speeches. He spends a part of each winter in Vail, Colorado. I played golf with him just the other day and we'd gone 3 holes before he remembered to take off his skis. Ford doesn't really have a lot of time for golf, but he squeezes every minute of it he can, and it's always a red-letter day for any tournament when the President is participating. The galleries idolize him, and for good reason. He's affable, congenial and in every way just a great guy. But he can go the other way, too. When John Curci of the Classic board asked him to play at the opening of Curci's Industry City Hotel in Los Angeles Ford agreed, even though he was troubled by a flare-up of the old knee injury he had suffered playing football at Michigan. During dinner Ford was resting the knee on a chair when a guy walked up and jovially slapped him on the knee. Ford, in deep pain, was furious. "Get your hands off there," he shouted, and I thought he was going to get up and punch the guy in the nose. He probably should have, too.

I don't suppose anyone has ever gotten more free advice about his game from the pros. Nicklaus once spent a couple of long sessions with him, trying to get more acceleration into his downswing. So many times I've seen pros come up to him during a round and say, "Why don't you try this? Move your hands back just a little." Or, "If you'd just open your stance a little, you'll free that left side." They see a lot of the natural athlete in the President and they're anxious to help him improve. But they've never been quite able to curtail that occasional wildness off the tee. Ford is the only man I know who can play four courses simultaneously. There are over fifty courses in Palm Springs, and he never knows which one he'll play until he hits his first drive.

The first time I ever played with him was shortly after he had become President. We had gone over to see Betty in the hospital at Bethesda, Maryland, and then we went out for a round at Burning Tree. He was a fair player at that time, I think about an 18, and he's certainly improved his game since then.

And he's done so much for golf. He's won just about every award there is. The World Golf Hall of Fame, at Pinehurst, North Carolina, owes him a special debt. When the Hall had its opening ceremonies in 1974, on that unforgettable day with the charter inductees honored and a team of parachutists hurtling out of the sky, Ford had just become President. He must have had a million items on his schedule, but he went down to Pinehurst to be with Hogan and Snead and Nicklaus and Palmer and all the stars, and it was his presence that provided the ceremonies with that extra reservoir of prestige.

Shortly afterward I played with the President at Burning Tree. I was staying in the Lincoln Room at the White House, and when I got up the next morning I casually looked through my golf bag. The 6-iron was missing. I was sure it had wound up in the President's bag, so I called down and asked where he kept his golf clubs. I was told they were in the sporting room.

Well, you've never seen anything like it. I went into that room and there must have been more clubs than in the Spalding plant. It looked like the bag storage room at the U.S. Open. I spotted his bag and there was my missing 6-iron. I don't know why he would have wanted it—it never hurt anybody.

I was ready for Gerald Ford's golf game because I had played many rounds several years earlier with Spiro Agnew when he was Vice President. Now there was a real wild man on the golf course. When Agnew yelled "Fore!" you never knew whether he was telling someone to get out of the way or if he was predicting how many spectators he would hit with the shot.

Actually it was exciting playing golf with Agnew. You never had to wait for the group ahead. They were all hiding in the bushes. I was his partner one day at Palm Springs, although I didn't realize it until my caddie handed me a blindfold and a cigarette.

A couple of weeks later we were playing again. There was a foursome of nuns behind us. The sisters must have heard all about Agnew, because they asked if they could pray through.

Then Ford came along and I became not only a friend but one of the survivors. I think Ford could have made it in show business . . . as anything but a knife thrower. But I enjoy playing with him. That element of risk gets my adrenaline flowing and adds twenty yards to my tee shots. You don't know what fear is until you hear Ford behind you shouting "Fore!" . . . and you're still in the locker room.

One day Ford asked me what term I used when conferring with Dwight Eisenhower.

"He wanted his friends to call him Ike," I said. "So I did."

"What did he call you?"

"He always called me . . . well, you know how upset you can get when somebody talks on your backswing."

Shortly after I started playing golf with Jerry Ford I thought it was time to take some lessons. Not golf lessons. First aid. But you know, the President has improved his game and now he plays at a golf club in Palm Springs that is so exclusive that the ball washer has a wine steward.

In 1977, playing in the pro-am of the Danny Thomas Memphis Classic, Ford got a hole in one. It made page-one news all over the country the next day. Danny allows one miracle there every year. But right after the ace, Ford returned to his old self. He took the ball out of the cup, threw it to the gallery and missed.

Whenever I play with Ford these days I carry thirteen clubs and a white flag. I try to win only enough from him to pay my extra insurance premiums. In one round at Eldorado in Palm Springs the gallery ended up with more dimples than his golf ball had.

But I jest. He's really a fine trap player. He seldom misses one. He drives well, too. He's never lost a golf cart yet.

One reason the Bob Hope British Classic drew such big galleries was that Ford went over and played in the pro-am the last three years. They love him in England just like they do in America.

At the pro-am dinner the first year he was there I told the British audience I wasn't sure how to describe his golf game. He's to golf what Prince Charles is to steeplechase riding. I guaranteed them one thing: Gerald Ford would put their National Health program to the test. And then I gave them a little tip—Ford's second shot is the one to watch. It means you survived his first.

Actually Ford had been in England on several previous occasions, but never for golf. The other trips were all peacetime visits. The Americans know he's a dangerous golfer because they chipped in to send him over.

My tournament in England was the first time Ford was allowed to play golf on foreign soil. We found a loophole in the SALT agreement. He played British golf on the 2nd hole. Two spectators got stiff upper lips. On the 3rd hole his caddie enlisted for service in Northern Ireland. He wanted at least a fighting chance. Why not? In America his Secret Service men are demanding combat pay.

We had great weather over there, but one day it got a bit British and I wore a thermal vest, wool shirt, three sweaters and a windbreaker. Ford was laughing because I finished my follow-through before my clothes had started my backswing. Big deal. On the 18th tee Ford put a ball through the clubhouse window. It wasn't easy. It was behind him. That's when I remembered that the Russians used to say if we were really serious about disarmament, we'd dismantle his golf clubs.

But what a great guy. He watched the 1981 U.S. Amateur finals on television and when Nathaniel Crosby won he called me, really bubbling with excitement. "It wasn't just his putting, Bob," he said. "That young man hit a lot of greens with his iron shots."

I had to agree. There hasn't been a Crosby with that much accuracy since Nathaniel's sister Mary Frances shot J. R. Ewing.

Ford was at Pebble Beach on the last round of the 1982 U.S. Open, when Tom Watson beat Jack Nicklaus by chipping in for a birdie on the 17th hole. The President and I got together the next day and he couldn't stop talking about that shot.

"Listen," I told him, "that ball traveled only twenty-seven feet. I hit a lot of shots twenty-seven feet. Sometimes with my driver."

"Yes, but do you realize the ball went twenty-seven feet and never hit anybody?"

Reminiscing about Jerry Ford reminds me that I've had the pleasure of playing golf with six Presidents—Ford, Ike, John Kennedy, Lyndon Johnson, Richard Nixon and Ronald Reagan. Reagan doesn't play much anymore, but he once broke 100 and that's pretty good for a man on horseback.

Kennedy could have been an outstanding player, bad back and all. He was an excellent striker of the ball. I don't think golf appealed all that much to JFK. He often appeared restless and detached on the course. I guess sailing and touch football were his games.

Another President who took his golf casually was LBJ. I played with him only once, in Acapulco. Darrell Royal, who was then the Texas football coach, played with us. I think LBJ enjoyed getting out that day, but he didn't seem to have much touch or feel for the game.

Nixon was a different matter. He played with a lot of gusto and enthusiasm, favoring the down-the-middle approach. Nixon never had the natural athletic instincts of Kennedy or Ford, but he got his game down to a 14-handicap and he took his rounds seriously.

I'll never forget the time Nixon came out to play Lakeside, and

I don't suppose George Gobel, or his wife Alice, will, either. Nixon was in the White House at the time. I was talking to him one day and he said he was coming out to California. I asked him to play with me at Lakeside. I suggested a foursome. He said, "Good, get Jimmy Stewart and Fred MacMurray to round it out." So I did.

The President's security people arrived at my home at 10 A.M. in a helicopter, buzzing in over the hedge surrounding the house. The neighbors thought it was a delivery from Chicken Delight. Nixon came two hours later, with Bebe Rebozo. We took them over to Lakeside. Nixon acted like he was campaigning, hugging and kissing everyone in sight. I told him, "Mr. President, you're already elected." I though it was pretty funny, but I didn't notice him laughing.

After the round we adjourned to the locker room. Gobel was there and so was Norm Blackburn, the Lakeside historian. Gobel passed by my locker and I said, "George, come here and meet the President." Nixon said, "Sit down and have a drink with us." Gobel replied, "I'd like to, but I'm supposed to meet Alice pretty soon. She'll never believe I was having a drink with the President of the United States."

Nixon laughed and said, "Well, go call Alice and I'll speak to her and explain it."

Knowing Alice and her freewheeling personality, we all held our breath. But they appeared to be having a nice conversation and then the President said, "You know, Alice, George will probably be a little late tonight." She said, "Oh, that's all right, I'm used to that."

Then Nixon told her, "I almost had a hole in one today. It was a brand-new ball and it's got my name on it. I'm going to wrap it up and have George take it home to you."

It was a nice thing for the President to do, and with that we all sat down and had another round of drinks.

I've always enjoyed playing golf with a President. The only problem is that there are so many Secret Service men around there's not much chance to cheat.

Class Struggle

THOMAS BOSWELL

Thomas Boswell has been a sportswriter and columnist for The Washington Post *since 1969. He was awarded the American Society of Newspaper Editors' first annual award for sportswriters in 1981 and has been nominated for the Pulitzer Prize numerous times. "Class Struggle" was originally published in Boswell's collection,* Strokes of Genius.

Golf is the gentle killer.

The air here at lush Doral Country Club in Miami is as soft as though the breezes blew Chanel No. 5. A single room can cost nearly $200 a day, and the $30 steaks in the Conquistador Room are two inches thick. The lakes are blue, the sand white, the grass a deep July green in March. An enormous flower bed in red and gold carnations spells out the word "Doral" in letters six feet long. In all of sports the Tour, the PGA Tour, comes closest to looking like the promised land. The hours are short—four hours, four days a week. The pay is huge—$30 million in 1986 purses. The career can last forty years—Sam Snead proved it. More than fifty players earned $150,000 on the Tour in 1985. For them the air is perfume, the steaks thick. For practice balls, they hit new Titleists.

But the tropical elegance of stops like Doral is a mask of the Tour, which is, in fact, pure laissez-faire capitalism and Social Darwinism placed behind a thick glass partition of good manners. The public does not have to listen to the screams. From outside, golf looks like a homogeneous world of prosperous pros living a luxurious life. That's one of the sport's great lies.

Actually, golfers are divided into three castes: the stars, the stalwarts and the starving. Nowhere in American pro sports do people who rub shoulders every day live such utterly different existences. Nowhere are the gaps between classes so great. Nowhere is it tougher to go from one level of the game to another—tough, that is, on the way up. Easy on the way down.

Nobody knows all this better than Jim Thorpe. In the last three years, he has lived all three lives: hobo, hopeful and hero. Let his experience provide a preliminary sketch of the golf tour's three starkly separate castes. As recently as the start of the 1983 season, Thorpe still drove to every event, even coast-to-coast—D.C. to L.A. at a gulp—like some migrant following the golf harvest. He'd often call a Pepsi and a pack of crackers a meal. At road's end, he knew which Days Inn charged $11.88 a night, which cost $12.88. That dollar mattered. "I was one-quarter hungry, one-quarter tired from driving, one-quarter lonely from missing my wife and daughter and the rest of me was burned out from the pressure of playing."

His first five years on tour, Thorpe won $200,000. Sounds okay? After expenses and his sponsor's cut, Thorpe's share was zero.

Far from being a rarity, Thorpe was the rule. Most of the 250 or so players on tour, then and now, are in this class. They'd make more money as fry cooks, feel less exhausted jockeying a jackhammer and spend less time away from home if they were in the merchant marine. "Prayers, hard work and believing in yourself" was all that kept Thorpe at it. That and his wife's silence. If she'd ever once said, "Why don't you just get a job?" he probably would've.

Finally, in 1983 and 1984, Thorpe moved into the Pack—that group of perhaps sixty to eighty players who have won a tournament or three in their lives and earn in the respectable neighborhood of $100,000 a year (more than half of which goes straight into Tour expenses).

These gents—with names like Inman and Halldorson, Fregus

and Hinkle, which barely tickle the edges of our sports consciousness—aren't much richer than good plumbers or electricians (and they have far less security), but they've got public identities and private hopes. At least they're contenders. "I finally started to see a little gravy," said Thorpe, who won tournaments in Houston and Boston, cashed in about $125,000 a year and became his own man. By early 1985, he had a nest egg and the beginnings of some peace of mind.

Most Pack players never leave this netherworld of grinding and striving, worrying and swing-fiddling, hedging against age and injury. By forty, they're history and back to a club pro job. Not Thorpe. At thirty-six, this son of a greens superintendent made the leap to stardom he'd dreamed of since he hit balls by the back porch light as a kid. Now, as Thorpe speaks, recalling this whole odyssey, he sits in a private villa at the Kapalua Bay Resort in Hawaii. He's flown in from New York with his wife and daughter. Tickets: $3,200.

Yes, he's one of the hottest golfers on earth. Over the last half of 1985, after the Fourth of July, in fact, Thorpe won a third of a million dollars in eleven events. He can afford room service now. Thorpe's a star. Or very close to it. He's one of the thirty to forty names who define the sport, draw the crowds and have a chance to become millionaires if they play their clubs and their angles right. Who are these fellows in the brahmin caste? Simple. They're the winners—the guys who average a victory a year in their primes. Check cashing is nice—for the Pack; that's their pecking order. But stars only go by the glory; they ask each other, "What'd ya win, buddy?"

Golf has always sold itself as a strict star system. Come see Snead, Hogan, Palmer, Nicklaus, Watson. First place gets the kiss; even the runner-up gets the kiss off. You want the names of the stars—*exactly?* Believe it or not, it can almost be done. The castes are that precisely drawn: Nicklaus, Watson, Trevino, Palmer (still), Strange, Wadkins, Peete, Thorpe, Floyd, Pavin, Sutton, Mahaffey, O'Meara, Stadler, Ballesteros, Langer, Kite, Zoeller, Green, Norman, Irwin, Bean, Nelson, Morgan, Miller, Graham, Crenshaw,

Pate, Player. Throw in a few fogies who still play occasionally and, at the moment, that's the lot. What's shocking is that, in a Tour locker room, this list would barely draw an argument. Everybody knows.

When you finally do start winning on tour, everything changes fast. "Now I get to a tournament, they got a car waitin' for me. An exhibition or clinic is lined up. I'm in the Pro-Am, meeting businessmen with connections," chuckles Thorpe, who was the number four man ($379,091) in golf in 1985. "I remember when nobody noticed me. They could care less. Now somebody's looking for me to give me a courtesy Cadillac. You can hear whispers, 'There's Jim Thorpe. He did this or that.' You go into a good restaurant and somebody walks over and takes your check. When you really need it, you can't get it. But as soon as you get halfway on top, when you're finally gettin' over, it just comes to you. That's the system. I told my wife today, looking out at Hawaii, 'I like this part of it. It's a great life.'"

And Thorpe laughs. Laughs like a black man who's labored his way up from hardscrabble hustlers' games, beating taxi drivers out of nickels and dimes on their lunch break. In three years, Thorpe has gone from the Days Inn to the rainbow's end. Almost before he got used to reservations at the Hyatt and three good meals a day, he suddenly had folks offering to rent him their lovely homes for the week that the Tour's in town.

"People tell me, 'Jim, now you got it made.' I know better. I know where I came from. Now I got to work three times as hard to stay where I am."

More than any other quality, it is this caste system that defines and sets the Tour apart, both for better and for worse. In other sports, one lifestyle fits all. For instance, the poorest major league rookie earns $60,000 a year and everybody travels in the same pampered-to-death style. You could go ten years without ever touching a suitcase, a steering wheel or a check. "Compared to football, basketball and baseball, I think you gotta say that golfers are the ones who play for the love of it," says Thorpe. "Guys in other sports, everything is taken care of for them. You could play a whole career in the NFL or NBA and still be a baby. To stay out here, you have to be an adult."

The PGA Tour is a Reaganomics meritocracy where performance is quickly rewarded and the rich get richer; but it's also a jock ghetto where economic and psychological pressures on the lower castes amounts to a cumulative edge for the entrenched haves. "The hardest thing is to *believe* that *you* can get to the top," says Thorpe. "Lee Trevino is the one who kept telling me, kept making me believe."

Jack Nicklaus comes to town in his private jet, stays at a mansion on a seaside cliff, practices alone on a deserted course and has a $400 million fortune behind him. How's a guy feasting on Pepsi and crackers gonna beat him? Anybody who thinks that pro golf is fair, that everybody really tees it up equal, has dustbunnies for brains. Yet does this system breed revolt? Hardly.

Ask pros in each caste if they think they get a fair deal, and, basically, they say they do. For instance, John Mahaffey has been from the bottom to the top, back to the bottom, back to the top, back down to the middle and now has returned near the top. "I've seen every side of this coin that they have out here," says Mahaffey, who's had serious injuries and a divorce, lost his confidence, changed his swing and changed his attitude. "I'd say our game is about as close to the American Dream as you can get. The harder you work, the more respect you get. Desire means *everything* out here. Isn't that what our economic and political system is about? Individual initiative?"

Ask players if they feel that snobbery or gamesmanship embitters feelings between the classes and they claim that, within the parameters of human nature, golfers act about as decent as you could expect. "This is going to sound corny," says Thorpe, "but the Tour seems to be pretty much one big happy family. Sure, certain guys are exceptions. But not many players act like they think they're above the rest. More likely, they'll talk about how we've got to look out for each other down the road or how to invest a dollar when you've got it. I've never seen a fistfight out here, never heard of a drug or drinking problem."

If there's one sadness that recurs, it's the way that the caste system separates friends. "You do lose touch with people that you care about," says Mahaffey. "It's not that you, or they, change so much as the way the Tour is structured. . . . I don't have the words for it, but it's just the situations you're put in."

"It just happens," shrugs Lanny Wadkins, who's been in the top ten money winners seven times yet has fallen out of the top fifty six times. "When you move up, you're going to stay at the nicer hotels, eat at the nicer restaurants and those other guys won't be able to." What's more shocking is the reception a player can get from the Tour world when he's been high and is set low. "You find out who your friends are," says Wadkins. "Some people didn't have much to do with me when I was down. I've got a long memory."

On tour, it can be out of sight, out of mind. Players from different castes seldom ever play together. The strugglers are dewsweepers or sundown beaters, playing very early or very late before the small crowds. The stars—i.e., tournament winners—are paired together in early rounds in an explicit system created to increase fan appeal. "It really is like I had suddenly joined a different caste," George Burns says of the aftermath of winning his first PGA event in 1980. "It rubbed off on me. What you see with Watson or Trevino or Floyd is their hearts. They're fighters."

If anything, golfers have inordinate sympathy for each other, even across caste lines. They know how their sport seems to lie in wait to destroy a man's confidence—not just to humble but to humiliate him. "I remember standing on the practice range next to Hubert Green back when he'd fallen out of the top 125 players," says Thorpe. "Everybody had written him off for good. We were both struggling then. He looked me in the face and, for no reason, said, 'Hubert Green *will* make a comeback.' Man, I could see it in his eyes."

You'd think that, if anything would annoy golfers, it would be a player who was "miscaste"—i.e., someone who got more or less of the gravy than their golf game deserves. This does exist and does cause some prickly feelings. But less than might be expected. A few players never seem to travel in the caste appropriate to their accomplishments: Gil Morgan, Bruce Lietzke, Larry Nelson, Miller Barber and Wayne Levi are recent examples. Sometimes it's because they exude what might be called negative charisma. Barber, Morgan and Nelson are among nature's noblemen. But they just don't have that sexy Palmeresque spark. Call them Mr. X, Mr. Y and Mr. Z. Sometimes, as in the case of Levi and Lietzke, the problem is a lack of major attention. When the "majors" roll around, they disappear. You get more name recognition for leading the Masters after two rounds than for winning the Pleasant Valley–Jimmy Fund Classic.

At the other extreme, a few men have stayed in the top echelons of the game without totally legit credentials. Chi Chi Rodriguez has only cracked the top twenty in money twice in twenty-five years on tour, but his humor, his trick-shot knack at clinics and his endless self-promotion have made him a popular Tour fixture. He has his detractors; others say he's just the sort of live wire the Tour lacks. Peter Jacobsen is such a brilliant mimic and such a charming fellow that it's been said that he's "a billionaire waiting to happen." Despite just four modest wins in nine seasons, Jacobsen has a superstar's outside income with more five-figure exhibitions than he can handle. Yet, he's seldom resented. Jerry Pate, haughty when he was on top, has done nothing for three years, yet he still plays a star role. Most players just shrug. Anybody who jumped in lakes after his victories was obviously never a shrinking violet.

"The gravy may still keep coming for a while after your game's gone bad," says Mahaffey, "but it disappears pretty fast once people catch on."

The most extreme case of total mis-caste-ing is Andy North. It's been axiomatic for generations that a fluke could win one Open, but never two. Another cliché bites the dust. In thirteen seasons, North has three wins; he's deep Pack material. But two of those wins were Opens. For years we'll read: "Other prominent pros who shot 73 yesterday include Andy North. . . ."

Golf's class structure has several wonderful oddities. One is the way an occasional college phenom can join the Tour as a star and have to play himself out of that category. Bobby Clampett has managed to go way back into the Pack, thanks to paralysis from analysis.

By contrast, every couple of years a lifelong journeyman is suddenly touched by a one-season benediction, as though to tease all the other Packers. In 1985 Roger Maltbie won $360,554—about as much as he had the previous seven years. In recent years, Rex Caldwell, Bob Gilder and Mike Reid have also pulled such top ten stunts, then relapsed.

Even more perverse is the way stars—in perfect health and still young—plummet to the poverty line in earnings. Bill Rogers and Ben Crenshaw are there now. Johnny Miller, asked years ago how he could go from number 1 on tour to number 111, said, "I had climbed the mountain I'd always dreamed of climbing—and I wanted to rest and enjoy it." It's taken Miller a decade to clamber back to the level of minor star. In a sense, there's been more dignity in his second climb than his first. "It's a little tougher every time, comeback after comeback," says Mahaffey. "It's so damn hard to get back up there."

Despite the obvious broadbrush structure of the Tour's class system, the stories at the individual level have an infinite level of detail.

Greg Powers, golf journeyman, is forty now. But, thinking back just a few years, he still remembers the most important day of his career—the day he escaped his caste—almost.

He woke before dawn that Sunday. Through the dark glass of receding sleep, his fanciful dream came back to him. Nicklaus and Tom Weiskopf were waiting for him on the first tee to play thirty-six holes on the final day of the Doral Open. The 7,000-yard Blue Monster was waiting. The national TV cameras were waiting. That gorgeous, towering scoreboard, showing Powers just a couple of shots off the lead, in prime striking range, was waiting.

Then, in a flash, Powers remembered it was all true. The chance to win more money, more recognition and more security than he had in his whole struggling twenty years of golf were all waiting for him. Three times he had worked his way up the golf mountain to the pinnacle of the Tour. Twice he had fallen to the bottom, losing his Tour card without ever leaving a ripple on the golf scene. This day, this tournament, would be his break. With two decent rounds, he could win enough cash to secure his card. And what if he won? Finally, his luck was turning.

At 8:12 A.M., Powers stepped to the tee. Nicklaus and Weiskopf had long, illustrious introductions. "Next to hit is Greg Powers," the announcer said. After a pause came: "The Tennessee sectional champion." Powers's first drive on the 543-yard-left-curving par-five was a sickening hook that careened lakeward until only ripples remained. "I was numb," Powers said.

Powers's mind gradually became a sort of groggy blur. After dropping a new ball into the dewy, tangled rough two club lengths from the lake, Powers gouged an iron shot out of the grass—and again into the lake. Nicklaus and Weiskopf looked away. Such visions can be contaminating. Powers lashed again. And again hooked into the drink. Three swings, three different clubs, three splashes. As the third ball went under, it might as well have been Powers who was drowning. "I thought, 'Oh God, I'm going to be on this hole all day. They're going to leave me here in this rough.'" When Powers took his third drop, the ball buried itself again in an impossible smothered lie. "Honestly," Powers said, "it passed through my mind that I was going to take a 20 on the hole, walk off the course and go back to bed." When the counting was done, Powers had used up all his fingers. His score for the first hole was 10. That's 10. Out of pity, the teenager carrying the threesome's scoreboard took down Powers's score, leaving only a blank hole in the sign next to his name. Eventually, Nicklaus explained to Powers that he need not have dropped his first ball in the wet rough, but might legally have dropped it in the fairway. "It helps to know the rules," Powers said. "That one thing would have saved me four shots. . . . It would have saved my whole tournament." His final check: $365.

Though locked in ten hours of combat with Weiskopf, Nicklaus chatted with Powers as though they were old buddies. When Nicklaus eagled one hole, Powers was so comfortable with him that

Powers laid out his hand, palm up, for a luxurious, fifties-style "gimme-some-skin" slap. "Jack calmed me down and told me at least I had a cheap greenside seat for his battle with Weiskopf," chuckles Powers. "But the truth is I never recovered any part of my game after that. After that . . ." Powers did not finish the sentence.

Powers has no illusions. A steady country club job awaits him in Nashville. But he keeps giving the Tour one more fling. Only young once.

Bob Eastwood, however, is different. He's still sure he is a great athlete. At age twenty-one he won the medal (first prize) in the qualifying school to get on the Tour in 1969. He was called "Bobby" Eastwood then, and people said, "That boy can ring up some low members." Nearly fifteen seasons later, Eastwood still traveled the country in a mobile home, trying to scrimp and make ends meet. Drive from California to Florida? Sure. "Some guys couldn't look at those four walls," he'd say. "They'd go crazy."

But Eastwood's vision of his talent held him together. For years his wife stayed back in Stockton as his two youngsters grew up. He thinks of his little boy playing with a sawed-off three-wood in the backyard. "I miss 'em," he says. "But I belong out here. I can play this game."

Eastwood has almost the same body as Nicklaus—huge legs, Popeye forearms, excellent golf size (five-foot-ten, 175 pounds). He starred in a half-dozen sports. Baseball scouts wanted him ten years ago. "My position? I played 'em all." But if it wasn't for bad luck, Bob Eastwood would have no luck at all. Take the year he made a hole-in-one at Doral. On Wednesday a $15,000 Porsche sat beside that fifteenth green—the prize for any man making an ace there. Did he win a Porsche to keep his mobile home company? Of course not. On Thursday the car dealership discovered it couldn't get proper insurance to cover the car. And withdrew it.

"I'm not surprised," said Eastwood. "I have one other hole-in-one on the Tour. They gave away a Mercedes on that hole the following year. I was a year too soon."

"It's lonely for most of us out here, even when we're on the course," explains Maltbie. "Nobody cares what you're doing. You can be very successful and nobody knows you. People pay to see Nicklaus. Even if you're in his group and have a huge gallery, hundreds of people are scrambling to the next tee after he putts out—even if you still have a three-footer. Face it, you can feel very alone in the middle of a whole lot of people."

Greg Powers never got his break, but, almost as it seemed too late, Eastwood did. In 1983–1984–1985, approaching forty, he put it together—sort of—over $500,000 in prizes and three titles, including the Byron Nelson Classic. "Incredible," he said. "It was just a matter of time for me to get everything together."

Only fifteen years.

Tom Watson was still on the practice tee at sundown. He had just missed the cut by three shots. Cynics in his gallery said he looked disinterested, like a man tired of golf and anxious to bug out. But Watson wasn't on a plane out of Doral. He was drilling two irons.

"Rik, can you come help me?" Watson said to Rik Massengale.

"Am I crossing the line?" The two pros stood for twenty minutes, Watson first hitting the ball, then turning to this relative unknown to get critique. "The club face feels like it's shut at the top of my swing. The swing's just not in one piece. The takeaway feels all wrong. See?" Watson said, almost pleading as he showed Massengale the angle of his wrist, the plane of his swing, the pronation of his wrists after impact. Massengale commiserated and then went back to his own bucket of balls.

Watson hit a dozen more balls. Massengale left. Watson spots an unknown tour rookie, Lee Mikles, who hasn't won as much money in his life as Watson has in one week. "Hey, Lee," Watson calls, "can you come watch me?"

No man is at peace with the game of golf. Always there is the nightmare of a tiny injury that will change the magic stroke, or the subtle aging of the body, or the hundred things that can make the mysterious golf swing disintegrate. "All the vital technical parts of the swing take place in back of you, or above your head," Maltbie says.

"It's terrifying to think of all the gremlins that can creep into your game. Our margin for error is infinitesimal."

The one inflexible law of the Tour is that the hot player of today is a better than even-money shot to be in eclipse six months later. "It's no illusion that we all seem to be on a roller coaster," says one player. "Dave Hill—a great student of the swing—won $117,000 one year and $17,000 the next. Think that doesn't scare people? It can happen to anybody."

The Tour's hundreds of have-nots are a constant—the rabbits ye shall always have with you. And a handful of Sneads, Hogans and Nicklauses span generations. But the Tour's great middle class, its most fascinating and agonized members, are the players in transit: going down, or fighting their way up.

"You become accustomed to good living," says John Mahaffey. "You scrimp and save on the way up as a kid. You don't mind staying at less-than-the-best motels, and cutting corners, and long drives between tournaments. You expect it. But once you make it, you take the good life for granted. When you crash, like I did, it's a lot harder to go through that scrimping and saving the second time. You are used to living high and spending fast. I didn't know what I had when I had it. I was a fool."

Golf is the gentle killer, teasing its pursuers, giving up its secrets, then taking them back without warning.

"Good times, bad times," says Maltbie, who's won five times in a dozen years. "They're both hard to grasp."

Once, incredibly, Maltbie won two weeks in a row. Could he be changing caste? The thought could unnerve almost any golfer. Maltbie, given a $40,000 first-prize check, had a few drinks and somehow let the prize fall out of his hip pocket at the bar at the Pleasant Valley Country Club. He was reimbursed, but the check is framed and mounted over that bar in Sutton, Mass.

"When I left the golf course, I had $500 in cash and a $40,000 check," Maltbie says. "When I woke up the next morning in another town, I went through my pockets and didn't have a dime."

You Don't Have the Responsibilities . . .

BETSY RAWLS

A member of the LPGA Hall of Fame, Betsy Rawls won fifty-five tournaments during her career—the last coming in 1972. After her playing days, Rawls served as LPGA Tournament Director for six years. Ms. Rawls then moved on to become the Executive Director of the McDonald's Championship—an LPGA event played near her hometown in Malvern, Pennsylvania, just outside Philadelphia. The following piece is from the book, Gettin' to the Dance Floor: An Oral History of American Golf.

My father was the only one in my family who played golf, and he taught me the basics. Then I started taking lessons from Harvey Penick at the Austin Country Club when I was in college at the University of Texas. For my first lesson Harvey charged me $3. Even then that wasn't a lot, but Harvey never charged a lot, so it wasn't because he knew me or anything like that. Anyway, I stayed out there with him for about an hour and a half. The next time I went out to him, when I got ready to pay he said, "No, I'm just telling you things I told you last week," and he never let me pay him again. I got a lot of mileage out of that first $3. I took lessons from Harvey for twenty years. He's the only teacher I ever had, and I owe a great deal of my success as a player to him, just as Ben Crenshaw, Tom Kite, and a lot of others do.

It didn't take me too long to become a good player, and one

reason, I think, is because I started a little later than most—at seventeen. I think you can do it easier at that age than at twelve or thirteen, because you're more mature and stronger. Also, I always thought well on the course. I was a good student. Phi Beta Kappa. I studied a lot, and that helped my concentration. Maybe it helps to have a very controlled, logical sort of mind to play golf. I studied physics in college, and my father was an engineer. Maybe there's something to that. Of course, you also have to just play a lot when you're young. You have to pay those dues. When I was in college it was hard to play much, because I had a lot of math. In summer, though, I played just about every day, round and round and round.

There is always the problem of women athletes being taken as tomboys, as being too masculine. But when I started out I can't remember there being any kind of stigma attached to women athletes in Texas, at least not to women golfers. You see, golfers weren't that way, much. Most of them I ran into were at country clubs and from the upper classes, so to speak, and knew how to behave. So that didn't seem much of a problem. Eventually I was given a membership at Austin Country Club, but at the start I played golf. I played with the boys except in tournaments, carried my own bag, did a little gambling—skin games, you know—and held my own. It was fun.

Maybe we weren't socially conscious back then. Of course, women golfers are different in that they wear skirts—*we* did, anyhow—and golf is not that physical a game; you don't have to be very muscular or big. If you watched women's basketball you'd get a much different impression of women athletes. A lot of women golfers are small and feminine-looking. So we never really fought that battle. We were always conscious of needing to dress properly and look and act ladylike, and we always did.

The feminist movement never really touched the women's tour, we were all just totally unaware of it. I think that's because we were so involved in playing golf and winning tournaments. We weren't interested in furthering women's rights. We felt we had everything, and nothing to prove. We had a golden opportunity to go out there and make money if we played well. We were treated well, and had nothing to gain from the women's movement, so consequently we pretty much ignored it.

I didn't pattern my swing after anyone in particular, because for quite some time after I started I never saw a real good player, man or woman. The first good player I ever saw was Byron Nelson, in an exhibition in Fort Worth. I was absolutely amazed. I had no idea golf could be played that way, that people could hit the ball so far. I was so green. At the first tournament I entered, the Women's Texas Open, at the Colonial Country Club—imagine playing your first tournament at Colonial? Good Lord!—I didn't know anything. I didn't know people had shag bags and warmed up before they played. I came from a little town in Texas. Arlington was pretty small then, and I had never even seen a golf tournament before. I just went out and played, and that was it.

Anyway, I qualified for the championship flight and won my first match. But I lost my second match, to Dot Kiltie. She was runner-up once in the Women's U.S. Amateur. Then I lost in the first round of the consolation matches. I did pretty well for my first tournament ever, but I was so mad that I lost. I just hated losing. After that is when I really started working on it. I gathered together some practice balls and went at it. Once you play in a tournament, you get hooked on that.

I played amateur golf for only about two and a half years, because I turned pro in 1950. Wilson Sporting Goods asked me to join their staff. They had Patty Berg and Babe Zaharias, and needed someone else to do clinics and play exhibitions. I considered the offer carefully and decided that golf would be more interesting than physics. I played professional golf for almost twenty-five years, and was in on the beginnings of the Ladies Professional Golf Association. The LPGA got started in 1950, and Wilson hired Freddie Corcoran to be tournament director. Wilson needed places for Patty and Babe to play. Eventually, MacGregor and Spalding, the other two major equipment manufacturers at the time, joined Wilson to help pay Freddie's salary. Fred booked tournaments, but that's all he really did; none of the promotional stunts he was known for when he ran the men's tour. We handled the day-to-day operation of our tour, did it all, and it was a kind of interesting situation. One of us kept the books and wrote out the checks, someone else did all the correspondence. I look back and can remember making rulings on other players in a tournament I was competing in. In this day and time, good gracious, you'd probably get sued for something like that.

We didn't have any staff, because we couldn't afford to hire people. That was the situation for a long time. I mean, the average purse in our tournaments was $3,000, perhaps $4,000—total. Five thousand was a good tournament in the early 1950's. Can you imagine that? But, you know, it didn't seem like a small amount. It was fine for us. We were happy to get that much, and didn't mind that the men pros were getting so much more for their tournaments. You see, we didn't compare ourselves to men pros, or expect as much.

How do I account for that feeling? I guess the men are more spectacular. They hit the ball farther, score better, are just better players because of their strength. It's simply a matter of strength. I think that's the only way they differ. Then, again, we could have our moments. One year six of us women pros were in England and played the British Walker Cup team, the country's best men amateurs. We beat them, and, oh, it was a black day in England for them! We played doubles in the morning and were behind by one point, but in the afternoon singles every woman won her match. We had Babe, Patty Berg, myself, Betty Jameson, Peggy Kirk, and Betty Bush. Well, those men were just stricken. They just couldn't believe it. We played at Wentworth, the "Burma Road" course, and from the same tees as the men—about in the middle of the members' men's tees. It was the funniest thing. The press made a big thing about it.

On our circuit at home, in the early days, we drove almost everyplace. We didn't have as many tournaments as they have now, so we didn't play every week. I got my own car my second year on the tour, a Cadillac, which everyone drove because of its weight and room for clubs and baggage. We would travel two in a car, and caravan. Caravaning was following each other on the road, usually two cars. It was fun. I got to see the country. We drove across the United States at least twice a year, and did a lot of sightseeing. Driving through the Rockies, we'd stop and have picnics. I know if I were starting out now I would never see the country, because I would fly everyplace. I would see the golf course, the hotel, the airport, and that's it. So today's players miss a lot, I think, by not driving. Of course, it's impractical to drive now, but I'm glad we did it.

In the beginning a woman could get on the tour by just showing up. She would apply to join the LPGA and come out and play. She was either good enough to stay on tour or she wasn't. Money was the only limiting factor. If she ran out, she had to go get some more or not play. People didn't turn pro back then unless they were good players, because the only appeal was golf. Nowadays there are other things that appeal to players—the life, the exposure, the endorsements, being on television. In the early days you just made out from the purse money, and the only reason you did it was because you loved to play golf.

When I first turned pro, there were only fifteen people playing our tour regularly. Then it went to about twenty, and gradually built up. Now, almost every good amateur turns pro. And back then the galleries weren't that big. But we didn't worry about that too much. We thought of the tour as more of a competition than a show. We thought of it as playing a tournament and producing a winner. The first prize would usually be around $1,000. We all decided at one of our meetings how much the winner would get, and then break down the remaining money places. There was no particular formula for that. I must have made up a hundred formulas over the years. We just figured what percentage of the total purse we wanted to give first place—it was usually fifteen percent—then go from there. It was an unwieldy process sometimes, because there were people who felt strongly about certain issues. Anytime you talked about money there would be vehement discussions. But, to everyone's credit, I can't think of any wrong decisions that were made.

We had some tournament sponsors in the first years who were kind of patrons and saw us through. The first was Alvin Handmacher, who made Weathervane suits for women. The next big one was Sears, Roebuck. But most of the tournaments were sponsored by local organizations, the Lions Club or Chamber of Commerce. They could afford to put one on because the prize money was low and it was nice for the community.

We had some sponsors who reneged on the prize money. There was one in Oklahoma City, I remember, but it wasn't Waco Turner. He had plenty of money and we never had anything to worry about with Waco. He put on two or three tournaments for us. He built his own course in Burneyville, Oklahoma, out in the wilderness. The course was so new when we played there the first time, and so badly built. I remember Bob Hagge and some other guy who was on tour with us went out to cut the cups, and the greens were so hard they couldn't get them cut. They had to hammer them out. So they didn't change the cups for the rest of the week. That was when Waco was paying so much for every birdie and eagle you made, and I remember having a good week. I won the tournament and made two or three eagles, which were worth $500 apiece. I walked away with all kinds of money.

Then there was Tam O'Shanter in Chicago, George S. May's tournament. That was the biggest event on our tour, the biggest purse we played for. It was very exciting, because you got to see everybody in the whole world, the whole golf world at least. There was a tournament for men and women pros and men and women amateurs. Four tournaments at once. It was quite a phenomenon. It's hard to find a tournament to compare with Tam O'Shanter in excitement. Everybody in the game was there, the money was terrific, the clubhouse facilities were special, and there were the biggest crowds. People came out and had picnics in the rough. First time I ever saw that. And it was fun to see all the top men pros and amateurs, and foreign players. I watched Sam Snead and Ben Hogan and other great men players. But I didn't get much of lasting value from their swings that I could use in mine.

The strength of my game was the short game. I could really scramble well, manufacture shots, play out of difficult situations. I always got a kick out of that. Driving was my weakest part, and whenever I did drive well I won tournaments. But nobody is ever going to be better than Mickey Wright.

Mickey was much better than Babe Zaharias. No comparison. Babe was stronger, and maybe a better athlete—she was so well coordinated—but Mickey had a better golf swing, hit the ball better, could play rings around Babe. See, I think Babe got started in golf too late. She didn't really take it up until she was past thirty. If she had started as a kid, the way Mickey did, maybe nobody would ever have beaten her. She was just that good an athlete. And Babe loved to win. Or she hated to lose is the better way to put it. She was absolutely the worst loser I ever saw. She wasn't a bad sportsman, but if things didn't go her way she could show her displeasure. She didn't like it when people crossed her. I guess that's often the way with great athletes.

The sponsors made all the decisions about running their tournaments in the early days, and I must say they were greatly influenced by Babe Zaharias. And Babe was not above saying she would drop out of a tournament if this or that wasn't done. She knew how much they really needed her, and they did. She was the draw, really. For instance, back in '51 we were playing someplace and Babe was leading the tournament. Patty Berg was second. They were paired together for the last round, in the last group, and Babe started out horrendously. So Patty caught her and passed her. Then it started raining. They were near the clubhouse at the time and Babe marched in there and told the sponsors it was raining and she wanted the round canceled. And they did it. They rescheduled for the next day. It wasn't even close to being rained out, or the course being unplayable. Well, Patty was absolutely furious, just livid. But Patty beat Babe the next day anyway. Played rings around her.

But I loved Babe. She was good to play with, fun to be around. She was very witty and kept the gallery laughing all the time. Wisecracks all the way around. Very uninhibited. She was a little crude, and some things she said shocked me a little because I was just the opposite, but the gallery loved her. There will never be another like her.

Sometimes we resented Babe for the way she was in cases like that rain-out. I didn't admire her tactics then, but I never really got angry at her. She was just that way. The thing I objected to more was that we had no control over sponsors being influenced in that way, that they could do whatever they pretty much pleased. I think the sponsors treated us in such a high-handed way for two reasons: because we were women, and because we weren't that big a draw and needed them more than they needed us. They felt they were doing us a favor, and didn't look upon us as great athletes. It was just a matter of having a nice little tournament; fun having the girls come to town, I guess. I didn't have a big problem living with that sort of thing, though, mainly because there was nothing to compare it with. If we had been able to look into the future and see how tournaments would be run and what kind of control the organization would have, I'm sure we would have been appalled. But back then we didn't know any differently. We had our hand out, and couldn't be too demanding.

In those early years the local greens superintendent or pro would set the cups and tee markers, and as a result we played tough courses. We would never play a ladies' tee. It was generally from the middle or the back of the men's tees. They just couldn't stand it for the women to score well on their courses. We played some monstrous courses, much longer than they play now. And pin placements were tough. But nobody ever thought of complaining. There was nothing wrong with long courses; everybody had to play them. It was when we got so concerned with our public image and the scores in the newspapers that we became concerned with long courses. But back then it didn't matter if you shot a 75, so long as you won the tournament.

But I remember Patty Berg shooting 64 at the Richmond Country Club in California—a tough course. I was playing with her, and to this day it may be the best round of golf I've ever seen played. Now the players come close to shooting 64, but on courses that were nothing like those we played in the early years. Those courses averaged 6,400 yards. Then, again, I didn't want any shorter courses. Mickey and Babe had an advantage on them, and so did I, although Mickey would have won on any golf course, any length. Anyway, the cream really came to the top on a 6,400-yard course. You just had to have a good swing to play it, or you'd have a 90.

In the early days there was not much of a future for women pros in golf after tournament life. There were very few if any club jobs available. But I don't think the really good players ever thought that far ahead. Patty Berg, Louise Suggs, myself, we had contracts with Wilson and MacGregor and had clubs made with our names on them, so we didn't have to worry too much. But when you got past the first five, it was a problem. I don't know that any of them were prepared for living without tournament golf. When you're playing the tournament circuit you think you'll always play and there will never come a time when you will have to do something else, quit and go to work. People become addicted to it. It's a very protected kind of existence. You don't have the responsibilities people have in the real world. You go from place to place, and nowadays sponsors take care of all your needs—they meet you at airports, provide so many services. You don't have to make beds, do wash, and such mundane things. People hate to give that up, even players who aren't having a lot of success, and I'm afraid a lot of them don't prepare for life after tournament golf. I had a lot of success, and can't imagine anyone staying out there as long as I did without winning.

It was a shock for me to quit the tour. I had withdrawal symptoms. It was traumatic. But that was mainly in making the decision to quit. Once I did it, I got so involved in the work of a tournament director that it never bothered me at all.

Now it's much easier for women to get club-professional jobs. They are in great demand. More women golfers want to take lessons from women pros. I get a lot of offers to take a teaching job. Women pros are admired now. The women's movement probably has something to do with that, and being on television. Women pros are admired now.

I won fifty-five tournaments as a professional. I won ten of them in 1959, and won a little over $26,000. But I don't feel any resentment at the amount of money the girls are playing for now. That's not why I played, for the money. If it was a lot of money I was after, I probably would have done something else. I thoroughly enjoyed playing and got a lot of satisfaction out of it. I take pride in being a pioneer that helped make today's tour possible.

The Missing Links

RICK REILLY

Rick Reilly is a senior writer for Sports Illustrated *magazine and has been named National Sportswriter of the Year five times. He has also authored several books, most notably* Missing Links, *a golf novel. Mr. Reilly lives in Denver, Colorado.*

The most important man in golf has a ball retriever in his bag, a score counter on his belt and a loop in his backswing, He buys three balls for a dollar and shows up at the course in jeans, Reeboks and a golf shirt that's so old it has no emblem. He's the foot soldier of the game, the guy who's up at four in the morning to pay $12 to wait three hours to play a six-hour round to lose $6 in bets.

No company wants him to wear its name on his visor, and nobody shines his cleats. Yet he's the guy who keeps the sport alive. He's the guy who lines up three deep to hit a bucket of almost-round balls off AstroTurf mats, which stain his irons an unnatural green. That's him in the back of the clubhouse, lying about his round and playing gin rummy on a white Formica table that hasn't seen a busboy's rag since Easter.

Lately he's been forgotten. Lately people have thought of golf as some kind of 18-karat Aaron Spelling production, people driving up in expense-account Cadillacs wearing La Mode du Golf shirts and tipping doormen 10-spots. Every new course is more glamorous and exotic than the last. And "greens fees" mean you have to buy a Jack Nicklaus lot overlooking the 18th green.

But golf can't change neighborhoods on us. Truth is, underneath all that, the heart of the game is still the shot-and-a-beer hacker, the golf guerrilla, the guy playing courses that move about as fast as a Moscow meat line, and smiling about it. Fuzzy Zoeller may shoot 66 at Augusta and then gripe about the greens, but the essence of golf is still the 14 handicapper who doesn't mind if the tees are rough. The fairways look like the aftermath of a tractor-pull and the greens aren't. He loves the game *for* the game. It's Saturday. He's playing golf. He's gonna gripe?

At Bethpage State Park on Long Island, golfers arrive at 2:30 in the morning in hopes of getting on the first tee by 6:30. Golfers who arrive at 7:30 are lucky to be planting a tee in the ground by noon. At Forest Preserve National in Oak Forest, Ill., players begin lining up at 3 P.M. *the day before* for a 6 A.M. tee time. They sleep in their cars. In Los Angeles, if you haven't called by 6:30 A.M. on a Monday for a tee time the next Saturday, you're usually shut out for that day on all 13 public courses. The switchboard opens at 6 A.M.

It's not uncommon for a round of golf to take almost seven hours. If you get around at all, that is. At Pelham Golf Course in the Bronx a few years ago, youths hiding in nearby woods robbed a man on a green of $65 and his credit cards. It is not known whether he then made the putt. When American Golf, a course management company, took over at Pelham, employees were surprised at what they found—dead bodies. Because of that, Kimble Knowlden of American Golf told *The New York Times,* "I try not to be the first one out on the course in the morning."

But warm bodies, too, keep flooding the Bronx's public links. Same as they do in Chicago and L.A. The country is four quarts low on reasonably priced golf courses for John Q. Public to play. The National Golf Foundation estimates that the number of golfers has grown 24%, to 20.2 million, over the last two years. To keep up with that pace, the foundation says, a course a day would have to be built between now and the turn of the century. Last year only 110 opened, and more than a third of those were private.

Still, for all of that—the ordeal of getting a tee time, the 20-minute waits between shots and the ungroomed greens—the public course golfer, one of the most abused sportsmen in America, pursues the game loyally and lovingly, as if he had invented it. And nobody's more loyal than the regulars at Ponkapoag Golf Club in Canton, Mass., known, for better or worse, as Ponky.

Overheard at a Ponky lunch table:

RALPHIE: "You know what my problem is?"
PETE: "No, what?"
RALPHIE: "With you fishes, I need a bigger wallet."
PETE: "Slob."
HERBIE: "What'd everybody make on that last hole?"
RALPHIE: "Four."
BROOKLYN: "Five."
PETE: "Other."
HERBIE: "Whaddya mean, 'other'?"
PETE: "Other. Like on TV, when they put up what all the pros have been making on the hole, right?"
HERBIE: "So?"
PETE: "So it says something like, '181 birdies, 300-something pars, 98 bogeys, 42 double bogeys and seven others.' Well, I had an 'other,' O.K.?"
JUICE: "I'll guarantee you, tomorrow I'm not shootin' any 'others.' Tomorrow, I'm throwin' a 72 at you slobs."
TOMMY: "Right. And I'm Seve."
JUICE: "Bet me?"
TOMMY: "Sawbuck?"
JUICE: "You got it."
TOMMY: "So, how do you guarantee it?"
JUICE: "After I hit it 72 times, I'm pickin' it up."

*   *   *

For the third time in history, the U.S. Open, which begins June 16, will be held this year at The Country Club in Brookline, Mass. For the 88th time in history, the U.S. Open will not be held at Ponky. Still, the two courses are only 20 minutes apart in Greater Boston, and it's easy to get them confused.

At The Country Club, for instance, you drive up to the clubhouse, where the boy meets you and takes your bag. At Ponky, you give a boy your bag only at gunpoint. At The Country Club, you change shoes in the locker room. At Ponky, most people don't change shoes. At The Country Club, the men's room is stocked with colognes, hair dryers and jars full of combs rinsing in blue disinfectant. At Ponky, you comb your hair looking into the metal on the front of the paper towel dispenser. At The Country Club, the greens are truer than any love. At Ponky, the greens look like barber-school haircuts. At The Country Club, lunch in the Men's Grille might begin with the vichyssoise, followed by an avocado stuffed with salmon salad. At Ponky, you can get a fried-egg sandwich for a buck and a quarter.

At The Country Club, the most esteemed tournament is The Country Club Gold Medal. At Ponky, it's the TV Open. (Each member of the winning foursome gets a TV—color, no less.) At The Country Club, the names are Wigglesworth, Peabody and Coolidge. At Ponky, they're Papoulias, Sullivan and Tomasini. At The Country Club, the members peruse *The Wall Street Journal.* At Ponky, they read the *Racing Form.* At The Country Club, most of the families came over on the *Mayflower.* At Ponky, most of the guys came over on the bus.

Ponkapoag endures 120,000 rounds a year over its two courses, and a whole lot of these are played by the regulars. Among them are Bluto, a construction worker with a high resemblance to Olive Oyl's suitor; Ziggy, who looks like the doorman in *The Wizard of Oz;* Little Eddie, a slightly pudgy accountant; Jimmy, a postal worker; Cementhead, a cement-truck driver; Socks, a contractor; Pappy, a high-tech engineer; and the Can Man, a retired cop who collects plastic garbage bags full of aluminum cans during rounds and hauls them saddlebag-style over his golf cart.

Then there is Bob DePopolo. If The Country Club has Francis Ouimet, winner of the 1913 U.S. Open, then Ponky has DePopolo, 57, inventor of the Triple Tripod Leg-Log putting stroke. To do the Triple Tripod, you get a five-foot putter that reaches up to your sternum (DePopolo insists he invented this extra-long putter, now popular on the Senior tour), stand with legs crossed, use a cross-handed grip and whack away.

DePopolo was a master of all things technical about golf, but he was most obsessive about the wind. In fact, the only ball he would play was a Titleist 8. He said the symmetry of the 8 caused less wind friction than other numbers. "For years," says Paul Bersani, a Ponky regular, "you could not buy a Titleist 8 in the pro shop. DePopolo had 'em all."

DePopolo gave up golf to tend to an ailing mother, but he had long since become a legend. One year he played the Catholic Youth Organization tournament, still held annually at Ponky. After winning his semifinal match on a Friday, he was eating a cheeseburger when a priest admonished him. "Son, what do you think you're doing?"

"Having a cheeseburger, Father," said DePopolo.

"Don't you know it's Friday?"

"So what?" said DePopolo. "It's a free country, ain't it?"

DePopolo, thus rooted out as a Protestant, was immediately disqualified.

Ziggy, a short, sturdy man in his mid-50's, gets constant abuse at Ponky for: 1) his toupee, and 2) the fact that in 25 years, he has never gotten the clubhead past his waist on the backswing.

SOCKS: "O.K., Ziggy, this is the one. Baby. Get those hands way up high this time. Way up!"

BLUTO: "Wait, Ziggy, wait! There's a divot on your head."
(Despite making a perfect practice swing, Ziggy still

strikes the ball with his usual foreshortened style.) "Beautiful, Ziggy. You did it that time."

SOCKS: "Ziggy, you could make a swing in a phone booth."

PAULI: "Without opening the door."

RUDY: "Remember that time Ziggy made that great shot out of the woods?"

PAULI: "Remember! I was *there.*"

RUDY: "Absolutely great shot. He was all bashed in there, in with the trees. Had no shot. Only he makes a great shot and he comes running out to watch it. Only his toupee is still hanging on one of the branches."

PAULI: "The Parks Department came, they thought it was a wombat."

ZIGGY: "Rot, you slobs."

Golf isn't the sport of choice at Ponky. The sport of choice is betting. Golf is just a convenient vehicle for it. At Ponky, they bet on whether the pro on TV will sink his next putt. They bet on how long it will take Russ, the cook, to make a two-minute egg. They bet with their partners, and they bet against their partners. They bet with guys playing two groups ahead and with guys three counties over. They bet while they're waiting on the tees. They bet on whether they can chip into the garbage can or off the ball washer. On a rainy day at Ponky, Pappy the Edgeman (so named because he always wants the betting edge) will take bets on a hole that consists of hitting a ball off the locker room floor, over a bank of lockers, out a door, onto the practice green and into a designated cup. Par is 3.

They'll bet you can't make a 4 on the next hole. They'll bet you can't turn the front nine in 42. Little Eddie will bet you that he can stack two golf balls, one on top of the other, ricochet the bottom one off a wall and catch the top one in his back pocket. (Don't take the bet.) Pappy, the snake, has bet people he can beat them putting with his wedge. (Don't take that one, either.)

Then there was the time Pappy bet Socks 10 bucks that Socks

couldn't make a 4 on the next hole. Socks made a 3. "Pay up, Edgeman," said Socks.

"What for?"

"You know what for. I made a 4."

"No you didn't. You made a 3." Took a while for Socks to get
over that one.

They bet for 27 holes on weekends, and they bet on their regular nine-hole game after work. They bet "sandies" (up and down
out of the sand), "greenies" (closest to the pin on par-3s), "barkies"
(hit a tree and still make par) and "Arnies" (make a par without ever
being on the fairway). Afterward, they'll bet on hearts, gin, whist
and poker until it gets dark, and then go outside, turn the car head-
lights on the putting green and have putting contests until somebody has won all the money or the Diehards start to wear out. In the
winter, when the course is closed, they'll get a pound of bologna,
some roast beef, a loaf of bread and some tonic and play cards in the
clubhouse, although they're not supposed to have a key. Loser has to
vacuum.

Golf is so much fun at Ponky that guys who are members at
country clubs come over for a most un-clubby kind of golf game.
Rudy Tomasini has been a member of Plymouth Country Club for
years, yet every afternoon Rudy shows up to play a 5 o'clock round
with the boys, and every day the boys give him the business.

> BLUTO: "Hey, Ziggy, what's Mr. Country Club doing here,
> anyway? Why does he want to play Ponky when he
> could be at the country club?"
>
> ZIGGY: "I'll tell you what he's doing. He's slumming, that's
> what he's doing. He's favoring us with his presence."
>
> BLUTO: "Must've run out of hors d'oeuvres over there or some-
> thing."

Most of the gambling is $5 stuff, but some of it isn't. Herbie
lost $18,000 one day at Ponky. Another gambler—we'll call him

Nicky—plays golf, the puppies, the ponies, the games, the lottery, anything. "You can always tell whether Nicky's had a good week," says Bluto. "If he's ahead, he's playing golf. If he's down, he's mowing greens." Today. Nicky is mowing greens.

> BLUTO: "Whaddya think Nicky made last year?"
> JIMMY: "I don't know. Hundred grand?"
> BLUTO: "Yeah. And he lost 110."

Sometimes the betting gets complicated. One day Georgie Conroy, a regular, was playing in a sevensome and had bets going with everybody. After madly scribbling down all his bets, he headed for the first fairway, where everyone found his ball. Everyone except Georgie, that is. They were just about to give up looking when somebody pointed back to the tee and yelled, "Georgie! There it is!" He had forgotten to tee off.

The boys have just found out that qualifying for this year's state amateur championship will take place at Ponkapoag.

> LITTLE EDDIE: "Can you imagine a guy from The Country Club coming here to qualify?"
> BLUTO: "Man, wouldn't you love to get a three handicap from The Country Club out there for a little $50 Nassau?"
> JIMMY: "I get a game with somebody from The Country Club, I start refinishing my basement."
> ANDY: "I'd just like to see the guy at the first tee. He's probably not used to guys yelling at him on his backswing."
> JIMMY: "Yeah, I played at Brae Burn [Country Club] one time, and I couldn't concentrate on the tee. Too quiet."
> SOCKS: "Wouldn't you love to see a guy from The Country Club try to get out of our rough? He'd come back into the pro shop with his attorney."
> CEMENTHEAD: "I dunno. They got some pretty mean rough out there for the Open, you know."

LITTLE EDDIE: "How do you know, slob?"

CEMENTHEAD: "Didn't I tell you? I *played* The Country Club the other day. Played it even par."

SOCKS: "Get out! You never."

CEMENTHEAD: "I did. I was working on a job on some property that's next to it. And, you know, I always carry that four-iron and some shag balls in the truck with me, right?"

SOCKS: "So?"

CEMENTHEAD: "So I realize I'm standing right next to No. 2. It's a par-3, like 185 yards away. I look around and I see that nobody's watching me, so I hop the fence. I tee it up and I just couldn't believe it. Their tees are better than our greens, Eddie! So I hit it and I hit it pretty good, but it catches up on the left fringe. Still nobody's looking, so I figure, what the hell, I'll go putt out. Their greens, you can't believe. I felt bad just walking on 'em. So I make par putting with the four-iron, and I guess I could've kept going because nobody was out there, but I decided not to. So that means I'm par for The Country Club, right? Take that, you muni hacks."

BLUTO: "Geez. Where do you play next week? Winged Foot?"

Sometimes the boys at Ponky hustle visitors, and sometimes the boys get hustled. One day Jimmy Sullivan, a 12-time club champ, and Pappy the Edgeman lined up a game with two guys from Franklin Park in the Roxbury section of Boston. One of the guys from Franklin Park walked with a limp and hit all his shots cross-handed. The Edgeman tried to keep from drooling. They upped the bet to $50 Nassau, with plenty of presses.

As they approached the 9th tee, Pappy was losing his bet, and Jimmy was two under par but still two holes down to his man.

Pappy and Jimmy lost big. Jimmy's opponent turned out to be Charlie Owens, now a star on the PGA Senior tour, a lifetime cross-handed player and a man who has walked with a limp for 36 years.

The latest hero of the publinks player is Tour pro Jodie Mudd, who won the 1980 and '81 U.S. Public Links championships. (To enter the Publinks, you can't have had privileges at any private club during that year.) But public courses are more famous for forging the great minority players—guys like Lee Elder, Lee Trevino and current Tour star Jim Thorpe—players who, in their amateur days, could not afford a country club and who probably would not have been afforded membership in one even if they could. But on municipal courses, these guys were *good.* In 1967, Charlie Sifford, a former Tour player, came to Palmer Park in Detroit, a famous hustlers' track, and lost four days in a row. He then left and won the $100,000 Greater Hartford Open.

Thorpe's legendary days were at East Potomac Park in Washington, D.C., when he was in his early 20's. He was unbeatable at Potomac and, therefore, unbettable. So Thorpe had to take his game on the road. Wherever he went, he would show up late, with his clubs falling out of his dilapidated bag and his tennis shoes untied and wearing a shirt with a hole in it. "But I was ready to play," he says. "I could play *anywhere.*"

Except at a country club. "I just didn't feel comfortable at a club," says Thorpe. "Everybody's shoes all spit and shined, clubs sparkling clean, everybody being so polite. Everybody saying 'Good shot.' I wouldn't say 'Good shot' to a guy if he holed out from 300 yards. I might say 'So what?' But I'd never say 'Good shot.'"

One time Thorpe set up a match with the best player in Flint, Mich. On the first day they played a public course, and Thorpe took him for $16,000. "I figured I'd catch a flight out that night," recalls Thorpe, "but at the end of the day, the guy says to me, 'What time we playing tomorrow?'" So the next day he took Thorpe to the Toledo Country Club. Thorpe's game wasn't the same. "Chandeliers hanging everywhere, real thick carpet," he says. "I just wasn't dressed for the part." Thrown off, Thorpe got him for only $1,000.

Thorpe is convinced that, all things being equal, a public course player can whip a country club player every time. "You take a 15 (handicapper) from a public course and a 15 from a country club," says Thorpe, "and that public course 15 is going to walk out with that guy's ass. A public course golfer learns to play all the shots. He has to roll his putts true just to give them a chance to go in. When he gets on nice greens, he can make everything."

On a public course almost any kind of, uh, gamesmanship is fair play. "I'll jangle the keys, rip the Velcro on my glove," says Thorpe. "Anything to distract the guy."

Thorpe tells a story about a match in Tampa between the best local hustler and the famous Atlanta-based hustler George (Potato Pie) Wallace. The two men came to the 18th hole with about $20,000 on the line. Potato Pie had driven safely, but his opponent had hooked his ball into the rough, and even the 20 or so spectators following the twosome were having trouble finding it.

"They'll never find it," Potato Pie whispered.

"Why not?" Thorpe said.

"Because I've got it in my pocket."

Just then, the opponent, standing 50 yards ahead of the search party, hollered, "Found it!"

Thorpe looked at Potato Pie and Potato Pie looked at Thorpe. "Well," Potato Pie whispered. "Looks like the man has got me this time."

Ponky etiquette: Jimmy is about to hit his drive on No. 10. The bets are flowing. The usual 10th-hole logjam crowd is hanging around. Just as he takes the club back, Socks, standing 20 feet behind him, interrupts.

SOCKS: "Hey, Jimmy. Am I safe back here?"

JIMMY: "Not if you keep that up." (Jimmy hits and now it's Wally's turn.)

LITTLE EDDIE: "Excuse me, Wally, but I just wanted to remind you—you haven't come over the top with your swing yet today."

WALLY: "Thanks, Bum."

LITTLE EDDIE: "You're welcome, Wally." (Wally hits without incident and Socks steps up.)

BLUTO: "O.K., everybody, pay attention. The pro from Dover is on the tee." (Socks hits it dead left into the woods.)

LITTLE EDDIE: "Now you got it, Socks. Those lessons helped." (Socks hits his provisional ball dead right into the woods.)

CEMENTHEAD: "Atta way to correct it, Socko."

BLUTO: "Hey, Socks, ever thought of taking up boccie?" (Cementhead steps up and splits the fairway.)

CEMENTHEAD: "I'm hitting it so straight, all I need is one pass of the mower and I'm in the fairway."

SOCKS: "Hey, Cementhead, this is Ponkapoag. All you get is one pass of the mower."

JIMMY: "Yeah, unless it's a weekend or holiday. Then you get no pass of the mower." (Lee steps up and hits a perfect drive.)

FREDDY: "What is it with this guy? Every time I bet against him, he swings like he's the poorest man in Boston. You need money that bad, you got to swing like Gene Littler, for Chrissakes?" (Now Little Eddie is up. He is partners with Socks today and has made two straight bogeys.)

SOCKS: "You're getting heavy, Eddie, you know what I mean? I'm not a frigging camel. I can't carry you forever." (Eddie shrugs, and then hits his drive into the trees.)

SOCKS: "Eddie, what the hell are you doing?"

EDDIE: "I'm screwing up, what's it look like I'm doing?"

SOCKS: "Eddie, do you understand the term 'fairway'?"

EDDIE: "Do you understand the term 'slob'?"

Almost half the tees have no grass on them. Only a few sand traps have sand; the rest are overgrown with weeds. The 150-yard markers aren't 150 yards from anything in particular. The greens are a quilt of dirt patches, weeds and long grass, all of which can make a straight putt do a 90-degree turn. "I had one putt today actually back up on me," said Bob Stone, who has been playing Ponky for 25 years. And there's no such thing as a putt dying in the cup at Ponky. The crew members are so inexperienced that when they yank a hole out of the green, they don't flatten the ground around it back down, so every hole has a crown. Only regulars know that to make a putt at Ponky, you've got to allow for the hump of the hole.

All of this is not how it was meant to be. The first 18 holes at Ponky were designed by the famous golf architect Donald Ross in 1933. Ponky now has 36 holes, which require at least 12 crew members to maintain them properly. Ponky has only five.

Problem is, Ponkapoag is run by the Metropolitan District Commission, an archaic arm of the Commonwealth of Massachusetts that operates in 46 towns, patrolling beaches, skating rinks, swimming ponds and pools, and two golf courses. Why the towns can't maintain these facilities themselves is anyone's guess. The MDC hires employees for the courses from within the MDC. As a result, most Ponky staffers have about as much expertise in golf-course maintenance as they do in 747 repair.

Ponkapoag's greens fees are cheap as dirt: $7 on weekends, $6 on weekdays, $3 for seniors on weekdays and $3 for anybody after 3 p.m. Given those rates and the course's overall condition, Ponky is crying out to be leased to a private management company like American Golf, which would raise the prices a little and improve the playing conditions a lot. But the MDC won't do it.

"If there are 25 jobs in a year at Ponkapoag," says former pro Ken Campbell, "then 25 different politicians can give the jobs out. They don't want to give that up." So Ponky becomes, as one Ponkian put it, "a summer drop-off spot for every politician's son, brother-in-law, cousin and niece."

Ponky's members are left, more or less, to take care of the course themselves. Many of them spend their off hours repainting 150-yard markers, digging weeds out of traps and using their own chain saws to cut down overgrown limbs and trees. They went so far as to buy flags for the pins and rakes for the traps. The rakes were stolen.

Even in the face of such ratty conditions, an act of sheer will is still needed to get a tee time. Unless you're a member of the Inner Club, whose members, for $30 a year, get guaranteed starting times, you must put a golf ball in a long green pipe to establish your position in the tee-off order for that day. Dropping a ball in the pipe at 6:30 a.m., when the pipe is first brought out, will get you a tee-off time at about 11. The only way to beat the pipe is to arrive at the course at 5 o'clock in the morning, sign in with the starter and wait for dawn. On some mornings the fog is so thick at sunrise that groups on the fairway must holler back when it is safe to hit.

So why put up with it all: the shabby conditions, the starting-time masochism, the six-hour rounds? Boston has public courses with shorter waits and better greens. Why do it?

Pete Peters, a dyed-in-the-polyester Ponkian, knows why. "If somebody came up to me right now," says Peters, "and told me, 'Pete, you can become a member of The Country Club today, free of charge. But if you do, you can't ever come back to Ponky,' I wouldn't hesitate a second. I'd stay right here. I'd stay here where I can get some action, have a lot of laughs, relax and be with my friends."

In fact, not only do hardly any of the guys leave Ponky once they become entrenched, they even aspire to what Al Robbins did. Al was a Ponky lifer, a man who played there on weekends when he worked and seven days a week when he retired. But for all his playing, he was still an ordinary hack. Then one day Al parred the 1st hole, picked his ball out of the cup, walked over to the 2nd tee, had a massive heart attack and died on the spot.

Nobody at Ponky grieved much for Al. If anything, the guys thought of him as a lucky stiff. Former pro Campbell remembers why.

"He always said if he ever shot even par on Ponky, he'd like to drop dead then and there," says Campbell. "He finally got his wish."

Chapter Seven

THE 1990S

O NE OF THE high points of the Nineties—and I'm loving the Nineties—was playing golf with *SI*'s black senior editor at Wykagyl Country Club, one of the clubs I used to play as a kid. For one thing, it was the first time I'd played with a caddie since the Sixties, effectively taking ten strokes off my game, and the caddie was white and the member black, to boot. Maybe things were changing after all.

My stepfather had to give up golf because of a vicious pain in his shoulder, and soon thereafter, without the joy of his life, he had a debilitating stroke. At the same time, my mother's mother, who'd moved to the old folks' home at Sawgrass, was on the slow road down. My mother had a difficult time of it, and though she tried to keep up her golf and her spirits, she played less and worried and smoked more. On a visit to Ponte Vedra while on the golf course with my mother—leave it to your kids to hit you when you're down—I got up the courage to talk to her about something I'd been blaming her for since I was grounded for taking out the car when I was fourteen—that is, the loss of my friendship with Dennis.

Dennis and I had made every day an adventure. We'd run track together, stole a bottle of bourbon and, after two or three swigs each, got drunk for the first time, got in trouble together, and still got some of the best marks in our class. We'd been sneaking out and driving our parents' cars for months before we got caught. It had been the most fun and joyous year of my life, and not seeing him hurt me deeply. When, just before I got hit in the head with the golf ball, I told Dennis I wasn't supposed to see him anymore, he transferred to another school. Semicoma was bad, but without my best friend to laugh and make mischief with, life, in a word, sucked. My interest in school and everything else did a slow dissolve. Sure, I put up a good front, but I was just walking through life.

So there I was playing Ponte Vedra's Ocean Course with my mother, and after talking about friendship and how important it was, I got up the courage to tell her how pained my high school years were. How could she have forbidden me to see my best friend? She listened through several shots and three cigarettes, and then she said, "You know, Sky, I don't remember telling you you couldn't see Dennis. If I did, I'm sure it was in the heat of anger, because I didn't know what else to do." She puffed on her cigarette, and then she said, "You know how important my friendships are to me, and always have been. You must know I wouldn't ever have knowingly forbidden you to see any of your friends."

All of a sudden the world looked different to me. How strange is life that we build dungeons for ourselves out of dust and spit, with walls we're sure will never come down.

In rapid succession, my stepfather and my grandmother died, devastating my mother, who by then was smoking at least three packs of cigarettes a day. Then, just as she was beginning to get back to life, my mother got lung cancer and died at the age of seventy-four.

It was because of that talk that I was able to stop blaming my mother for something that, for whatever reason, was clearly my own doing. And it was only on the golf course that I could have wiped the slate clean and deepened my relationship with my mother by speaking with her about friendship and love and what had happened so many years before. There's something about the wide open spaces, the public yet private forum a golf course provides, the formal informality that couldn't have been found in her house or mine, or in a restaurant or on the beach or anywhere else.

My mother was raised in boarding schools and graduated with honors from the University of Texas when she was twenty. But she was of that generation that got married, had kids, and used her intelligence on crossword puzzles, mystery novels and conversation with her friends.

It took years for me to realize that one of the things that attracted my mother and my father to each other was the extreme loneliness they had felt as youths. My father had been orphaned by the time he was twelve, and my mother had been dumped with one relative or another until she was eight, when she went off to boarding school, while her parents lived around the world courtesy of the U.S. Navy.

Golf sustained my father and gave him a kinship with the long-dead father who had taught him the game and whose clubs he kept in our attic. What my father taught my mother on their honeymoon at Pinehurst was that golf can ease the pain and suffering. No matter how bad their lives got, my parents played together and with us. And now, when I play, I see my mother dropping her cigarette before taking each shot, the look of consternation on her face when her shot went wrong, the wan smile when she hit it well. I see my father's club head going spastic and his hips wiggling before each straight shot. But more, in the open air on lush green grass in wide open spaces, as I attempt to make the simple motion to swing the club to hit the little white ball that defiantly sits before me, I experience a joy and a sorrow and a kinship that I've felt only in stone churches listening to unseen cloistered nuns singing a Bach or a Mozart Mass.

And trust me, a good golf course is a might bit easier to find than cloistered nuns who sing like angels.

Playing Through Racial Barriers

RHONDA GLENN

Rhoda Glenn is a respected golf writer and correspondent who was an accomplished amateur golfer in the 1960s. This piece from Glenn's book, An Illustrated History of Women's Golf, *appeared in this form in* Sports Illustrated.

One day last summer, during my visit to Golf House, the United States Golf Association (USGA) museum and library in Far Hills, N.J., curator Karen Bednarsky showed me a letter she had recently received. It was from JoAnn Overstreet, whose mother, Ann Gregory, had died earlier in the year at age 77. Overstreet wrote that her mother had been a fine golfer, and she wondered if the USGA would be interested in Gregory's trophies.

"Did you know Ann Gregory?" Bednarsky asked me.

Yes, I knew Ann Gregory. I used to play against her. And I also knew that on Sept. 17, 1956, Gregory had teed off in the U.S. Women's Amateur at Meridian Hills Country Club in Indianapolis—and so had become the first black woman to play in a national championship conducted by the USGA.

There would be other good black women players: Eoline Thornton, of Long Beach, Calif., played in the 1958 Women's Amateur; Althea Gibson, Wimbledon and USLTA tennis champion, took up the game seriously at age 32 and in 1963 became the first black to play on the LPGA tour; Renee Powell of Canton, Ohio, turned pro in 1967. But Gregory was the first black woman to compete on the national scene, and she might have been the best.

"She was a determined and confident golfer," says Powell, "and she was such a warmhearted, inspirational individual that she helped me by her example, by the kind of person she was. Not enough people know about Ann. She set the stage for every other black female who came into golf after her."

I first met Ann when we were both contestants in the 1963 Women's Amateur in Williamstown, Mass. She was by then a veteran who mingled easily with the other players. But there had been an embarrassing moment earlier in the week.

Polly Riley, who was playing in the tournament, was unpacking her suitcase in her hotel room when she glimpsed Gregory, dressed in white, walking past in the hallway. Mistaking her for a maid, Riley called out, "Hey, can you bring me some coat hangers?" Moments later, Gregory, smiling, came into Riley's room and handed her a bunch of hangers.

"I saw then that she had on golf clothes," says Riley. "I was terribly embarrassed. We laughed about it many times, although that type of thing must have been very difficult for her."

Gregory endured a lot worse. Golf's delicate rituals, however, allow no room for vengeance, and from some deep well of character Gregory was able to forgive the indignities. "Racism is only in your mind. It's something that you overlook or you look at it," she said when I interviewed her for a book I was writing on the history of women's golf. She was 76 then, though she exuded the vitality of a much younger woman, and was playing in the 1988 USGA Senior Women's Amateur. Neither of us knew that it would be her last appearance in national competition.

"Racism works best when you let it affect your mind," she said. "It was better for me to remember that the flaw was in the racist, not in myself. For all the ugliness, I've gotten nice things three times over. I can't think ugly of anybody."

*   *   *

By 1956 there had been few real social advances for women in golf. The creation of the LPGA in 1950, spearheaded by Babe Zaharias and Patty Berg, opened the door for women professionals. But when Gregory stepped onto the 1st tee at Meridian Hills six years later, the burning issue in the women's game was dress codes rather than integration. In 1954 the U.S. Supreme Court had ruled on the landmark case of *Brown v. Board of Education,* banning racial segregation in public schools. In December 1955, the Reverend Martin Luther King Jr. had led the bus boycotts in Montgomery, Ala.

In contrast, the women's amateur circuit of the 1950s was a sort of enclave of golf debutantes. The players were fresh faced, young white women who vied for silver cups on a tour of private clubs and exclusive resorts. The era produced great players, among them Mickey Wright, JoAnne Carner, Marlene Streit, Barbara McIntire and Anne Sander. But following the circuit was expensive, and while a few had jobs, many players were well-to-do.

The opposite was true of Gregory, who was born in Aberdeen, Miss., on July 25, 1912, the daughter of Henry and Myra Moore. Her parents died when she was a child, and she went to live with a white family, the Sanderses, for whom she served as the maid. In '38 she married Percy Gregory, and they moved to Gary, Ind.

"That family cried like babies," Gregory said of her leaving. "They said people in the North were so cold and that I didn't deserve being treated like that. I said, 'Mrs. Sanders, you've prepared me very well for mistreatment.'"

The new Mrs. Gregory was a good athlete. She took up tennis and soon won the Gary city tennis championship. In 1943 she joined the Chicago Women's Golf Association (CWGA), a black organization, and took golf lessons from Calvin Ingram, a good black player who worked at a Chicago club.

It wasn't long before she was winning amateur tournaments, including the CWGA championship, the Joe Louis Invitational in Detroit and the championship of the United Golf Association (UGA), a national organization for black players. Those events drew little or no notice in most major newspapers, but black papers hailed her as "The Queen of Negro Women's Golf," and in 1947 George S. May, a golf promoter in Chicago, invited her to play in his open invitational tournament, the Tam O'Shanter. She was the only black woman in the field.

"Mr. May told me if anyone said anything to me, to let him know," Gregory said. "No one did. The galleries were just beautiful to me. But I was lonely. For a whole week I didn't see any black people.

"My neighbors drove up from Gary to see me play the final round and, when I saw them, that's the only time I felt funny. It just did something to me to see my black friends among all those white people, and I cried."

The Gregorys lived in a comfortable house in Gary, where Percy worked for U.S. Steel. Ann was a caterer for the University Club, served on the Community Chest and United Fund committees, and in 1954 became the first black appointed to the Gary Public Library Board.

In 1956 the Chicago group became the first black organization to join the USGA, thereby making Gregory eligible for its championships. She immediately entered the 1956 Women's Amateur and drove to Indianapolis with Jolyn Robichaux, a friend from the CWGA.

"We were so excited about the idea of her being in the championship that we didn't notice any problems," says Robichaux, who lives in suburban Chicago. "Ann was the type we needed to break that barrier. She was outgoing, told jokes and was compassionate and encouraging to the other golfers. They immediately liked her. Joe Dey, the executive director of the USGA, did everything he could to see that her participation was pleasant."

The Associated Press noted the historic day: "A starting field of 105 players, including the first Negro in its history, was paired Saturday for match play in the 56th USGA Women's Amateur. . . ."

But there was no escape from prejudice. Gregory's first opponent, Carolyn Cudone, a Curtis Cup player from West Caldwell,

N.J., recalled a parking attendant telling her father, "Your daughter better win today, or you'd better not come back to this parking lot."

"Every reporter in Indianapolis was there," recalls Cudone. "You couldn't stir them with a stick! She must have been nervous as a wet hen, because as we left the tee, she said if she didn't count her strokes right, it wasn't on purpose."

Cudone had her hands full. Making several escapes from bunkers, Gregory gained a 2-up lead, then began to drive wildly. Her lead collapsed, and she narrowly lost the landmark match, 2 and 1.

"My husband said I didn't have a snowball's chance in hell," Gregory confided as she shook Cudone's hand. "I guess I fooled him."

In 1957 Gregory returned to the Women's Amateur and advanced to the third round without incident. Subsequent appearances didn't go so smoothly.

When she arrived at the 1959 championship at Congressional Country Club in Bethesda, Md., trouble was brewing. A UGA event was under way in Washington, D.C., and black members were angry that Gregory had chosen instead to play in a white tournament. And Congressional simply didn't want her. In a flare-up of prejudice, the club banned her from the traditional players' dinner on the eve of the championship. Dey broke the news.

"I told Joe Dey it was no big deal," Gregory said. "I said, 'I realize the money I paid to enter the tournament didn't buy stock in the clubhouse. I'll eat me a hamburger and be just as happy as a lark, waiting on tee number 1.' I didn't feel bad. I didn't. I just wanted to play golf. They were letting me play golf. So I got me a hamburger and went to bed."

One of Gregory's best performances in national competition followed. In the second round she faced the Georgia state champion, Mrs. Curtis Jordan.

The Georgia player, heavily favored by the gallery, dashed to a 2-up lead. Gregory, meanwhile, enjoyed her own fans. With Frank Stranahan, an Ohio professional, cheering her from the sidelines she began to rally. She squared the match on the 17th. On the home hole, she hit a clutch shot, firing a three-iron over a pond to the putting surface. When Jordan hit her ball into a bunker and bogeyed, Gregory had two putts to win the match.

"I stroked my putt, turned my head away and heard the ball fall into the cup," she remembered. "All of the people began to applaud for me. When I made that deuce to win, my caddie turned a somersault. The club fired him for that. When I asked for my caddie the next day, the caddie master told me he had been fired."

Gregory lost her third-round match, 6 and 4.

"After I lost, the club president invited me into his office," Gregory recalled. "He told me that I had exhibited myself as one of the most beautiful ladies to ever walk that golf course, and that I was welcome to play there anytime I was in that area.

"I thought, He's got to be crazy! I would never come back there to play after all of the things they put me through."

There would be other incidents. When she played in the 1960 Women's Amateur, in Tulsa in August, the manager of a white hotel would not honor her reservation and sent her to a shabby black hotel with no air-conditioning. Ann and Percy sat on the hotel steps eating ice cream until she was tired and cool enough to sleep.

At home in Gary, Gregory played at Gleason Park, a public course. Only whites were allowed to play the 18-hole layout at Gleason Park, while blacks had to make do with a nine-hole course. One day in the early 1960s, Gregory slapped her money on the counter and announced that she had outgrown the short layout.

"My tax dollars are taking care of the big course, and there's no way you can bar me from it," she said.

She teed off and played without interference. Soon Gary's black golfers began to make tee times on the longer course.

In 1971 Gregory nearly won the U.S. Senior Women's Amateur, at Sea Island (Ga.) Golf Club. In the final round of stroke play, only one woman stood between her and a national championship, her old rival and friend Carolyn Cudone. Cudone parred the last hole to beat Gregory by a single stroke.

"Ann was a lady and she could play," says Cudone. "She was a fine competitor. She played the game as you wanted to see it played."

When I last saw Ann, in 1988, I asked for photocopies of her tournament records. Instead, she shipped her scrapbooks to me. I leafed through them, moved by the life that unfolded in yellowed newspaper clippings. On one page she had pasted her invitation to a 1963 tournament in the South. I, too, had saved my invitation to that tournament, but I knew that Ann's invitation meant so much more.

She teed it up during a difficult era, against odds that few of us can ever know. She endured painful slights with warmth, humor, courage and good sense. More than most of us, she cherished the game, and in the end, she honored it. I knew Ann Gregory. She was simply a golfer. A very fine one.

The American Way of Golf

TOM WATSON

Born in Kansas City, Missouri, in 1949, Tom Watson soared into the golf spotlight by winning the British Open in 1975. He would win that major tournament four more times to go along with his two Masters victories and one U.S. Open title. Watson also captured two Player of the Year honors and was the PGA tour's leading money winner from 1977 to 1980. He wrote this brief but interesting piece for the Op-Ed page of The New York Times.

Golf has changed slowly through the decades, yet it is growing phenomenally, nationally and internationally. There are more players from more segments of society, more new courses, more women and more better opportunities for young and old to learn the game. That's all good; golf is healthy (and healthful), wealthy and still wise.

Yet 1991 has been a troubled and historic year. For the past century, golf in America has been largely the sport of the privileged, a game for white Protestant men to learn and master at private country clubs. Most such clubs have had restrictive and highly secret membership policies. Jews, Hispanics, blacks, single women and others who sought the comforts of a private club with its pool, dining room and lush golf course, not to mention elevated social standing and potential business contacts were left to fend for themselves.

Golf didn't care. The game produced its great champions: Bobby Jones, Hagen and Nelson, Hogan, Palmer and Nicklaus.

Each was white, none was Jewish and each was accepted by the public and the privileged. The game flourished.

Then last August, at our P.G.A. championship at the Shoal Creek Country Club in Birmingham, Alabama, the inevitable happened. The club's founder was quoted, or misquoted, as saying after an interview that blacks were not allowed to play at Shoal Creek because "that just isn't done down here."

Suddenly, the closet door flew open. Why should a major golf championship, in this day and age of social advances, be played at a site where such discrimination toward fellow Americans prevails? The unspeakable had been spoken and the reaction was swift and sure.

The furor took the story from the sports pages to the front page: corporate sponsors of the tournament telecast withdrew their $2 million in advertising. In rapid order, Shoal Creek agreed to open its membership, and the PGA Tour stated that its tournaments would be played only at clubs that agreed to membership policies that did not discriminate on the basis of race, gender or religion.

(Because of the new P.G.A. policy, a few golf courses are no longer available for tournament play; the members chose not to abdicate control over their policies.)

Then, last last year, I resigned from the Kansas City Country Club where I had played golf since I was 6 years old. I had heard that my club had denied membership to a popular and distinguished business leader, Henry Bloch, who happened to be Jewish, the only possible reason for rejection. My decision to resign was a matter of personal conscience, brought to the forefront all the more because my wife and children are Jewish, though I am not.

At least two conflicting forces are involved in this snarling issue of privacy and openness. First, Americans cherish their freedom of choice, assembly and their individual rights to say, do and think anything they want within the law. On the other hand, and equally fundamental, we presuppose the merit of the Golden Rule and equal rights for every citizen. We abhor bigots and bigotry, hypocrisy and repression.

Truly American, I am in conflict with myself. The Bloch family certainly belongs, and indeed now does officially belong, among the members of my former club. It was painful for my family and me when I resigned to protest the Blochs' initial rejection, the secrecy of that decision and the lack of explanation for it.

Still, I fervently support the right of any group of people to band together in private association, just so long as they choose to admit their own discriminatory practices. There are significant differences among us. I see nothing wrong with private clubs, be they for men, women, Jews, blacks, Catholics, Hispanics, Asians, whomever. Just let them own up to it, not hide it.

There is no doubt in my mind that public posture and private practice are replete with hypocrisy. How many executives defiantly withdraw their advertising dollars in support of a civil rights protest only to leave the office and relax at a discriminatory private club? Should any club recruit one black member just to integrate the membership, obey P.G.A. policies and retain its televised tournament?

Perhaps someday Capitol Hill will establish quotas: religious quotas for my old club, gender quotas at the all-male Butler National Golf Club near Chicago and racial at Shoal Creek. To aid the economically disenfranchised, we have found that legislation is vital to equality. But let's not wait for government or the P.G.A. or a corporate sponsor to dictate what they think we ought to do.

Let's discriminate right now, each one of us, privately, between what is right and what is wrong. At work, at the country club, at home with the children (especially at home with the children), let's make our own personal choices that help, rather than hurt. And let's start soon.

A Cultural Backwater

MARCIA CHAMBERS

Marcia Chambers is a journalist and legal expert who wrote The Unplayable
Lie: The Untold Story of Women and Discrimination in American Golf,
from which this piece is excerpted.

Golf is booming in the United States. What used to be a sport accessible only to the wealthy at exclusive country clubs is now accessible to millions, and its popularity is at an all-time high.

Women, playing for both recreational and business reasons,
comprise the fastest-growing segment of the golf population. They
now make up roughly five million of the 24.8 million golfers. And a
huge number of them are teenagers, the next generation of career
women, says the National Golf Foundation. Overall, women account for about 37 percent of all new players since 1993.

Yet many women golfers find themselves subject to forms of
discrimination and prejudice unparalleled in almost any other part
of their lives. At many country clubs they cannot hold a property
right in the membership, even though their money may be paying
for it. They have no right to vote in club affairs, no real say in the
governance of club life. Desirable weekend tee times are often unavailable to them simply because they are women, even if they have
paid the same membership fees as a man. And when they wish to top
off a round of golf with lunch, they may find that the only place

open is a men's grill, to which they are denied entry. Even at the public courses they may find that no matter how good their game, they are treated unfairly.

Women now run their own companies, go to war, become doctors and lawyers and bankers. But the golf world and, especially, the world of the private country club have not dealt with these changes. The women who inhabit the private country club world, in particular, find themselves in a cultural backwater, constrained by arcane rules left over from a largely forgotten age. These old conventions are frustrating, especially for the new breed of working women, married or single, in business or the professions, women who expect the same rights on the golf course as they have elsewhere.

Unfortunately for today's women golfers, the sport they love, which has been growing here for a century, has always been deeply connected with the country club world of elitism and exclusion. Golf began in this country as one of the several enjoyable outdoor pastimes of the very rich. It did not develop as a sport of the people, as did baseball or, later, basketball, or even football, which had its roots in colleges and universities. Golf developed as part of the world of private leisure, first on the estates of the very wealthy and soon after at the private country club with its spaciousness, its acres of woods and grass.

Unlike most other sports, though, golf in the United States has had women participants from the beginning. The wives and daughters of members were always at the private country clubs where golf was played, because their main social life was there, and some went on to become competitive golfers as well. Several participated in a national women's championship as early as 1895. The first winner came from Shinnecock Hills Golf Club, on Long Island, New York, which is coincidentally the site for the centennial celebration of the men's United States Open Championship in 1995.

But for most of these women, most of the time, their role at the club was virtually always as guest or "associate," not as a full partner in the enterprise. If a woman had a son, he was embraced, taken in with great enthusiasm as a teenager. Daughters were not. Membership was unavailable to them unless they married, and then it was transferred to their husbands. Divorce spelled expulsion for either a mother or a daughter. Father and son remained. Unmarried women need not apply.

At the country club, golf joined such other elite sports as hunting, riding, shooting, and sometimes cricket, as part of the leisure life of the affluent. But of all these activities, only golf really caught on widely and spread throughout society, carrying some country club attitudes with it. As early as 1895 there was a public course in Van Cortlandt Park, in the Bronx, New York, and by the 1930s there were seventeen public courses within forty miles of Times Square. The Depression took its toll, of course, but by the mid-thirties Chicago had ten municipal courses, and there were several in Los Angeles and San Francisco.

After the Depression and World War II, public golf grew at a remarkable rate. Today there are nearly nine thousand public courses, including resort golf courses that cater to vacationers. Indeed, far more courses nowadays are public than are private, and many resort and upscale golf courses offer women a respite from the degree of discrimination they often encounter at the private club.

Within the private country club world today, there are some 4,500 courses. What was once a province restricted to the very rich has opened to the middle and upper middle classes. The country club has become a place for all the family, a literal home away from home that can be used by husbands and wives, parents and children, with restaurants, bars, swimming pools, tennis courts, lockers, and other amenities.

To an important degree, the world of golf has also become a stable feature of corporate culture in the United States. Many of the exclusive private country clubs are populated by men who make their living as corporate executives, from middle-level managers to the top CEOs of Fortune 500 companies. For them golf is a social and recreational activity, but it is also a way of entertaining clients, returning favors, and rewarding successful employees. The culture of the golf club world has always been heavily dominated by the males who are leaders in corporate and community life and who often assume leadership roles in their local country clubs as well.

But there is a world of difference between the modern corporation, which must respond to the issues of the day, and the insular, gated, and protected private country club that allows an escape from those issues. Removed as such clubs are from mainstream life, they have retained bylaws that are surprisingly similar to those they had when they were founded. Often today one finds private clubs whose values seem frozen in the social milieu of the mid-1920s, when many clubs were started. That was a different America, a place where women were just beginning to emerge as persons with equal claims to citizenship. The 19th Amendment to the Constitution, which gives women the right to vote, was not ratified until 1920.

When the first country clubs began, in the late nineteenth century, they were established by and for white male Anglo-Saxon Protestants. They were exclusive, of course. They rejected Catholics and Jews and Italians. The question of a black member was never even considered; it would have been unthinkable. The bylaws of many private country clubs specified "Caucasians Only."

Not surprisingly, many of these prohibited groups started their own exclusive clubs, allowing in others like themselves and treating the rest of the world as outsiders. Sometimes they even made distinctions within broad ethnic categories, as when certain Jewish clubs accepted German Jewish members but kept out Eastern European Jews.

This has begun to change. These days many formerly all WASP country clubs have a few Jews, Catholics, or Italians. Even black males are now admitted, an advance that few black executives ever thought possible but that came about after Alabama's Shoal Creek, the host of the 1990 PGA Championship, was criticized for having no black members. So the old barriers are slowly, slowly crumbling, not always for altruistic reasons but often to avoid unwanted legal complications.

But the old clubs still share one brand of exclusion in common: the exclusion of women, married or single, as full, voting, and shareholding members. This form of exclusion of women seems to know no religious or ethnic boundary.

The world around the country club has changed dramatically, of course. The civil rights movement of the early sixties, the social upheavals of the late sixties, the movement for gender equity in the workplace have transformed the society. If the world of golf were starting fresh, without the cultural weight of old traditions, a different set of policies might have evolved. But golf is still responding to the roles set for men and women in a bygone era. This is one reason that, increasingly, legislatures and courts are stepping into this terrain, passing laws and making judgments that may redefine the rights of country clubs and their members.

Many of these clubs' members, men and even some women, resist having these issues thrust upon them. They feel that because these are private clubs, the courts and legislatures should stay out of their affairs. Their policies are "internal matters," they say. But the issue of fundamental fairness for the women associated with these clubs can't be sidestepped.

In some of the most elite private institutions of our society, those conflicts are now being played out over who has the right, and when, to use a long club to hit a little ball into a barely bigger hole. They are being played out not among strangers, but among friends and colleagues, even husbands and wives, parents and children, those with whom we have our most intimate relationships. That basic expectations such as recognition and respect are undercut for the sake of such seemingly trivial pursuits says much about human nature and our fundamental relationships: male to female, husband to wife, parent to daughter or son.

What goes on in the small world of the private clubs wouldn't matter very much to anyone except its members if it weren't for the fact that the world of golf engages so many influential people, people who are the leaders in their nation, their cities, their towns, their companies. These are people who are among the best-educated in the country—legislators who make state and national laws, executives who manage large and small corporations, judges who sit on state and federal courts. In the past their private and public lives were separate, but now they are becoming blurred. The discriminatory aspects of the club world, the belief that some are entitled to withhold rights and privileges from others—even when the "others" are wives, daughters, mothers, and female colleagues—inevitably have some impact on all of us. When wives and daughters find advancement in their careers curtailed by restrictive policies aimed at them, then they rightly ask, Is it fair?

Some of the leaders of private country clubs, a disproportionately influential group, still support and practice behavior that many others in society believe to be unjust. The story of their treatment of women is sad, funny, and instructive. It reveals much about why discriminatory practices are so difficult to change, particularly when they are intertwined with marriage, friendship, social lives, and power.

The men who control country club life and support such policies may say it's simply tradition, that it has always been done this way, that it is simply an instance of exercising their First Amendment right of association. They are used to the idea of all-male sporting activities. Many of them were raised in all-male prep schools and colleges. What they are less likely to say is more to the point: these traditions serve their interests and they like it this way.

Despite these inequities at private clubs and the occasional "chill" in the air at public courses, a diverse group of women are taking up the game. Many find the game intoxicating. Few other competitive sports take place in such open territory, and every golf course is different. Each has its own length, texture, easy holes and hard holes, features that give it what golf-course architects describe as its "signature." The golf course can be a place where one can bask in the warmth and beauty of nature while also deeply immersed in a sporting competition with others.

Golf is also a game for a lifetime. Most sports are part of our youth and succumb to the inevitable as we age, but golf can be enjoyed throughout life. It may simply require a higher handicap.

The handicap, which allows golfers of unequal ability to compete on equal terms, is undoubtedly the feature that most distinguishes golf from other sports. Any golfer who plays with some frequency can submit scores to a state handicapping association and, after the scores are adjusted in various ways, will get a handicap that expresses, roughly, how many strokes that player will need to be given if he or she is to shoot a round of golf in par. Par itself is a bit mystical, but essentially means what an excellent golfer would shoot if he or she played very well and took two putts on every hole. Golf is traditionally played at eighteen holes, and if Player A has a handicap of, say, fourteen and Player B has a handicap of twenty, A will have to give B six strokes, one each on the three hardest holes on the front nine and similarly on the back nine, and then they will be able to play quite evenly.

The system assumes a basic honesty among the competitors—that they will not turn in fraudulent scores—but assuming that, this system allows people of unlike abilities to compete on equal terms. Try this in any other sport and it tends not to work or feels artificial, but in golf it allows a boss to compete with his salesmen, a client with his supplier, even (dangerously) a husband with his wife. When added to the natural beauty of golf courses and the lifetime of playing, handicapping gives golf a rare advantage over other forms of sport competition.

For these reasons, more than one in every ten Americans play the game, and as many as two million try it for the first time each year. Successful women are a large part of this current growth. They have a maddening variety of golf courses from which to choose, including desert courses and mountain courses, seaside courses and inland courses, short courses and long courses. One of the fascinations of golf is that it can be played in such an incredible variety of settings on very different surfaces, with different types of grass and sand.

They can also choose between public and private courses. The "public" in "public courses" refers not to ownership, but to who is allowed access. Public courses form the largest category of golf courses in this country, nearly 70 percent of the more than 13,440 golf facilities in the nation, and they include municipal courses, privately owned public courses, and expensive resort courses. The private courses range from the ultra-private and very exclusive to still-private but easier access family courses.

It is the elite private courses of the country that have been the scene of most of the legal battles over women's rights. This raises the natural question: Why put up with restrictive rules of membership and access at private courses? Why not stick to public places? It's a fair question, and not as easy to answer as it might have been years ago.

In the past there was a greater gap between the public-course world and the private-course world than there is now. The private course experience was restricted to persons of at least moderate wealth, and public courses, with their heavy play and low budgets for maintenance, often had to use rubber mats for teeing grounds and other cost saving devices that reduce the enjoyment of the game. There were exceptions, but generally the gap between public and private was great.

Now it is far less so. The gap has been closed from both directions. On the private side there are still elite clubs, but they are joined by a number of country clubs that are less exclusive and less expensive. And on the public side, golf entrepreneurs have come to realize that there's a vast amount of consumer dollars ready to go into golf at public facilities, if they have decent courses and policies. So although you can still find the fairly primitive local nine-hole layout, you also have extraordinary new resort courses where they no longer worry about skin color or gender, where, as one person put it, their only color concern is green—as in dollars.

At the same time, public courses are not immune from the gender biases that operate in golf's private world, but when gender bias creeps in it is more as a matter of male attitude and belief, and seldom a matter of club rules and bylaws. Public courses officially are not allowed to discriminate. But that does not mean there aren't drawbacks. Women golfers complain about rangers and starters who treat them poorly. They grumble about slow play by men, often resulting in six-hour rounds; they mutter about the amenities. They hate queuing up at 3:30 A.M. to get a tee time at the local public course.

Not all public courses are in this category. One remarkable woman, Nancy Oliver, saw the potential of upscale public golf courses for executive women and launched the highly successful Executive Women's Golf League. Her leagues and others like it are now giving thousands of women players a positive golfing experience. Still for a variety of reasons, including the desire to entertain clients, many of these women want the kinds of amenities that only a private club can provide.

"Then they call me up," says Ms. Oliver. "They are astonished. They say they spoke to the membership committee of the club or to the president or to someone and that person has told them they can't join because they are women. They say I led them down the primrose path but I forgot to tell them about the big bad wolf."

But the big bad wolf has been around a long time.

Tiger Woods at the Masters

RICK REILLY

This second contribution by Rick Reilly originally appeared in Sports Illustrated *in 1997.*

Short and pudgy, he pushed through the crowd, elbowing and worming his way, not stopping for any of the cries of "heyyy, watchit!" as he went. At last he popped through to the front and craned his neck down the line, wide-eyed, hoping to see what he had come for. As Tiger Woods strode past, Jack Nicholson slapped him on the back and grinned, same as everybody else.

It didn't matter who you were; if you were there the week everything changed in golf, you just had to reach out and touch a piece of history. Almost 50 years to the day after Jackie Robinson broke major league baseball's color barrier, at Augusta National, a club that no black man was allowed to join until six years ago, at the tournament whose founder, Clifford Roberts, once said, "As long as I'm alive, golfers will be white, and caddies will be black," a 21-year-old black man delivered the greatest performance ever seen in a golf major.

Someday Eldrick (Tiger) Woods, a mixed-race kid with a middle-class background who grew up on a municipal course in the sprawl of Los Angeles, may be hailed as the greatest golfer who ever lived, but it is likely that his finest day will always be the overcast Sunday in Augusta when he humiliated the world's best golfers, shot 18-under-par 70-66-65-69-270 (the lowest score in tournament history) and won the Masters by a preposterous 12 shots. It was the soundest whipping in a major this century and second only to Old Tom Morris's 13-shot triumph in the 1862 British Open.

When Tiger finally slipped into his green champion's jacket, his 64-year-old father, Earl, drank in a long look and said, "Green and black go well together, don't they?"

So golf is trying to get used to the fact that the man who will rule the game for the next 20 years shaves twice a week and has been drinking legally for almost three months now. "He's more dominant over the guys he's playing against than I ever was over the ones I played against," marveled no less an authority than Jack Nicklaus, whose 17-under Masters record of 271 had held up for 32 years. "He's so long, he reduces the course to nothing. Absolutely nothing."

It was something to see the way a 6'2", 155-pounder with a 30-inch waist crumbled one of golf's masterpieces into bite-sized pieces. The longest club he hit into a par-4 all week was a seven-iron. On each of the first two days he hit a wedge into the 500-yard par-5 15th hole—for his *second* shot. Honey, he shrunk the course. Last Saturday his seven birdies were set up by his nine-iron, pitching wedge, sand wedge, putter, nine-iron, putter and sand wedge. Meanwhile, the rest of the field was trying to catch him with five-irons and three-woods and rosary beads. When Nicklaus said last year that Woods would win 10 green jackets, everybody figured he was way off. We just never thought his number was low.

Said Jesper Parnevik, who finished 19 shots back, "Unless they build Tiger tees about 50 yards back, he's going to win the next 20 of these." (Memo to former Masters winners: Get ready for a whole lot of Tuesday-night champions' dinners you can supersize.)

Woods's performance was the most outstanding in Augusta National history, and that figured, because he stood out all week. He stood out because of the color of his skin against the mostly white crowds. He stood out because of his youth in a field that averaged

38 years. He stood out because of the flabbergasting length of his drives—323 yards on average, 25 yards longer than the next player on the chart. He stood out for the steeliness in his eyes and for the unshakable purpose in his step. "He may be 21," said Mike (Fluff) Cowan, his woolly caddie, "but he ain't no 21 inside those ropes." Said Paul Azinger, who played with Woods last Friday and got poleaxed by seven shots. "I just got outconcentrated today. He never had a mental lapse."

It was a week like nobody had ever seen at Augusta National. Never before had scalpers' prices for a weekly badge been so high. Some were asking $10,000. Even after it was all done, a seemingly useless badge was fetching up to $50 outside the club's gates. Never before had one player attracted such a large following. Folks might have come out with the intention of watching another golfer, but each day the course seemed to tilt toward wherever Woods was playing. Everybody else was Omar Uresti. Never before had so many people stayed at the course so long, filling the stands behind the practice range, 1,500 strong, to watch a lone player hit thrilling wedge shots under the darkening Georgia sky. It was the highest-rated golf telecast in history, yet guys all over the country had to tell their wives that the reason they couldn't help plant the rhododendrons was that they needed to find out whether the champion would win by 11 or 12.

Away from the golf course, Woods didn't look much like a god. He ate burgers and fries, played Ping-Pong and P-I-G with his buddies, screamed at video games and drove his parents to the far end of their rented house. Michael Jordan called, and Nike czar Phil Knight came by, and the FedExes and telegrams from across the world piled up on the coffee table, but none of it seemed to matter much. What did matter was the Mortal Kombat video game and the fact that he was Motaro and his Stanford buddy Jerry Chang was Kinatro and he had just ripped Kinatro's mutant head off and now there was green slime spewing out and Tiger could roar in his best creature voice, "Mmmmmwaaaaannnnnggh!"

By day Woods went back to changing the world, one mammoth drive at a time, on a course that Nicklaus called "much harder than the one I played" when he delivered his 271.

What's weird is that this was the only Masters in history that began on the back nine on Thursday and ended on Saturday night. For the first nine holes of the tournament the three-time reigning U.S. Amateur champion looked very amateurish. He kept flinching with his driver, visiting many of Augusta's manicured forests, bogeying 1, 4, 8 and 9 and generally being much more about Woods than about Tigers. His 40 was by two shots the worst starting nine ever for a Masters winner.

But something happened to him as he walked to the 10th tee, something that separates him from other humans. He fixed his swing, right there, in his mind. He is nothing if not a quick study. In the six Augusta rounds he played as an amateur, he never broke par, mostly because he flew more greens than Delta with his irons and charged for birdie with his putter, often making bogey instead. This year, though, he realized he had to keep his approach shots below the hole and keep the leash on his putter. "We learned how to hit feeders," Cowan said. Woods figured out how to relax and appreciate the six-inch tap-in. (For the week he had zero three-putts.) And now, at the turn on Thursday, he realized he was bringing the club almost parallel to the ground on his backswing—"way too long for me"—so he shortened his swing right then and there.

He immediately grooved a two-iron down the 10th fairway and birdied the hole from 18 feet. Then he birdied the par-3 12th with a deft chip-in from behind the green and the 13th with two putts. He eagled the 15th with a wedge to four feet. When he finished birdie-par, he had himself a back-nine 30 for a two-under 70—your basic CPR nine. Woods was only three shots behind the first-day leader, John Huston, who moved in front at 18 by holing a five-iron from 180 yards for eagle and then dropped from sight the next day with a double-par beagle 10 on the 13th. Playing in the twosome ahead of Huston, Woods had eagled the same hole after hitting an eight-iron to 20 feet, vaulting into the outright lead, one he would never relinquish.

By Friday night you could feel the sea change coming. Woods's 66 was the finest round of the day, and his lead was three over Colin Montgomerie. Last year's two Goliaths in the Masters drama—Nick Faldo and Greg Norman—had blown the cut, Faldo 20 shots behind Woods and Norman 15. For Norman, even a pretournament session with motivational speaker Tony Robbins didn't help. Next year: Stuart Smalley. *I'm good enough, I'm shark enough and, doggone it, people fear me!* "I guess I should start hating this bloody place," Norman said as he left, "but I can't."

Saturday was nearly mystical. As the rest of the field slumped, Woods just kept ringing up birdies. He tripled his lead from three to nine with a bogeyless 65. You half expected him to walk across Rae's Creek. Even when Masters officials warned him for slow play on the 14th, he kept his head.

That night there was this loopiness, this giddy sense, even among the players, of needing to laugh in the face of something you never thought you'd see. A 21-year-old in his first major as a pro was about to obliterate every record, and it was almost too big a thought to be thunk. "I might have a chance," said Paul Stankowski, who trailed by 10, "if I make five or six birdies in the first two or three holes." After playing with Woods on Saturday, Montgomerie staggered in looking like a man who had seen a UFO. He plopped his weary meatiness into the interview chair and announced, blankly, "There is no chance. We're all human beings here. There's no chance humanly possible."

What about last year? he was asked, a reference to Norman's blowing a six-shot lead and losing the Masters to Faldo by five. "This is very different. Faldo's not lying second, for a start. And Greg Norman's not Tiger Woods."

Ouch.

Only 47-year-old Tom Kite, who would finish second in the same sense that Germany finished second in World War II, refused to give up. He was a schnauzer with his teeth locked on the tailpipe of a Greyhound bus as it was pulling into beltway traffic. *How can you be so optimistic when Woods is leading by nine shots?* "Well," said Kite, "we've got it down to single digits, don't we?"

But Kite did not leave Augusta empty-handed. As the captain of a U.S. Ryder Cup team that will try to reclaim the trophy from Europe this September in Spain, he suddenly has a one-man Ryder Wrecking Crew on his hands, for Woods wiped out his playing partners from overseas: England's Faldo by five shots on Thursday, Scotland's Montgomerie by nine on Saturday and Italy's Costantino Rocca by six on Sunday.

The last round was basically a coronation parade with occasional stops to hit a dimpled object. There seemed to be some kind of combat for mortals going on behind Woods for second place, but nothing you needed to notice. Nobody came within a light year. Rocca and Tom Watson each trimmed the lead to eight, but mentioning it at all is like pointing out that the food on the *Hindenburg* was pretty good. Woods went out on the front nine in even par, then birdied the 11th, the 13th and the 14th and parred the 16th with a curvaceous two-putt. "After that, I knew I could bogey in and win," he said. That's a bit of an understatement, of course. He could've quintuple-bogeyed in and won. He could've used nothing but his putter, his umbrella and a rolled-up *Mad* magazine and won.

He wanted the record, though, and for that there was one last challenge—the 18th. On his tee shot a photographer clicked twice on the backswing, and Woods lurched, hooking his drive way left. On this hole, though, the only trouble comes if you're short or right, and Woods has not been short since grade school. He had a wedge shot to the green—if only he could get his wedge. Fluff was lost. "Fluff!" Woods hollered, jumping as if on a pogo stick to see over the gallery. Fluff finally found him as the crowd chanted, "Fluff! Fluff!" It was not exactly tense.

Still, Woods needed a five-footer for par, and when he sank it, he threw his trademark uppercut. The tournament he had talked about winning since he was five, the tournament he had watched on tape almost every night in his little suburban bedroom all those years, the tournament he had wanted more than all the others, was his, and the dream had only just begun. He was now the youngest man by two years to win the Masters and the first black man to win any major.

He turned and hugged Fluff, and as the two men walked off the green, arms draped over each other's shoulders in joy, you couldn't help but notice that Chairman Roberts's Rule of Golf Order had been turned happily upside down—the golfer was black and the caddie was white. "I've always dreamed of coming up 18 and winning," Woods, still a little shocked, said after slipping on the green jacket. "But I never thought this far through the ceremony."

So golf is all new now. Everything is a fight for *place*. *Win* seems to be spoken for. If you are the tournament director of a PGA Tour event, you better do whatever's necessary to get Tiger Woods, because your Wendy's–Shearson Lehman Pensacola Classic is the junior varsity game without him. The Senior tour seems sort of silly next to this. A babe in swaddling pleats with a Slinky for a spine and a computer for a mind has just won a major by more shots than anybody this century. How does he top this? The Grand Slam?

"It can be done," he said, unblinking.

"The bigger the event, the higher he'll raise the bar," Azinger said. "He's Michael Jordan in long pants."

Of course, much more than golf was changed at Augusta National last week. As Woods made his way from Butler Cabin and an interview with CBS, he brought his phalanx of Pinkerton guards and other escorts to a sudden stop. Out of the corner of his eye Woods spied Lee Elder, the man who at 39 had finally won a PGA Tour event, the Monsanto Open, earning his invitation as the first black man to play the Masters, in 1975, the year Tiger was born. Woods knew Elder's story, knew about Teddy Rhodes, too, the star of the black golf circuit in the 1940s, who might've won here if he'd had the chance: and of Charlie Sifford, who outplayed Masters champions like Doug Ford and Gay Brewer regularly on the Tour but never qualified to play here; and of his own father, who was the first black man to play baseball in the Big Eight and was often forced to stay in separate hotels and eat in separate restaurants, apart from his teammates. Tiger knows all the stories he never had to live, so he stopped and put a giant bear hug on Elder. "Thanks for making this possible," Woods whispered in his ear, and then the parade swept on. Elder had tears in his eyes.

At the very end Woods made it into the elegant Augusta National clubhouse dining room for the traditional winner's dinner. As he entered, the members and their spouses stood and applauded politely, as they have for each champion, applauded as he made his way to his seat at the head table under a somber oil painting of President Eisenhower. But clear in the back, near a service entrance, the black cooks and waiters and busboys ripped off their oven mitts and plastic gloves, put their dishes and trays down for a while, hung their napkins over their arms and clapped the loudest and the hardest and the longest for the kind of winner they never dreamed would come through those doors.

Leaping Lucifer

HARVEY PENICK

The former longtime pro at the Austin (Texas) Country Club, Harvey Penick is regarded as one of the finest golf instructors ever. Mr. Penick has honed the skills of first class women golfers such as Betty Jameson, Betsy Rawls, and Mickey Wright. He has also brought along a great number of top male players—many of whom he worked with during his thirty-two years as coach of the University of Texas golf team which won twenty-two Southwest Conference titles. His popularity skyrocketed in his later years, partly due to the fact that two men whom he started in golf—Ben Crenshaw and Tom Kite—became major successes on the PGA Tour. Mr. Penick also authored an enormously popular series of books on golf, including The Game for a Lifetime, *where this piece originally appeared.*

There was a loud thunderstorm during the night.

Lightning cracked a limb off one of the giant oak trees that helped to make our golf course near Riverside Drive such a joy. We had many oaks I couldn't wrap my arms halfway around. They called our country road Riverside Drive because it followed the course of the Colorado River through the southeast part of town, but the road had been a cattle trail, and our golf course had been a dairy farm. A golf course needs water and good soil. The rolling farmland was excellent soil, and the thunderstorm was bringing us water. That night four or five inches of rain pounded the roof of our house a few yards from the twelfth tee.

Lord knows, we needed the rain. I never in my life complained about rain. Texas always needs rain, even when its flooding. All natural-born Texans who have been on earth a while have endured long spells of no rain and have learned that a lot of rain always beats a drought.

At first light, I watched from our kitchen window, looking down the fairway to the green of the par-3 twelfth as the rain stopped. I knew the lone creek that meandered through the course would be churning along out of its banks, and the caddies would be swimming in the ponds that formed in the swales. It would be at least noon before we could open for play.

There was plenty of work to do at the club, but I decided the rain had given me freedom to slip off and hit a bag of balls. I had a couple of lessons to give in the afternoon, and I wanted to practice my trick shots that I showed off in clinics and in exhibitions at baseball parks. Some of my pupils, especially the girls, would ask me to hit trick shots for them, and I needed to keep my touch.

I put away my polished shoes and my trousers with the fresh-pressed creases that I ordinarily wore to the club, and dressed in old clothes that wouldn't be ruined by the mud. By nine o'clock, my shop duties were under control, so I sneaked out to the tenth fairway with a bag of balls. I wanted to practice, not draw a crowd and wind up doing a show.

I dumped a mound of balls in the wet grass, paced off 145 yards down the fairway, and dropped the shag bag to be used as my target.

I had been hitting 7-irons for about five minutes when I noticed someone was leaning against a pecan tree, watching me from under the dripping branches.

A muddy Cadillac was parked on Grove Road, which runs beside the tenth fairway. I was already losing my hearing, and wasn't aware the Cadillac had arrived.

"They told me up at the club that Harvey Penick might be down here," the fellow called from under the pecan tree branches.

"That's me." I was really wanting to practice, but this fellow was nobody from around Austin, and he caught my eye because he looked a little bit like the movie actor W. C. Fields.

Walking toward me, the fellow said, "I heard Harvey Penick is a classy dresser," as if my clothes made him doubt he was talking to the right person.

I addressed the ball with my clubface upside down and backward. It appeared impossible to hit a shot from that position. But I whacked a neat little draw that bounced up next to the shag bag.

"Good trick. I saw the Fat Man do it in Florida. You spin the grip in your hands faster than my eye can follow it. Very nice," he said.

I looked the fellow over again. Bill Mehlhorn had told me about a big money player in Florida named the Fat Man.

"What's your name?" I asked.

"At my home club the boys call me Leaping Lucifer."

I smiled at that, but he didn't.

The fellow's nose wasn't as large as the movie actor's, but his face was flushed and plump with the expression of an angry baby. He was wearing a white silk shirt under a yellow cashmere sweater, and his trousers were creamy wool. He had on brown alligator shoes exactly like the pair I had left in the closet at home that morning. He was about the same age I was at the time, about fifty.

"I was hoping to get a lesson from you," he said. "I've driven all the way from New Orleans."

I said I could fit him in later in the day. He shook his head.

"I was hoping you could do it right now," he said. "I'm driving back this afternoon. I have a game at the club tomorrow morning. Please, pro, can I get my sticks out of the trunk? Tomorrow is my birthday, and I want to win."

"I don't promise I can help you," I said.

Before the words were out of my mouth, Leaping Lucifer was slogging across the fairway through the mud toward his Cadillac. I watched him open the trunk and wrestle with a leather bag that was big enough to carry three boys and a dog.

"Just bring your 7-iron," I yelled.

But he was already staggering back across the fairway, bent under the weight of the bag full of clubs, his alligator shoes squishing in the wet earth with each step. Mud was splashed all over his slacks and sweater. When he planted the bag beside me, it must have lowered three inches into the ground.

"Tomorrow's your birthday, is it?" I asked, to start him talking. Whatever demon had caused him to drive from New Orleans to Austin to seek help from a stranger, it might reveal itself if he talked about his life.

"Yeah. My fiancée is throwing a big party at the club tomorrow night. She organized a birthday tournament for me tomorrow afternoon."

"She sounds like a wonderful person," I said.

"I'm playing two guys a thousand bucks three ways, and five hundred with the other," he said.

I said, "I think you've come to the wrong teacher."

"I checked you out. You're the one. Dutch Harrison told me."

I said, "I'm happy to try to help you with your swing, but I've been known to fail, and I want no responsibility for what you win or lose at the tournament tomorrow. You'd better try a different pro."

"I didn't come to you because of the gambling money!" he cried, earnestly enough to make me believe him. "I came because I'm tired of being laughed at! Especially tomorrow! I don't want to be laughed at in front of my fiancée on my birthday!"

"What is it about you that is supposed to be so funny?" I asked.

"It's my golf swing!"

There was such misery and pleading in his voice that I told him to take out his 7-iron and address a mud clod as if it were a golf ball. His left hand grip was very weak, rolled almost under the handle. With his right hand, he held the club like a sledgehammer. Otherwise, his address was all right. He stood to the clod in a plain way, as I like to see.

"Make a few practice swings," I said.

He swung the club back and around at shoulder height, like a baseball bat. I was about to inform him that a true practice swing is always aimed at some spot on the ground so that it will imitate golf, but curiosity made me move on quickly to placing a golf ball on top of the mud clod.

"Hit it," I said.

The violent motion that followed startled me into dropping my club.

Maybe I can compare it to a man with an axe attacking a charging wild beast.

The fellow slashed his right shoulder and arm viciously toward the clod, and at the same time he lunged forward far past the ball—and yet, there was an explosion of mud, and I saw his 7-iron shot flying about six feet off the ground and slicing a little to bounce some ten yards short of my shag bag.

As a teacher with many years of experience, I have seen all sorts of leapers and lungers, but Leaping Lucifer was in a class by himself.

The most amazing thing about his swing was the exquisite timing that was necessary for him to produce a straight, usable, halfway decent 7-iron. Despite his plump cheeks and his middle-aged body, Leaping Lucifer was very talented as an athlete, or else he had just now been very lucky.

"Do it again," I said.

I stepped back a few feet to escape the shower of mud from his clubhead and his feet as he leaped and bashed the ball, his head finishing waist high and two feet in front of his left leg.

But the ball landed within thirty feet of the first one.

"Can you hit your 7-iron like this consistently?" I asked.

"Yeah, pro. Pretty much. I don't hit the ball far, but I'm straight. Long carries over water or some kind of swamp or gully, those things kill me. I avoid those courses. I like a course where I can hit run up shots."

Remembering Lucifer all these years later, it occurs to me that he couldn't finish the first two holes at our Pete Dye golf course on the bank of the river we call Lake Austin. Lucifer's worm burners would never cross our ravines and water hazards. Most golf courses built in the 1980s went away from the old-fashioned ground game and forced players to hit the ball high. It would require a lifetime overhaul for Lucifer to hit a shot of much height. He could probably make it around the Old Course at St. Andrews with a score reasonably close to his handicap, and he could have finished a round at our Hancock Park or Riverside Drive courses, but his card at our new Austin Country Club would be a couple of X's followed by a brisk stroll back to the clubhouse.

"Are you going to help me?" he asked.

"What would you like me to do?"

"You can teach me to keep my head behind the ball so I look a little more stylish."

What he was asking for would take months, if it could be done at all.

"How often do you play golf?" I asked.

"Every Wednesday afternoon and usually on Sunday."

He was probably a doctor or a dentist. As a teacher, I had his best interest at heart, as I would expect from a doctor or dentist who was treating me. But this was like waiting until your disease was incurable or your teeth were falling out of your head before you went to see a professional.

"Do you practice your golf?" I asked.

"I hit a few balls before I go to the tee, just to warm up."

"What is your handicap?" I asked.

"I'm a 16."

I must have looked surprised that it was so low, because he misunderstood and scowled at me.

"I used to be a 12," he said. "But I was much younger then."

"How long have you swung at the ball this way?" I asked.

"Probably twenty-five years. I didn't take up the game until I could afford to join a country club."

He realized his alligator shoes were buried in the mud, and he pulled his feet free and moved to a patch of ground that was a little more solid. I knew he was waiting for me to do something wonderful for him, but I had already mentally discarded the things I would ordinarily do for a player who lunges. I would have started with his grip, but fixing this fellow's grip would have only made matters worse.

Leaping Lucifer glanced at his wristwatch.

"Just a couple more questions," I said. "These men you will be playing with tomorrow, can you beat them?"

"Yeah. All of them outhit me a long way off the tee, but with my handicap I win a lot more than I lose."

"Are you a good putter?" I asked.

"One of the best. If I need to sink a six-foot putt on the eighteenth green to win, I'll make it."

As the golf coach at the University of Texas, I told my boys to beware of the opponent who had both a bad grip and a bad swing, because chances are he repeated his mistakes consistently and had learned how to score. This was my diagnosis of Leaping Lucifer. Anything I did in one lesson to change his grip or his swing would destroy what he already believed and would cause him to lose all his bets tomorrow, a sorry birthday present.

"Listen, pro, I'd like to get started here," he said. "It's a tough twelve hours back to New Orleans."

I needed to give this fellow some kind of gift, something that would make him feel better about himself without ruining the only good thing about his swing, which was that he did it the same way over and over with impeccable timing.

Reflecting on the situation, I remembered Leaping Lucifer had not asked me to improve his golf game. He had asked me to make his swing look stylish, that's all. It was vanity. He had been swinging this way for twenty-five years, and he had been laughed at for probably as long. But he was a winner, so he had borne the burden of his opponents' wisecracks because he was taking their money.

Now his fiancée had entered the picture, and tomorrow was his birthday. He didn't want to be laughed at in front of her.

"You're a very lucky man," I said.

"Yeah?" He eyed me suspiciously. "How?"

"Well, you've got a new Cadillac car and a cashmere sweater and a woman who wants to marry you, plus you've made it through life in apparent good health for another year."

"Skip the sermon, pro. Let's talk about my golf swing. What are you going to do about it?"

"Nothing," I said.

"You give up, huh? It's that bad, is it?"

I took off my hat and scratched my head.

"In fact, I wouldn't touch your swing because you are a golfing genius. Your swing is not funny, it is unique to your particular genius. You play golf only once or twice a week, and you don't spend hours on the practice range. To keep your game going at a 16-handicap level, and win money from your opponents with it, you must be a genius."

He was liking what he was hearing. It was making sense. Sure, I told him, if he had time to put in long practice sessions and play several days a week, as most of the best players did, he could get his game down into the high 70s. Good a putter as he was, his scores would only get better.

Leaping Lucifer was smiling at me now.

"If they laugh at you tomorrow, you just wink at your fiancée. She's a smart woman. She'll see that they're really laughing at themselves because they aren't good enough to beat you. You and your fiancée can have a fine laugh while you're counting your winnings."

"Ah, pro," he said, "I see what you mean. What do I care if these losers laugh? I'm the one who wins the game."

"One more thing," I said. "It's a tip for tomorrow and now on. When you hit pitch shots to the green, use your sand wedge, and grip it high on the handle, which prevents chili-dipping, and hold tight with the pinky and ring fingers of your left hand so the blade won't turn over. This will take three strokes off your game tomorrow."

This advice couldn't possibly hurt, and it would help if he remembered to do it. This was something technical enough for him to put his mind on it and feel he had learned something.

"Hey, great, thanks," he said brightly.

He wiped the mud off his right hand and stuck it out. I shook it.

"How much do I owe you?" he asked.

"Send 20 percent of your winnings to the Salvation Army," I said. "I hope your wedding is blessed forever. And say hello to Dutch Harrison for me."

I turned back to the pile of balls at my feet. Behind me I could hear the clanking and puffing as he heaved the heavy bag over his shoulder, and then the slurping of those beautiful alligator shoes sloshing through the mud on the fairway as Leaping Lucifer marched again to his Cadillac.

The Cadillac backed up and made a U-turn on Grove Road and I watched the sprays of water thrown up by its wheels as he drove happily off toward New Orleans.

I faded a 7-iron that landed with a loud plunk against the shag bag. I laughed and wiped my hands with a towel. It was a great morning to be alive and be teaching, and there were another fifty balls to hit before I would need to go back to the shop. That warm, easy feeling is hard to explain, but it is better than riches to me.

Going Back

JOHN GARRITY

We end this collection with this piece by the author who contributed an introduction to this collection. He is the senior writer on golf at Sports Illustrated.

The trip starts, as it always does, with a good-natured difference of opinion. "They hate me coming," the old man says. "They can't stand to see me drive up that Magnolia Lane."

And his son, a tall man of 50 with a sand-colored mustache, gives his practiced response: "It's just the opposite, Dad, if you ask me. They treat you as if you won the tournament last year."

The crunch of gravel underfoot and the retreating storm clouds in the eastern sky are the harbingers of dawn. The son is holding the keys to the old man's car—a 1977 Cadillac with rust spots on the trunk and a National Rifle Association decal in the rear window. Shoe boxes and clothes cover the backseat, but the 51-year-old green sports jacket is safely stored in the trunk. "Where's the jacket?" the old man asks.

"I packed it," says the son.

Minutes later, with the younger man at the wheel, the old Caddy pulls away from Keiser's Golf Range, in Copley, Ohio, outside Akron, and onto Cleveland-Massillon Road, heading south.

*   *   *

The old man insists it's about money. Every April, he says, he has to drive down to Augusta and attend the champions' dinner. Otherwise, he won't get the check for $1,500. "Can you believe they make an old man drive all that way?" he grouses.

The son says it's not about the money, which is given to every past Masters winner who goes to the dinner. And if you had seen the old man the day before, trying on the green jacket and proudly showing off the *Herman Keiser* sewn inside over the wallet pocket, you would have had to agree. But the old man remembers the Great Depression, and at 82 he's not comfortably fixed. As the Cadillac passes the Loyal Oak Golf Course, just minutes up the road, he looks longingly at the silky fairways and frost-covered greens. He sold his partnership in the course some years back, in 1961. The proceeds dwindled. Now he lives on income from some investments and a small Social Security check, sleeping winter nights at his daughter's house and summer nights in a dormer apartment above the range office.

When he slipped the jacket on, his son asked, "Do you remember who put it on you when you won?"

The old man frowned. "Was it Hogan or Snead? Who was it?"

"Nelson," said the son. "It's always the winner from the year before."

Now the sun is a red ball on a wooded ridge. The Cadillac slides onto Interstate 77 and searches for a constant speed amid the cars and big rigs finding their way out of Akron. In the passenger seat the old man sits contentedly, wiggling his toes in his brown leather shoes. His son, one of the old man's four children, tends to lead the conversation. They talk about the son's teaching job at a golf school in upstate New York. They talk about the old man's daughter, son-in-law and three young grandsons, who left for Augusta two days ago in a van. They talk about raccoon hunting and the old man's dogs.

But the conversation always comes back to 1946 and Augusta. For a half-century the old man has replayed that week—the funny conversations with bookies and chums, the angry exchanges with club members and tournament officials. Ben Hogan, his implacable and awe-inspiring foe, has few lines in these remembered dialogues, but the legendary Bobby Jones and the imperious tournament chairman, Clifford Roberts, loom large.

Some memories are so sharp they could have happened yesterday: his final-round approach shot around a pine on the 10th that missed the trunk by an eyelash and wound up six inches from the hole . . . the two bookmakers ("the fat guy from New York and the little guy from Texas") who lent him money on the weekend so he could bet on himself . . . his run-in with sportswriter Grantland Rice, who said he was playing too slow, in the third round, which ended, the old man says, when he threatened to wrap his putter around Rice's neck. . . .

WELCOME TO WEST VIRGINIA, interrupts a sign at the Ohio River bridge. A few minutes later the Cadillac exits the freeway and rolls into Parkersburg for gas. "You have to understand," his son says, working the pump. "There was big money on Hogan at 4 to 1, and Dad was five strokes ahead after two rounds."

And you have to understand, too, that the Masters, in those days, was less a solemn major-cum-flower-show and more a high-stakes Calcutta. Club members, some with up to $50,000 on Hogan, might have been hoping that the leader, a 20-to-1 long shot from Springfield, Mo., would have car trouble or contract food poisoning. Unseen forces did, in fact, switch his third-round starting time without telling him—he almost missed his tee time—and someone arranged a change of caddies.

"Oh, yeah, they gave me a 13-year-old kid," the old man says, returning to the car with a bag of potato chips and a can of Dr. Pepper. "By the second hole he was dragging my clubs. I stopped and demanded a real caddie." No experienced caddies, he was told, were available.

Opening the passenger-side door, the old man says, "I am going to drive some. If not, let me out, and I'll hitchhike."

* * *

It's not like the old days. I-77 has tamed the mountains and by-passed the coal towns, making West Virginia safe and scenic. The Cadillac growls up grades with no effort, leaving the father and son with little to do but listen to LeAnn Rimes on the radio warbling her admonition not to lose "the light in your eyes." The younger man says, "That Bobby Locke must have been the greatest putter who ever lived." The old man says, "I might have put Horton Smith ahead of him." And the old man pictures Locke, the great South African player: "Knickers and long hair, called everybody Laddie. From the sand he'd pick the ball off like it was on a tee. He said, 'I don't like the splosh'"—Locke-talk for the explosion shot.

As the sun climbs, you almost expect to see a vintage Plymouth or Packard roar by in the passing lane, an adult arm out each window, cigarette sparks bouncing on the pavement. The Tour moved by automobile in the old man's day, and the names of cherished travel companions are always on his lips—Johnny Bulla, Duke Gibson, Bob Hamilton, Chandler Harper (who teamed with the old man to win the 1942 Miami Four Ball), Jug McSpaden, Byron Nelson, Henry Picard. A family friend back in Akron had spoken with feeling of those pioneers, telling how they doubled up in dollar motels and crossed deserts in caravans. "One time," the friend said, "Herman and Ky Laffoon and Bob Hamilton drove from the West Coast to Miami and had 15 flats along the way."

"How many flats?" the old man asks. "Well, I don't know."

The old man is more definite about the classic travel tale starring Laffoon—definite, he says, because he and Hamilton were in the trailing car. "We're going along, and I say, 'Look out,' 'cause there's sparks under his car like maybe the tailpipe's draggin', and we're afraid it's going to catch fire or blow up. I catch up and get him stopped, and Ky holds up this putter he's been draggin' out the window. He says, 'See this putter? It's too heavy, and I'm takin' some weight off it.'" The son, in a later telling, has Laffoon saying, "I'm just grinding down a wedge." That's the version he remembers from his childhood in the '50s, when his father cut back his golf and worked as a club pro. The stories enthralled the youngster, who had his father's given name and was known in the family as "our Masters baby." (When the old man came back from the war in 1945, his wife said it was time to have a child. "When I win a big tournament," he joked. The boy was born on Feb. 1, 1947—barely nine months after the '46 Masters.) He loved the way his father yelled "Boom!" when he was telling about the right rear axle that broke on his '34 Plymouth during a drive back from Canada.

But now, as the Cadillac slides out of the mountains into a broad farm valley, he finds himself mentally editing the old man's stories—putting the right club in someone's hands, correcting the year, rescuing the critical detail.

The stories mean a lot to him.

Around noon, the Cadillac plunges into the East River Mountain tunnel, coming out in Virginia. Wytheville gets the nod for lunch, and the two men pick a Bob Evans Restaurant just off the highway. The old man orders turkey with mashed potatoes and then holds his left wrist while clenching and unclenching his fist. Asked if he hurt something, he says, "No, I just exercise it. I've got a little arthritis." Smiling, he adds, "I don't know why. I'm only 82."

The cap he's wearing—black, with THE TRADITION printed on the crown—also requires some explanation. The Tradition, a Senior tour event held the week before the Masters, in Scottsdale, Ariz., has its own champions' dinner, to which winners of all the majors are invited. Even the old man's fear of flying can't keep him away from that dinner, which, he notes with enthusiasm, pays $3,000—twice what the Masters pays. "I'm going to wear this hat all week," he chortles. "That's a great tournament."

The Masters may not be on his hat or in his heart, but it's certainly on the old man's mind. As they eat, the two men replay the final hole in '46, which the old man figured he had to par to avoid a playoff, although a bogey did it.

"Hogan was charging, and you could hear the applause behind you," the son says.

The old man nods. His playing partner that day was Nelson, who was the perfect sportsman and an ally. An excited crowd climbed the hill behind them, while club members with money on Hogan waited at the green, distressed. He describes his shot from the fairway, how it hit the flag and "ricocheted right about 12 or 15 feet."

"Is that all?" the son interrupts.

"Maybe 30 feet," the old man allows.

"Everyone says you hit a four-iron on your last approach, but it was a seven-iron." The son turns in his chair. "They've got Dad's seven-iron in a glass case at Augusta National. You can still see the ball mark from that last shot—right in the middle of the face."

The old man smiles, remembering how it felt to beat Hogan. He left Augusta, he says, with $2,500 for winning and perhaps $1,000 more from the bookmakers. He left, as well, with a thousand eyes looking daggers at his back.

The afternoon miles go quietly, with country and western music on the radio and long pauses between stories. Spring has come to North Carolina, laying lavender blossoms on the median and turning the hardwoods pale green. The Cadillac stops in Statesville for gas, barrels through downtown Charlotte around four o'clock, and exits onto I-20 West. The day's drive ends at 5:15 p.m., at a Days Inn in Columbia, S.C., about 70 miles shy of Augusta. In the motel office the old man opens his wallet and lays out $99 for two nights, ignoring his son's offer to pay. A sign on the counter reads ABSOLUTELY NO REFUNDS AFTER 15 MINUTES.

In their room the old man discusses his plans for Tuesday: coffee, drive to Augusta, check in, breakfast or lunch on the veranda, walk a few holes, sit for hours under an umbrella with his daughter's family . . . and finally, the champions' dinner. Afterward they will return to this room, the young man and the old, and early the next day, 24 hours before the tournament gets under way, they will head back to Akron. The door is open, and the nose of the Cadillac is visible just beyond the threshold, its bumper a mirror in the sunlight, the engine clicking as it cools.

"I don't know where they came up with that 'dark horse winner' stuff," the son says, still thinking of '46. "I've never liked that. You were the ninth-place guy on the money-list, and you lost a playoff to Hogan earlier that year in Phoenix."

"Hogan was the greatest player in the world," the old man says. "In that Phoenix playoff we tied two holes, and then Hogan went over the green on the third. I had 12 or 15 feet for birdie, and he pitched the son of a bitch in. Of course, I missed my putt."

The two men are silent for a moment. "We won't start too early," the younger man says. "You don't want to get too tired."

The journey ends, as it always does, in bumper-to-bumper traffic on Augusta's Washington Road. "Park, five bucks," the old man says, reading a sign by the roadside. "That's cheap, if you stay all day."

He has his windbreaker on and the Tradition cap. His eyes follow people on foot, while his son works his way into the left lane, ready to turn at the gatehouse. And finally, they see the sign at an opening in the tall hedgerow: MEMBERS, PLAYERS, HONORARY INVITEES.

The son waits for oncoming traffic to clear and then turns in. A uniformed guard steps up on the passenger side and bends forward. The old man lowers his window and says simply: "Herman Keiser."

The guard smiles. "All right, Mr. Keiser. Go right on in."

The Cadillac rolls forward, under the canopy of magnolias— but slowly, like a processioner at a wedding. The son leans over the wheel and looks up at the arching branches. He says, "It doesn't get any better than this."

In a wavering voice the old man concedes the point. "It is beautiful, isn't it?"

On this they're in complete agreement.